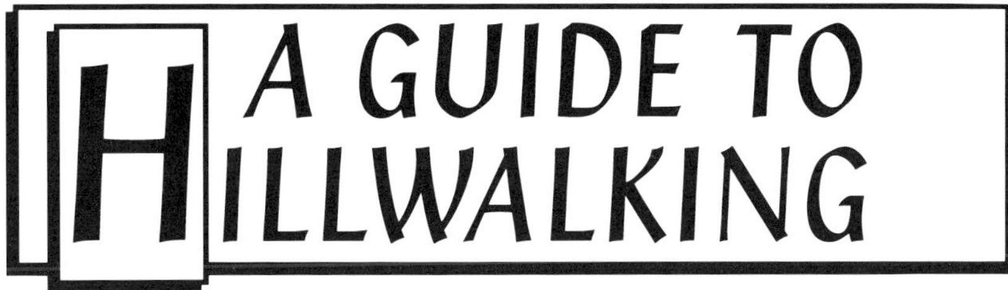

A GUIDE TO HILLWALKING

Chris Townsend

The Crowood Press

First published in 1996 by
The Crowood Press Ltd
Ramsbury, Marlborough
Wiltshire SN8 2HR

British Library Cataloguing-in-Publication Data

A catalogue record for this book is available from the British Library.

ISBN 1 85223 958 1

Picture Credits
All photographs by the author
All line-drawings by Nada Price

Printed and bound by WBC Book Manufacturers, Mid Glamorgan

Contents

Acknowledgements

This book is based on years of hillwalking – on my own and with others. I have learnt much from my companions, hence my thanks to Chris and Janet Ainsworth, Mark Edgington, Dave, Di and Robin Fuller, Graham Huntington, Andy and Jill Hicks, Alain Kahan, Alex Lawrence, Lynne Metcalfe, Al Micklethwaite, Scott Steiner, Rowena Thorn, Fran Townsend, John Traynor and Steve Twaites.

I should particularly like to thank my partner and regular hill companion Denise Thorn for her patience in allowing me to drag her out into the mountains on days of foul weather in order to take photographs. Denise also read the text of the book carefully and made many useful comments and suggestions.

As an outdoor writer I have also gleaned a great deal from magazine editors, other writers, gear designers and other professionals I have been in contact with. I have also been able, as a gear tester for outdoor magazines, to use a much wider range of equipment than would otherwise have been possible. Too many companies and individuals deserve my thanks to mention them all here but I would particularly like to mention Akzo (makers of Sympatex), Judy Armstrong, Frank Bennett of Troll, Martin Bergerud of Lyon Equipment, Bill Birch of Dark Peak, Alastair Bramwell, Chris Brasher of Brasher Boots, Hamish Brown, Nick Brown of Nikwax and Paramo, Camera Care Systems, Mark Carr of Buffalo, Rab Carrington of Rab Down Equipment, Morgan J. Connolly of Cascade Designs, Gordon Conyers of Tor Outdoor Products, Oliver Cooper of Terra Nova, Laurie Grey of Lowe Alpine, Hamish Hamilton, John Hunt of Sprayway, Ray Jardine, Tim Jasper of Rohan, John Keighley, Tony Lack, Steve Laycock of Pertex, Ken Ledward, Peter and Pat Lennon of Mountain and Wildlife Ventures, Stefan Lepkowski, Duncan MacDonald, Cameron McNeish and John Manning of TGO magazine, Mike Parsons of Karrimor, Carlton Reid, John Skelton, Roger Smith, Brian Thomson of Highland Guides, David Udberg of Mountain Range, Walt Unsworth, Jim White of Vango, Alan Waugh and Ken Rawlinson of Phoenix Mountaineering and Tony Woods of Craghoppers.

The opinions and recommendations in this book are my own, and I know that many of the above-mentioned people will disagree with some of what I say. Any errors or omissions are my responsibility too.

Introduction:
The Joys of Hillwalking

Once you have started walking down the right road, you begin, sooner or later, to dream of truly wild places. (Colin Fletcher, The Complete Walker)

Walking in the hills is an exciting, adventurous and fulfilling activity. By climbing hills walkers can escape the restrictions of lowland footpath walking and revel in the freedom of wandering where they choose. Hillwalking also means entering the wilds and leaving behind the tamed, civilized flatlands. At its best it means moving into the natural world and feeling part of the moors and mountains. The form of the land; the forces that have shaped and are shaping it; the patterns of stream and lake; the patterns of the weather, storm and sun, cloud and wind; the animals, birds, plants and rocks are all open to the hillwalker. Learning about this world and how to be part of it is to my mind an essential part of hillwalking.

My hillwalking experience began with school outings on which we climbed Snowdon, Scafell Pike, Kinder Scout and other peaks accessible on Sunday coach trips from Merseyside. For someone brought up on the flat Lancashire coast, where 50ft (15m) sand dunes were the biggest hills for some distance, these mountains were a revelation. Ever since, climbing hills has been the standby of my outdoor life and what I do when I have a day or even half a day to spare. I have learnt that hillwalking can mean more than just ascending to summits. Walking through high passes and remote valleys can be just as challenging and gives a different perspective to familiar scenes, while staying out night after night in the mountains greatly enhances the experience of wild places. In winter I often travel by ski, more efficient than walking when the snow lies deep, or take ice axe and crampons to tackle the icy slopes, a very different form of walking to that of summer. In winter the short daylight hours

Hillwalking takes you into wild and spectacular places. This is Loch Avon in the Cairngorms.

The grandeur of mountains in winter. On the summit of Skierfe in Sarek National Park, Lapland.

and the difficulties imposed by snow and ice limit the distance that can be travelled. Pure hillwalking, with few obstacles, takes place between May and October when the long days are taken up with wandering the high tops, visiting favourite peaks by different routes and searching out new hills to climb.

The majority of hills in England and Wales and the most popular hills in Scotland (such as Ben Lomond and Ben Nevis) have well used, clearly marked ways up that novice hillwalkers can easily follow, except perhaps in winter. Further afield marked routes through and up the hills can be found in many countries. Of course in many areas such as the Alps and Himalayas technical climbing skills and equipment are required to reach most of the summits but there are still some hills that can be walked up and many high mountain paths that can be followed by competent walkers.

For me real hillwalking as opposed to path following begins when such pedestrian motorways are left behind and I strike out on my own. The less popular hills in England and Wales (yes, there are still some) and the majority of those in Scotland have only a few narrow paths – if any at all – making them excellent for the adventurous walker to explore. Even the most popular hills have routes people rarely use. I once went up Helvellyn, arguably the most climbed hill in the UK, at Easter yet by picking my route carefully I managed to avoid the crowds, only encountering others on the summit.

Peak bagging – the climbing of all the summits in a range or country or above a certain height – has become much more popular in recent years and has therefore been subject to much criticism by those who consider themselves above what they term as mere list-ticking. I am happy to confess to being a peak bagger, though since I completed my round of the 277 Scottish Munros – 3000ft (900m) summits as listed in Munro's Tables – in 1981 I have not been so single-minded about it, no longer charging up new peaks regardless of the weather. Instead I take a more leisurely approach to collecting hills, being as interested in new ways up tops I have already climbed as in ticking off new summits. I have also spent many satisfying summers walking long distances through mountain ranges in places as far apart as Norway and Canada rather than climbing the peaks. I am convinced, though, that by collecting peaks I have visited areas I might otherwise have neglected and had superb hill days that I might have spent mooching about in the valleys without the goal of a

Competent hillwalkers can explore mountains the world over. This is the Grand Canyon in Arizona.

On the High Level Route in the French Pyrenees, a superb mountain walk for experienced hillwalkers.

new peak to spur me on, especially in stormy weather. Climbing all the peaks in a country or mountain range also gives a depth of knowledge and experience lacking in those who climb just a few chosen summits. Do explore the hills thoroughly, perhaps camping out overnight at times or walking a through route and using public transport or two cars, one at either end, rather than dashing between the hills by car and zooming up each one by the quickest route from the nearest road. Hillwalking is about travelling in the hills, not standing on summits.

To enjoy the freedom of the hills safely a few skills are required, the main one being navigation, and a few items of essential equipment are required, most notably suitable footwear and waterproof clothing. Without the ability to use a map and compass the walker is restricted to the popular, well-frequented paths marked by cairns and delineated in countless guide books. And even on these a sudden clamping down of mist on a featureless top – especially if combined, as it so often is, with heavy rain and a strong wind – may make even the clearest path fade away and become very hard to follow. I can remember once needing a compass bearing to find my way off Bleaklow in the Peak District in a thick mist even though I was by the summit cairn and my way off coincided with the Pennine Way long distance path.

In this book I have described the techniques and equipment needed for safe hillwalking. Overall, it is not a difficult or dangerous pursuit but the enjoyment of it – and pleasure is the only reason for going hillwalking – can be immeasurably enhanced by having the right skills. Hillwalking is not about equipment or techniques, of course. These are just the means to the end. Hillwalking is about feeling part of the

Even in the Alps there are peaks accessible to hillwalkers. Signing the summit book on the Secharspitze, Austria.

Camping is a superb way to really experience the hills.

wilds, about escaping the artificiality of modern urban life, about remembering that we are part of nature, about feeling really alive. It is also about the excitement of struggling through a storm, the joy when the mist clears and a vast spectacular mountain landscape suddenly appears at your feet, the pleasure in the physical work of climbing upwards, of using the body as it was meant to be used.

In the pages that follow these reasons for going hillwalking may seem to disappear in the welter of information on gear and techniques. The reason for concentrating on these is so that when you are out in the hills you can take them for granted, knowing that your waterproofs will keep out the rain and that if the mist comes down your compass skills will ensure you do not get lost.

Going cross country makes hillwalking a real adventure. On the Moine Mhor in the Cairngorms, Scotland.

1 An Introduction to Equipment

No elaborate equipment is needed for mountain-walking in summer. Any old clothes will do – grey flannel bags or plus-fours, or shorts if it is warm, golf-stockings, an open shirt, sports jacket or golf-jacket, and a spare sweater or pullover. (C.F. Kirkus, Let us Go Climbing!, 1941)

Hillwalking does not require much in the way of equipment. Overall it can be an inexpensive activity. You can spend a great deal on gear, but there is no need to do so and an inability to afford the latest jacket or electronic navigation device should not prevent anyone heading for the hills. What you wear or carry is not important as long as it does what is required of it. Whether you look like a 'proper' hillwalker does not matter in the least, though it is surprising how many people judge other walkers by their gear.

BASICS

Competence in the hills means having good judgement and techniques, not the latest jacket. If a piece of kit works for you, however unfashionable it may be, then use it, regardless of what others may say. A few specialist items are needed for safe walking, though. Of major importance are good quality footwear and waterproofs. Slips due to inadequate footwear regularly top the list of causes of mountain rescues while getting cold and wet can lead to the potentially fatal chilling of the body known as hypothermia. Other specialist clothing will make you more comfortable but is not essential.

You will also need a small rucksack to carry your gear in plus a few safety items such as torch, bivvy bag, map and compass. A wide choice of equipment is available for walking but not all of it is really suitable for serious hill use. To make sure you get the right gear go to a specialist outdoor retailer who can give good advice.

Green gear

Hillwalkers have a far closer relationship with the natural environment than most people and in general are very concerned about what is happening to it. Yet how many people consider the effects of the gear they buy? Making gear consumes resources – non-renewable resources in the case of synthetics, now the major component of most gear – and the industrial processes involved cause pollution.

There are a number of ways concerned walkers can minimize the effect they have. The first is to wear gear out or, if it is replaced while there is life left in it, sell it or pass it on to someone else or a charity shop. Of course, when gear is 'worn out' depends in part on how much repair work you are prepared to do. If this is a chore you would rather not undertake many manufacturers will mend items. Shoecare of Preston offer a repair and cleaning service for clothes and packs as well as footwear. A good book on this is Annie Getchell's

The Essential Outdoor Gear Manual).

Caring for gear properly extends its useful life and ensures it works well. There are many products for caring for clothing and footwear but Nikwax specialize in this area and also take care that their products do not in themselves cause environmental damage. They make waterproofing and cleaning treatments for all types of footwear plus wash-in waterproofing agents for all types of clothing. I have tried most of them and found them to work very well.

When shopping for new gear you can look for items that contain recycled materials, as an increasing amount do. Some garments are made from 100 per cent recycled fleece while many boots contain recycled materials, especially in the sole.

Two schemes that are growing in popularity in Germany and will hopefully take off elsewhere are vauDe/Akzo's Ecolog Recycling Network and W.L. Gore's Balance Project. Both schemes allow for products to be returned to the shop when finished with so they can be recycled and turned into new gear. To enable this to be done all the components of Ecolog products are made from 100 per cent polyester. Garments and sleeping bags are being made like this and rucksacks and tents will probably follow (rucksacks made from 100 per cent recycled materials are already available in United States). The recyclable waterproofs and fleece jackets work just as well as standard items.

Many companies are now involved in environmental activities. At its lowest, but still welcome, level this may just mean using recycled packaging – and not all do even that. Some companies do much more. A donation from every boot or item of clothing sold by the Brasher Boot Company goes into environmental work, and has helped to fund the purchase of some of the most spectacular and wild parts of Scotland. Patagonia also put funds into environmental projects and use their excellent catalogues as forums for environmental education and campaigning. Other companies are starting to do more as well. If these are supported the rest should get the message and become involved too.

Colour

Bright colours in the hills can reduce the sense of wildness and environmental harmony. One orange tent beside a mountain tarn can draw the eye and dominate the scene while distant walkers are often first seen due to a flash of red or yellow. Such brightness will be quickly noticed by wildlife too, which is why birdwatchers and naturalists usually wear soft browns and greens.

Fabrics make a difference too. Smooth shiny synthetics stand out far more than cottons or polycotton blends of the same colour and a bit more than rough-textured synthetics with a dull finish. It is not always the item that looks bright close to that stands out most at a distance.

Some people like brightly coloured hill gear, arguing that it is cheerful and optimistic or that it is needed for safety. With regard to the latter not everyone in a group needs to be visible at a great distance. Indeed, except in emergencies no one needs to be. And in a crisis orange bivvy bags, hidden in the rucksack most of the time, stand out well. I prefer to be inconspicuous when walking and I would rather others were too. The only exception is when snow covers the hills as then anything but white clothing stands out, and all colours look black at a distance. Because I test gear I am sometimes sent bright items to try. The more garish clothing I have sometimes found so embarrassing to wear that I have only had the nerve to do so in bad weather in places where I am unlikely to meet anyone else! I have also occasionally taken a colourful jacket on long walks in very remote wildernesses such as Canada's Yukon Territory for safety reasons but I would not do so again as I was not happy wearing such gear. My own preference is for browns, greens and greys for both clothing and rucksacks. It is true that a red item stands out well in colour photographs and can prevent a figure from blending in too much. This does not have to be a shiny nylon item, and so need not be too obtrusive.

2 The Foundations of Walking: Footwear

At night the shoes are dried by hanging them upside down on stakes before the fire … or, fill a frying pan with clean pebbles, heat them (not too hot) over the fire, put them in the shoes, and shake them around after a while. (Horace Kephart, Camping and Woodcraft, 1917)

Footwear is undoubtedly the most important part of the walker's outfit. Blisters and sore feet probably ruin more walks than all other causes put together, including bad weather. Footwear has to do a great deal. Its main function is to protect and support your feet, stopping them slipping on steep, rough or wet terrain and preventing them twisting on rough ground or being bruised by rocks. In cold or wet weather footwear should also help keep your feet warm and, as far as possible, dry. It should be comfortable to wear too, ideally feeling as good at the end of a walk as at the start.

How much equipment you need depends on how long you are out. The author on a 12-day trip in the Grand Canyon.

WEIGHT

A commonly quoted figure is that 1lb (450g) on your feet equals 5lb (2.3kg) on your back. This is because every time you take a step you lift the weight of your boot and during a day you take thousands of steps. My stride is about 2½ft (75cm) long so I take about 2000 steps per mile (1200 steps per km). This means that if I wear boots weighing 4lb (1.8kg) I lift 80,000lb on a 20 mile walk (or 36,000kg on a 32km walk). That is why I do not wear heavy boots! Instead I usually wear shoes or boots that weigh between 1½ and 2½lb (675g and 1.1kg), roughly halving the weight I lift with my feet. When I do try heavier boots, usually for magazine tests, I find that my feet tire much more quickly.

I found out that heavy footwear is tiring long before I came up with any figures, once walking for weeks through the mountains and deserts of southern California with my 5lb (2.3kg) boots in my pack and 1½lb (675g) running shoes on my feet as that was much more comfortable and less tiring than the other way round. Once through the snowbound High Sierra range, where the boots were needed as I had to use crampons, I sent the boots home and replaced the running shoes with some slightly more robust trail shoes weighing about 2lb (900g), in which I completed the last 1000 miles (1600km) of my 2600 mile (4200km) walk from Mexico to Canada along the Pacific Crest Trail. Since then I have always preferred lightweight footwear, wearing sports sandals or walking or running shoes in summer and the lightest, most flexible boots the rest of the year. Only when there is snow on the hills do I use medium weight boots. Different makers classify boots differently but I regard boots up to 2½lb (1.1kg) as light, between 2½ and 3½lb (1.1 and 1.6kg) as medium, and above 3½lb (1.6kg) as heavyweight. Shoes should weigh 2lb (900g) or less.

ANKLE SUPPORT

The main argument in favour of heavy footwear and for wearing boots rather than shoes is that they provide ankle protection. While boots with stiff high ankle cuffs do provide ankle support most walking boots have low, soft cuffs that give little if any support. This does not matter, as what is required is for the foot to be centred over the sole of the shoe. This is done by a solid piece of material, usually synthetic, called a heel counter that cups the heel and keeps the ankle in place and stops it twisting from side to side. I once tried a pair of fairly high leather boots without heel counters and found my ankles turning over constantly. As good off-road running shoes, trail shoes and even the best sports sandals have heel cups you do not need boots for ankle support.

Regular walkers usually have strong ankles – even if they deny it! Strengthening exercises can be done if you feel your ankles are weak but the best way to strengthen them is by walking over rough ground. Hillwalking is ideal for this.

The only time boots with ankle support are useful, though not essential, is on steep snow when you may need to kick into the slope with the edges of your boots. Boots with stiff ankles and soles can give support in this situation.

FLEXIBILITY

Feet are wonderfully supple and complex, able to adapt to the roughest of terrain. In summer I sometimes walk barefoot across grassy ground or over boulders, revelling in being able to feel the texture of the vegetation or the stones and marvelling at the security given by instantly knowing what is under my feet. Once you constrict your feet inside shoes or boots they are less able to move naturally. The stiffer the sole the more your feet are held in one position and the more energy is wasted trying to make the boots flex with your feet. I think that stiff soled boots are also more likely to lead to injury as you cannot easily adapt to rough terrain; instead you are forced into placing your feet the same way with each step, leading to repetitive shocks that are transmitted to your ankles, knees and hips, especially on steep descents. With flexible footwear you can place the whole of your foot on the ground and avoid the jarring caused by walking downhill on your heels. This also gives greater stability.

For these reasons I prefer very flexible footwear and avoid shoes and boots with shanks or stiff midsoles unless I am venturing on steep, icy terrain where I might need to use crampons. There is an idea that stiff soles protect the sole of the foot against stones and rocks. They may indeed do so but a better way is by having thick shock-absorbing but flexible midsoles that will also cushion the feet when walking long distances on hard surfaces. Such midsoles may be EVA, polyurethane or rubber and may be injected into the sole or inserted in the form of wedges. I always look for them as they really add to the comfort of footwear.

DESIGN FEATURES

Materials

Leather is the traditional material for footwear and the most durable. One-piece leather boots are very long lasting as there are no seams to split. Fabric boots and shoes, usually reinforced with suede or leather in places, are usually lighter and more flexible and so more comfortable to wear. They are also cooler in warm weather. Some are now suitable for winter walking and crampons can be fitted to them, though most boots designed for walking on snow and ice are still made from leather. Plastic is used for mountaineering boots, a category only of interest to those walkers who want to tackle easy winter climbs.

Shoes do not usually have linings. In boots the linings are usually of a non-absorbent, quick drying synthetic material though some models still have leather linings. Most boots have padding behind the lining, at least on the tongue and at the ankles. Too much padding makes a boot very warm, which might be fine in midwinter but is one reason many people find their boots causing blisters and soft feet in summer. I prefer to have the minimum amount of padding.

An increasing number of boots and even some shoes have linings made from a waterproof breathable fabric. These make the boots fully waterproof, at least when new, though in my experience they last only a few weeks before they start to leak. They also make boots hotter and slower drying.

Construction

Most footwear is made by heat bonding the uppers to the soles with glue. Only the heavier more traditional boots have welt-sewn construction with visible lines of stitching where the upper has been sewn to the midsole. And even with these boots the outsole will be glued on. Some footwear does have

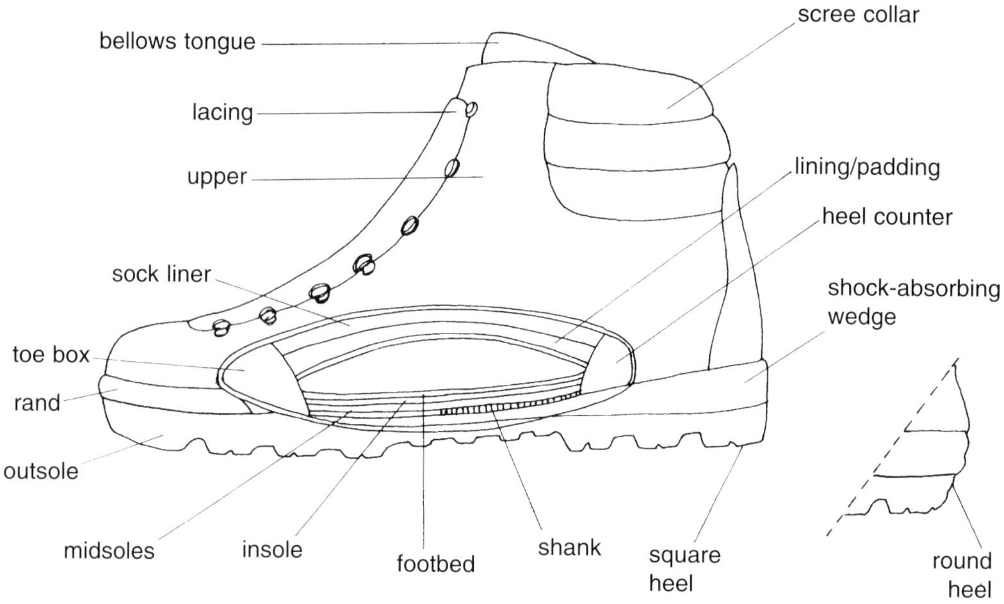

A lightweight boot.

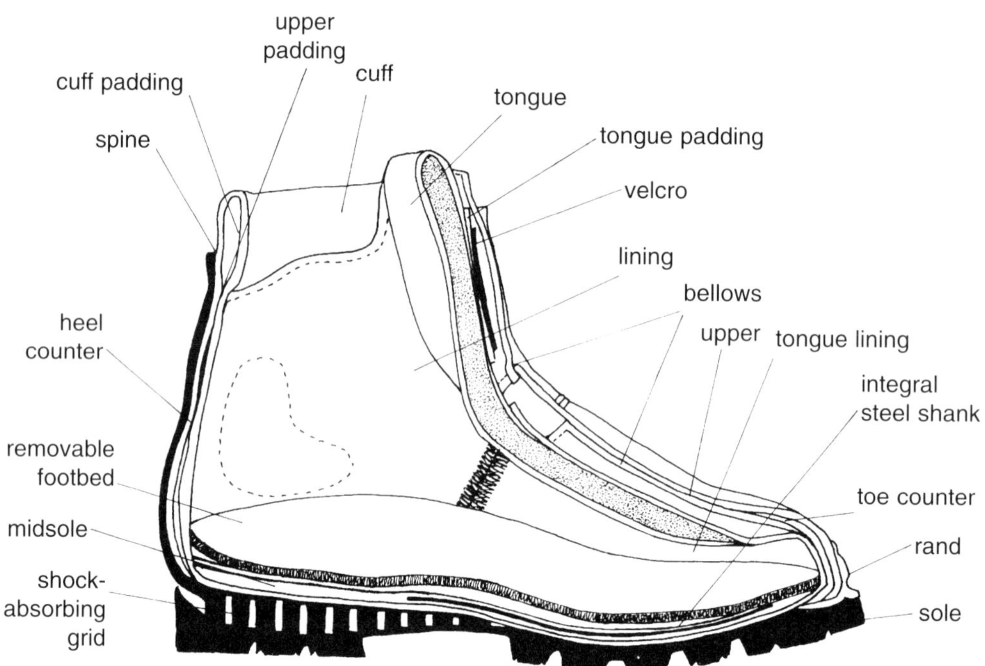

A winter mountain boot.

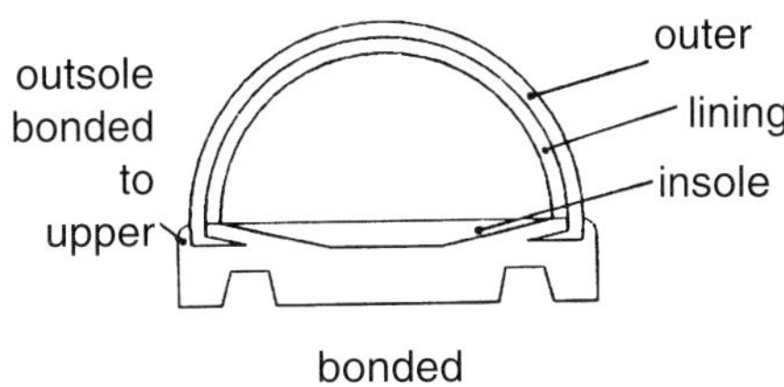

bonded

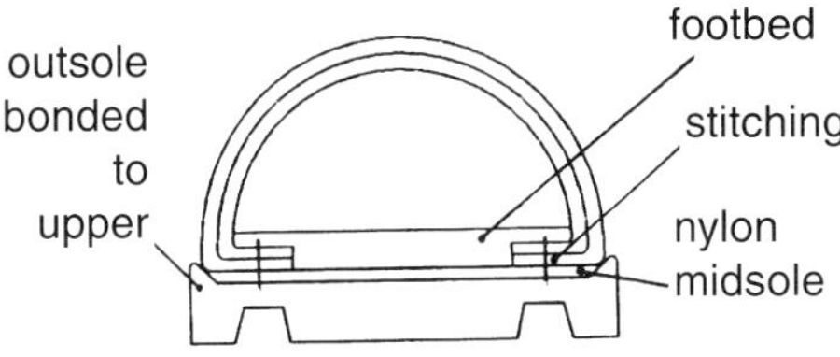

modified Blake (littleway) stitched

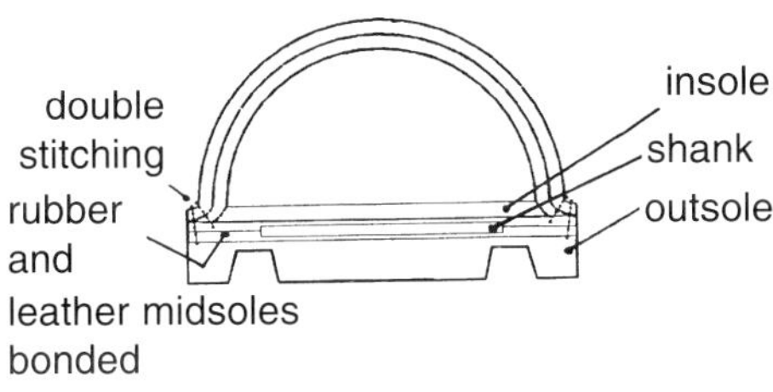

Norwegian welt stitched

Methods of boot construction.

stitching inside where the uppers are turned in and stitched to the midsole. This is called Blake-sewn construction.

All footwear is made on a last – a lump of material roughly shaped like a human foot. This determines the shape of the boot or shoe. Traditional lasts have flat bottoms; more modern sprung or anatomic lasts have curved soles that follow the shape of the foot as it bends when you push off it at the end of a step. Footwear made on a sprung last has a curved sole – sometimes called a rocker sole – that really does match the forward roll of your foot, making walking less tiring.

Insoles, Midsoles and Outsoles

Removable footbeds or insoles help support the foot inside the boot and are more comfortable than flat soles. Most boots have them. They can be taken out for drying when wet and replaced when worn out. I sometimes remove mine towards the end of long, hot days if my feet are starting to feel swollen and cramped in my shoes. Changing to thinner or thicker footbeds can also be done to adjust the fit of footwear. If your boots or shoes are lacking in cushioning and you regularly get sore feet you could try footbeds made from a shock absorbing material as these do add to comfort. Unfortunately many of these also add weight and, often, heat. The best I have found are made from a soft, flexible rubber-like material called Poron 4000. Eagle Rock is one brand. These footbeds cushion well but unlike similar insoles are not hot when the weather is warm as the material is fairly breathable.

Below the footbed lie the midsoles. Most boots have at least two of these, shoes often just one. In boots a thin plastic or nylon midsole usually lies under the footbed to add stiffness. These midsoles are graded to give the same stiffness in different sizes of the same boot. They are also available in different grades of stiffness from very flexible midsoles for lightweight boots through to almost rigid ones for winter climbing boots. Sometimes this midsole is bonded directly to the outsole. Boots of this construction can be very hard underfoot due to the lack of cushioning. As said above, the best footwear has midsoles made from thick shock absorbing materials. In boots these may lie between the nylon midsole and the outsole. In shoes they are usually directly under the lining. In an increasing number of designs the outsole and the cushioning midsole come as a unit with a rand running round the sides of the footwear to cradle the foot and protect against scuffing.

Nylon or steel shanks are still found in some boots. Depending on their length these give half, three-quarters or full length stiffness. While needed in boots designed for prolonged crampon use or Nordic mountain skiing, shanks are not required for hillwalking. If you do want a degree of thickness a graded nylon or plastic midsole is better as it flexes along its length rather than making part of the sole rigid and leaving the rest soft.

The number of sole patterns available is now legion. Most seem to work well. For scrambling, soles made from sticky or high-grip rubber work very well. Most boots and shoes can be resoled and for safety this should be done before the soles wear too much. How long soles last depends on the thickness

of the tread, the type of rubber used and the terrain you walk on. Road walking wears down soles fastest – soft, boggy ground slowest. Even the thinnest, softest sole should last 500 miles (800km) – many will be good for 800 to 1000 miles (1300 to 1600km).

Tongues

The tongue is not something people think much about when choosing footwear but it is something that is often cursed when problems occur. A good tongue should stay in place in the centre of your upper foot and not slip to one side. If it is sewn in at the edges, which is useful as it aids water resistance, the material should fold neatly when you tighten the laces.

Where tongues cause problems is usually at the base where they are sewn to the main uppers. The stitching here can rub every time you bend your foot,

A selection of boot soles.

causing sore spots and blisters. When buying boots you can check for this by putting your hand in the boots and feeling what the finish under the tongue is like at the base and also by bending your feet in the boots and looking for pressure at that point.

Lacing

A combination of D rings and hooks is the standard fastening on most boots. Some shoes have these too though many still use eyelets. I prefer to have several rows of hooks as these can be easily opened for putting on and taking off footwear. D rings are more awkward to use. A new idea from Asolo is mini pulleys through which the laces run. I have not used these in the hills but I have tried a pair of boots with them on and I did like the way the boots were held snugly and evenly round my feet and the ease with which the tension could be minutely adjusted.

With any system you can vary the tightness by adjusting the laces. With boots that have stiff ankles some people do not put the laces through the top hooks as this gives more ankle freedom. They can always be used when you need more ankle support for crampon use.

Laces are usually made from flat or round nylon or polyester and these days rarely break so I no longer carry spares. Round laces last a bit longer than flat laces but are slightly more likely to work loose. Overall there is little to choose between them.

Cuffs

Most lightweight walking boots have soft rolls of padded material at the ankle or soft padding inside the leather or fabric outer. These cuffs give little support but do help in keeping out small stones and dirt when laced up tightly. If you want some ankle support you need a stiffer cuff made from thicker leather or with some form of reinforcement built in

TYPES OF FOOTWEAR

The correct choice of footwear depends on the season and the ground conditions. Too many walkers buy boots designed for Himalayan peaks rather than Pennine peat bogs. Stiff soled climbing boots with rigid ankles are excellent for balancing on tiny rock edges or front-pointing up vertical ice. They are not suitable for walking.

In warm weather sports sandals are excellent, making hot, sweaty, aching feet a thing of the past. I have worn sandals for many summer walks including scrambles like the Carn Mor Dearg arête on Ben Nevis and also for trekking in the Himalayas and backpacking in the Rocky Mountains and the Grand Canyon. Good sandals have deep treads, well-cushioned midsoles, heel straps that hold the ankle firmly in place and raised or rimmed edges that prevent the toes slipping forward and bruising on rocks. There is an increasing number of makes.

Perhaps the best summer footwear is the off-road running or fell running shoe. They are very lightweight, flexible and cool with thick shock absorbing soles and deep treads, and are suitable for all types of terrain other than steep snow and ice. I have frequently walked long distances in running shoes, often with heavy backpacking loads. Beware of road running shoes, as these often have shallow treads that will not grip on slippery terrain and wide soft midsoles that can cause the feet to rock alarmingly from side to side on rough ground.

Sports sandals are a good choice for hot weather walking.

Very similar, though slightly heavier, are trail shoes. These sometimes have stiffened toes, so you can kick the occasional rock without hurting yourself, rands round the edge that help protect against side impact from stones and slightly heavier and thicker soles. Most offer no real advantages over running shoes but some have the same sticky rubber as is used for rock climbing shoes. These are superb for scrambling as the grip is astonishing.

Shoes do have one big disadvantage: they are not at all waterproof. In warm weather this is not a problem as wet feet do not really matter as long as you can keep them dry overnight. I would rather have cool, wet feet than hot sweaty feet. Even in cold weather wool socks changed regularly will keep your feet warm while moving. Having said that, there does come a point when your feet start to become painfully cold. This is where lightweight leather or fabric boots are useful and I usually wear these between October and May. They should weigh no more than 2½lb (1.1kg) and have thick cushioning midsoles and soft ankles cut low at the back to avoid pressure on the Achilles tendon. Such boots will keep your feet drier for longer than running shoes, much longer if they have waterproof or breathable linings that have not yet been punctured or torn, although a couple of days

Lightweight fabric boots are suitable for three season use.

Mediumweight fabric boots with a waterproof/ breathable lining suitable for use in wet and cold weather.

Lightweight leather boots can be used year round but are best suited to cool weather walking.

in really wet weather will have them sodden unless you wear gaiters as well. When wet they take longer to dry than running shoes. There are many models but do check the weight – some makers have funny ideas as to what is a lightweight boot.

Finally if steep hard snow or ice means crampons may be needed I wear medium weight boots with relatively stiff soles. Again I look for cushioning midsoles but this time for higher, stiffer ankles as these help when using crampons on steep ground. You can always loosen the laces at the ankle when walking on flat terrain.

Midweight boots suitable for use with flexible crampons.

Heavyweight winter mountain boots suitable for prolonged crampon use.

THE FIT

Whatever weight or style of footwear you choose a good fit is crucial. Ill-fitting footwear can cause endless problems no matter how technical the features or sophisticated the design. Shoes and lightweight boots are more forgiving than heavy boots but I can tell you from painful experience that badly fitting ones can still make a mess of your feet.

It is worth taking a long time fitting new footwear. As feet swell during the day it is best to try on footwear late in the afternoon, preferably after several hours of walking, even if it is only on a shopping trip. Most stores can provide thick socks for you to wear when trying boots but it is better if you take your own.

Many outdoor shops now have foot measuring devices. These measure width as well as length and can really help in getting a good fit so it is worth asking if a store has one.

If you cannot have your feet measured start by trying on boots in your normal shoe size. The same size can differ between makes so your usual size is only a guide. Width matters too. As only a few boots come in different widths you may have to try on several pairs to find the right one for you. If your toes feel pinched the boots are too narrow; if your foot can slide from side to side they are too wide. Both can lead to blisters and sore feet. Where the boots are widest matters too. Many people, myself included, have long insteps that mean the widest part of their foot is just behind the toes. But many boots are widest further back, narrowing at the toes. If your feet are not measured you just have to try on a series of boots until one feels right.

A good fit should be snug but not too tight. With the boots unlaced you should be able to slide a finger down the back when your foot is pushed towards the toe. If you cannot the boots are too short and you will suffer sore toes, especially on descents. If more than one finger fits down the back the boots are too long and your heel will probably move in them, causing blisters, and your foot will slide about, leading to a feeling of instability.

Once you have approximately the right length and width the boots can be laced up. Once this is done there should be very little heel movement up and down or side to side – 1/4in (6mm) at most. If there is any more movement blisters are likely. The tension of the laces can be varied to achieve a firm but not too tight fit across the top of the foot and around the ankle. If you cannot wriggle your toes easily the boots are too tight. You should also be able to put all your weight on one foot without it feeling under pressure across the instep.

Different thicknesses of footbeds and socks can help if boots do not fit correctly and may be necessary for one foot if your feet are very different in size (everybody's differ to some degree). You should always fit your larger foot, because you can pad out the other boot or shoe if necessary, but there is nothing you can do for a boot that is too small.

If you have real problems you could have boots made for you. This can be a very expensive option but Altberg offer a reasonably priced service (see Useful Addresses section).

BREAKING IN

Traditionally boots needed many days of wear before they felt comfortable or some drastic treatment such as filling them with water and walking them dry. Modern boots are softer, lighter and more foot-shaped and do not need much if any breaking in. If you often get blisters or sore feet or have not done much walking for a while it is probably advisable to do a few short walks in any new footwear before setting off on a long tough hike. The heavier and stiffer your footwear the more breaking in it will require.

CARE

Footwear will last longer if looked after properly. This means rinsing off mud after use and keeping leather supple and water resistant by treating it with a waterproofing wax. Paint or spray proofing treatments are available for fabric boots too. I particulary recommend Nikwax's Aqueous Leather waterproofing as it is unique in that it can be applied when footwear is wet.

Wet boots should be dried slowly,

whatever the material. Too much heat can dry out leather and suede too much so it cracks and may also damage the glues that hold the midsoles and outsoles on. Stuffing footwear with newspaper and leaving it in a warm room is best. Footbeds should be removed and dried separately. Do not put footwear too near heaters or fires of any kind. Huts, hostels and hotels in hillwalking areas often have drying rooms for wet footwear and clothing. These are usually very hot so if you do put your footwear in them it is best to take it out before it is completely dry to avoid any damage. I keep my footwear out of such places unless it is dripping with water.

SOCKS

While most people select their footwear carefully, knowing that a badly fitting pair could mean sore and blistered feet, not many pay such attention to their choice of socks. Yet, although obviously less crucial to comfort than your footwear, socks do make a difference and some types perform and last better than others.

Wool

Socks have four functions. These are to help cushion your feet from the hard ground, to absorb the moisture given off by your feet and carry it away from your skin, to minimize friction from your footwear and to insulate your feet from the cold and, to a lesser extent, heat. Wool performs these functions better than anything else and is still unequalled for socks. Some synthetics may work well at one or more functions but none will do all four like wool. Cotton does all of them very badly and should be avoided for walking socks. In particular it soaks up water and then

takes ages to dry, chilling your feet in the process.

Wool is not the most durable material, especially when constantly rubbed, so socks usually have nylon added to reinforce the toes and heel. This is the accepted view and one I followed until 1990 when I used good quality all-wool socks on a 1000 mile (1600km) walk through Canada's Yukon Territory. These proved harder wearing than any other socks I have ever had, making me wonder why nylon is added to most wool socks. I suspect the reason is the quality of the wool. The best wool blend socks use wicking synthetics such as polypropylene rather than plain nylon, which does not transmit moisture very well. For that reason I would avoid socks with less than 50 per cent wool if the rest is just nylon.

Construction

There are three styles of thick sock. The most common is the loopstitch construction where the inside of the sock is made up of soft, fluffy terry towelling type loops. These are very comfortable, especially when new, and cushion well. They need to be washed regularly if they are to stay so, preferably after every day's wear. This is what day walkers normally do anyway but it is not so easy for backpackers or those on hut to hut tours who may need to wear the same pair of socks for several days in a row. Then loopstitch socks can matt down to a hard, sweaty mass, especially under the soles. Like this they do not provide much warmth and they are uncomfortable to wear. Restoring the fluffy loops is just about impossible whatever washing powder or conditioner you use so I no longer wear loopstitch socks on long trips.

The second type of sock is the old

fashioned knitted Ragg wool one. These provide a bit less cushioning than loopstitch models when new and do not feel quite so luxurious. They can be worn for days on end without the performance declining and they soften up well when washed.

Both Ragg wool and loopstitch wool socks have been around for a long time, but have now been joined by a more complex design. These socks come in a bewildering array of styles, each designed for a particular activity.

The main difference between these designs and traditional socks is in the use of different densities and different materials over different parts of the foot to give extra shock protection and warmth where required and to maximize the wicking away of moisture. Most of these special socks are a blend of wool and wicking synthetics. Some are 100 per cent synthetic, which is good for those who are allergic to wool.

A useful feature found on many socks is a rib-knit leg. Wool and some wicking synthetics carry moisture upwards along their fibres from inside the boot to outside where it can evaporate. Ribbing is said to help this process.

The best socks I have found are Extremities Mountain Toesters, which are made from 49 per cent Merino wool, 49 per cent texturized polypropylene and 2 per cent Lycra, with a triple density loopstitch construction. The lower part of the sock, including the toe and the rear of the ankle, is very thick for warmth and impact protection, the top of the foot and the calf is less thick while the upper rear of the sock is relatively thin for minimum bulk. The cuff is ribbed. They are the warmest, hardest wearing cold weather socks I have ever worn and have kept my feet warm in temperatures down to -27°C (-17°F). Mine have been worn without being washed for eight days at a time and they have stayed warm and comfortable. No other socks I know will do this.

In warm weather I prefer thinner socks. I forego wool in favour of wicking synthetics as thin wool socks just do not last. There are quite a few so-called liner socks around that work well in running shoes. Slightly warmer and thicker are double layer socks – as the name suggests, these are really two socks sewn together at the toe and cuff. There are a number of makes, some 100 per cent synthetic, others a wool and nylon blend. The idea is the same as wearing two pairs of socks: to reduce friction between your feet and your footwear. I have found them surprisingly warm even when damp, though not adequate on their own for the coldest winter weather. They are cool enough for warm weather use. The comfort is very good and they are ideal for wearing with running shoes, trail shoes and lightweight boots. They remove moisture quickly, keeping the feet dry in warm weather. They are also very light – about 2oz (55g) per pair – and thus excellent for carrying as spares.

Length

Socks come in various lengths. If you wear breeches then knee-length socks are essential. Calf-length socks are good for use with boots if you wear shorts or long trousers. I like to turn the tops of my socks over my boots when wearing shorts as this keeps debris out. The shortest ankle high socks are fine with shoes but tend to work down inside boots.

How Many Pairs?

When heavy boots were standard wear year round wearing two pairs of thick socks at a time was recommended, presumably to minimize rubbing from the stiff leather. Today this is no longer necessary unless your boots are slightly too big. My feet are on the wide side so I have always worn only one pair of socks.

A compromise is to wear one thick pair and one very thin inner pair, usually made from a wicking synthetic material though there are silk versions available. I have tried both polypropylene and silk liner socks under thicker pairs. For me they made no difference whatsoever to how comfortable, warm or dry my feet felt but some walkers do find liner socks worthwhile.

Keeping Your Feet Dry

Where liner socks come in is in very wet conditions where keeping water out of your footwear is impossible. If it is cool enough for wet feet to be a problem or you are worried about blisters you can put plastic bags (bread bags will do) over your liner socks, then your thick socks and finally, if you have them, another set of plastic bags. If you have only two plastic bags you will have to accept wet outer socks. To keep water out of the plastic bags it is best to seal the tops with elastic bands. What wearing plastic bags does is create a vapour barrier that keeps your feet warm and dry.

There are socks made from waterproof or breathable fabrics available and these do work, at least when new. Most are quite expensive, though, and not that durable. The best are called SealSkinz and are made from a laminate of a nylon outer, a waterproof breathable membrane and a Coolmax, or, for cold weather, Thermax wicking inner. Unlike most waterproof socks they are cut like a proper sock and designed to be worn next to the skin or over a thin liner sock. I have used them in quite cold, wet conditions and found them warm and waterproof with only a trace of dampness inside at the end of a long day. They are not as comfortable or as cushioning as thick wool-based socks but if wet feet are a concern they are certainly worth considering.

Care

Socks should be washed regularly. Turning them inside out before you do so helps restore the inner fluffiness, which is the bit that matters. Fabric conditioners also make a big difference to the softness and I always use one.

Eventually all socks develop holes. Often the fibres clump together to form hard knots in places too. From experience I know that both of these cause blisters and sore spots. Darning holes, unfortunately, only produces rough edges that also rub the feet and so is not worth doing unless you want to wear old walking socks for everyday wear.

3 Clothing for the Hills

On wet days I put on one of two pairs of skin-thin bits of protective clothing, made of artificial fibre, that were supposed to be waterproof. They gradually leaked. (John Hillaby, Journey Through Britain)

Staying as warm and dry as possible is very important for safe and enjoyable hillwalking. As the weather can change rapidly and you can encounter warm sunshine and cold rain within hours, sometimes even minutes, of each other clothing has to be adaptable. This means dressing in layers rather than in one thick jacket. In this layer system each layer plays a different role. The layer against your skin is known as the inner or base layer. It is also often called thermal underwear – though this is misleading as its main purpose is to remove moisture from your skin as quickly as possible, a process known as wicking.

The middle layer consists of the garments that keep you warm such as wool pullovers, fleece jackets and down vests. The outer or shell layer must keep out wind, rain and snow and is the most important layer. If it fails your other layers will not work well. The second most important layer is the one next to your skin so it is in warmwear that compromises can be made. Soft fluffy fleece tops may be very comfortable but an old woollen sweater will still keep you warm if worn between a wicking base layer and a good waterproof shell. Wear a cotton T-shirt and a leaky shell and your fleece will not seem so good.

Dressed for a cold, windy day. The walker is wearing gaiters, thick windproof breeches, a waterproof/breathable jacket and pile lined windproof mitts. Under these garments she is wearing a thick base layer and a mediumweight fleece jacket with thin liner gloves on her hands and a bob hat under her jacket hood. In her rucksack she has a down jacket, overtrousers, spare hat, gloves and socks.

BASE LAYERS

Clothing worn next to the skin should transport or wick away body moisture – whether liquid sweat or the invisible perspiration vapour we give off all the time – as quickly as possible. By doing so it helps keep the wearer warm and comfortable. Modern synthetic fabrics are very efficient at doing this. As well as transporting moisture away they also dry very quickly if they do become soaked. Natural alternatives that also work well are silk and wool but not cotton, which absorbs moisture, feels wet and cold next to the skin and takes ages to dry. Except in hot summer weather, cotton should never be worn next to the skin.

Fabrics

There are several different synthetic base layer fabrics available and to make choosing one even more difficult each comes in a different thickness. Generally, lightweight fabrics transport moisture most quickly and are excellent for very energetic pursuits and warm weather as well as being suitable for wearing under other layers in the cold and when less active. Mid-weight fabrics are slightly warmer with tighter weaves and are good for year round use. The heaviest fabrics, often called expedition weight, are quite warm and are designed for cold weather use. Combinations of different weight garments can cope with widely differing temperatures. I often wear expedition weight garments over light or mid-weight ones in winter, a combination that, under a windproof outer shell, copes with most conditions while I am on the move.

Polypropylene is the original wicking thermal fabric. The latest weaves wick as well as anything else, do not stink like the original stuff did and can be washed at far higher temperatures than any other synthetic.

Polyester is the most common base layer material, available in a number of different types. In itself polyester does not wick moisture as it is hydrophobic: it pushes water away. There are two ways of making it wick moisture. One, as in Malden Mills' Polartec 100, used by many makers, and Capilene, exclusive to Patagonia, is to treat it chemically so it wicks efficiently. This treatment also means it does not easily pick up body odours. I have found treated polyester comfortable to wear and quite efficient though the treatment does eventually wear off. You can tell that has happened when you start to feel sticky in a garment as it traps moisture against the skin.

Other polyesters such as Thermax, Thermastat, Thermal Dynamics, Dryflow and Coolmax are structurally altered so they wick moisture, and some also have hollow fibres to trap warmth. In theory the wicking ability of these should last the life of the garment as it cannot wear off. Certainly I have never known one of these garments to cease working.

All the above fabrics come in various weights. Only available in expedition weights are Polartec PowerStretch, which is really a lightweight pile, and Paramo's Parameta S. Both of these have soft, brushed inners which help speed the movement of moisture away from the skin and smooth outers that spread the moisture for rapid evaporation and also keep off breezes.

Chlorofibre, a type of PVC, is used in Damart thermal underwear. It is warm and wicks well but needs great care as it shrinks at the slightest hint of heat. Easier to look after is Rhovyl/Modal, a combination of Chlorofibre and Modal (a natural material) in a 70/30 mix. It is a very soft mid-weight material with the most pleasant feel of any of the base layer fabrics. It works well too.

Viloft is a 50/50 polyester and viscose mid-weight fabric. The high proportion of viscose, a natural material, makes Viloft more absorbent than other fabrics, enabling it to cope with large amounts of sweat and I have found it wicks well. The viscose also makes this a pleasant soft fabric to wear. It is slower drying than 100 per cent synthetic fabrics, though.

Tactel nylon is usually used as an outerwear fabric, but is used by Sub Zero in two different weights for base layer garments. The expedition weight is extremely comfortable and quick drying and can be worn for long periods without it smelling.

Moisture Transfer

All these fabrics wick moisture away from the skin rapidly enough to keep me dry most of the time and go on doing this for several days without being washed. In really humid conditions and when working really hard some sweat is retained in the fabrics. However, all the materials dry very quickly and any cold, clammy feeling does not last long.

For hillwalking I do not think there is much to choose between the different fabrics despite the various graphs put out by makers, each showing their fabric performing best. The thinnest weaves and lightest garments work best in warm weather, mid-weight and expedition weight versions being too hot.

Once the temperature drops, though, the heavier fabrics work very well. Expedition weight fabrics, especially Powerstretch and Parameta S, wick moisture away quickly even when working hard and dry very quickly when damp. Except in warm weather these are now my favourite fabrics for wearing next to the skin.

Design

Over the years I have developed a strong preference for garments with stud fastened or zip up collars. They are comfortable in a much wider range of temperatures than simple crew or polo neck designs as they can be ventilated easily, while in cold weather you can seal in heat at the neck, a very efficient way of retaining warmth. If you do start to overheat you can cool down quickly by opening the collar. In summer I prefer crew neck designs that can be opened at the neck, again for ventilation. I also like short sleeved tops when it's warm as they make good T-shirts, but few are available with opening necks.

Fit is also important. Sizes vary greatly between makes so do not take stated sizes for granted. I have small, medium and large sizes that all fit me! If you intend wearing mid or expedition weight garments over lightweight clothes make sure they are roomy enough. Length is important too – it is not conducive to comfort or staying warm if your shirt pulls out of your trousers every time you stretch or bend – so check the garment carefully if you have a long back.

WARMWEAR

How much warmwear you need depends on the time of year and the weather. A spare garment should always be carried in the rucksack for wearing at rest stops and in case of emergencies. In summer I rarely wear a

warm top at all when moving, even in wind and rain, and so usually just carry one lightweight sweater in the rucksack. Once the days shorten and temperatures start to drop I add another thicker top, knowing that I may well wear the thinner one to walk in at times.

My preference is for pile and fleece tops as these fabrics are very warm for the weight, hard wearing, quick drying and very comfortable. Many people like wool sweaters and shirts, and it is really a personal choice. Avoid cotton sweatshirts as these are heavy and can soak up a lot of moisture. They then weigh even more and take ages to dry.

Designs are also personal. Shirts, sweaters and jackets are all available in all fabrics. High collars are useful in cold weather and a few pockets are handy for odds and ends and to stick your hands in when they are cold but really any design will do.

Whatever the fabric or design the thickness determines the warmth. The old advice that several thin layers are better than one thick one still holds true. Fleece and pile come in several weights

as do wool sweaters. The thickest may be fine for pulling on at rest stops in winter but are usually too warm to walk in most of the time. The thinner weights are more versatile. I usually carry a thin fleece top in summer and add a medium weight one in autumn, winter and spring plus a down top (see below) in severe cold.

The choice in fleece and pile clothing is bewildering with a myriad makers offering an ever-changing array of brightly coloured garments. There is not that much difference between the different types of fleece, however. The least expensive non-branded fleeces are not quite as durable as the more expensive makes but they are just as warm. Most fleeces come in a range of weights and this is where the real difference lies. Obviously the thicker the fleece, the warmer it is but also the heavier and bulkier.

There is one option in fleece worth pointing out. Most fleece is made from polyester, itself derived from petroleum oil. An increasing amount of the polyester used for fleece is recycled from used soft drinks bottles. I have a recycled fleece jacket and it is impossible to tell the difference between it and one made from 'new' fleece. As with other recycled products recycled fleece is far more environmentally friendly than that made from virgin fleece. The quantity of recycled fleece in a garment can vary from 50 to 100 per cent. Whatever the amount, it is worth looking out for.

Most midwear fabrics are not windproof as they are designed to be worn under shell garments in stormy weather. But windproof fleece does exist. This may simply be a fleece top with a windproof shell or lining or, more sophisticated, a garment consisting of two layers of thin fleece with a very thin windproof membrane stuck between the two. Both sorts are a compromise between a shell and a midwear garment and can be worn as the outer layer in all but the most severe weather. They are not as versatile as non-windproof midwear garments, and for most of the year I prefer one of the latter. In really cold weather windproof midwear does have a place as you can pull it on over your shell garment without worrying about the wind cutting through it. Some windproof warmwear is designed to function without need of a shell even in blizzards (see 'Replacing the layer system' below).

Down Clothing

For real cold the best clothing is filled with down. When I began walking a down top was a luxury item, far more expensive than any other garment. This is no longer so and a lightweight down top suitable for UK winters costs no more than a fleece jacket and less than most breathable waterproofs. Nothing comes close to down for warmth. Even the lightest down top is warmer than the heaviest fleece. Down is low in bulk too and takes up little room in the rucksack.

Down works best in the dry cold of midwinter, although it is suitable in any chilly weather as long as it is kept dry. Many down garments now come with breathable weather resistant outers but they are not fully waterproof as the seams cannot be taped. Most also come with their own stuffsacks, but these are rarely made from waterproof fabric. I carry my down top in a waterproof stuffsack with taped seams.

Except in the most bitterly cold weather down tops are too warm to wear when walking unless you really feel the cold. At rest stops they are ideal and they are also a good safety item to have in case of an unplanned night out.

I would suggest getting a down top in a size large enough for it to be worn over your waterproof jacket. That way you do not have to go through the heat-losing, time-consuming hassle of removing your outer jacket, putting on your warmwear and putting your outer jacket back on whenever you stop and then reversing the procedure when you set off. Down clothing is fairly windproof and will repel snow and wet mist. It needs protecting only in heavy rain and if it is raining it is probably too warm for down anyway.

For hillwalkers the simplest down garments are best as these are the lightest and lowest in bulk. Jackets designed for Himalayan mountaineering are heavy and bulky. Features to look for are hand-warmer pockets, adjustable cuffs and hems and high collars. Hoods are not usually found on the lightest garments but this is not a problem. A warm hat is more versatile.

Three styles of down top are available: vests, pullovers and jackets. The first are the lightest and lowest in bulk, ideal for carrying as extra warmwear when you are not sure how cold it will be. They are easy to pull on over a waterproof too. The advantage of pullovers is that they are usually slightly lighter than jackets and the fit is often better. They are not as versatile, and they are the most awkward design to put on over a waterproof.

LEGWEAR

Long Trousers

For decades hillwalkers wore wool breeches in cold weather and cotton moleskin or whipcord breeches in summer. Those natural fabrics were displaced in the 1980s by brushed stretch nylon and polycotton. These have been joined in recent years by synthetic microfibre fabrics.

For several years now I have worn microfibre trousers year round and have found them far superior to polycotton. Mostly I wear them on their own but in cold weather I put on long johns underneath, a combination I have found excellent for winter hillwalking and for ski touring in strong winds and temperatures well below freezing. When I do not wear them I carry long johns in winter just in case I need them. Long trousers lined with wicking synthetic materials are very warm and excellent for winter use but cannot be split for warmer weather walking.

Microfibres are extremely fine fibres, usually of nylon or polyester. The yarn fabrics are made from is labelled according to the weight in grams of a 10,000m length, which is known as the decitex, and the number of filaments required to make this decitex: 167f30 polyester describes a yarn of which 10,000m would weigh 167 grams and be made up of 30 filaments. The decitex

per filament is then 167 divided by 30, which is 5.57. A microfibre is a fibre with a decitex per filament of one or less: 10,000m of filament will weigh no more than one gram.

Microfibre fabrics are much softer and more pleasant to handle than standard synthetics, making them suitable for next to the skin wear. As they are less absorbent, quicker drying and far more durable than cotton or polycotton they are also ideal for outerwear. Microfibres are also windproof and very water resistant. While all microfibre fabrics are lightweight they are not all the same. There is some variation in weight and thickness. Heavier fabrics are warmer, more durable and more wind resistant than lighter fabrics but in hot weather can be slightly clammy. In those conditions shorts are better than long trousers anyway.

Designs

Breeches are still available but fast disappearing. Most of those in use were bought some time ago as few clothing ranges feature them now. Brushed stretchy polyester or nylon track suit style trousers are popular with many walkers but I have never liked them as they are not windproof and do not usually have many pockets. They are good for scrambling as they move easily with you. Microfibres and polycotton are windproof and come in more conventional trouser designs with as many pockets as you want. As some styles are aimed more at the high street than the hill trying pairs on is a good idea. For hill use trousers should be fairly loose fitting so you can move easily in them. In particular check that they do not bind above the knee when you take high steps.

Waterproof or breathable trousers

A summer walking outfit: sunhat, wicking tee-shirt, shorts.

and salopettes are now so comfortable that in cold weather I wear a pair of Paramo ones as my standard legwear. They are warm enough in most cold conditions, though on one New Year trip in Norway when daytime temperatures rarely rose above -20°C (-4°F) and were often below -25°C (-13°F) I wore Powerstretch pile tights under them.

Shorts

In warm weather shorts are far preferable to long trousers, giving greater freedom of movement as well as being much cooler. I wear them at every opportunity. They are useless against biting insects, of course, and you can quickly get cold in them in rain or wind so long trousers should always be car-ried in the rucksack. Any shorts will do, but as with long trousers they should not impede leg movements. I like shorts with built in briefs as these are more comfortable when you pull long trousers over them as the wind gets up or the midges emerge.

UNDERWEAR

After years of wearing standard department store underpants made from cotton or cotton and synthetic blends, a few years ago I tried some Tactel nylon briefs and found them far more comfortable as they wicked sweat away and dried quickly when I sat on wet ground without my overtrousers. Gone was the cold, clammy feeling I had become used to, and I will not go back to cotton underpants.

For the same reason bras made of synthetic materials, especially wicking ones, would be better than cotton. I am told that sports bras are the most comfortable for hillwalking.

WATERPROOFS

The choice in waterproofs is vast, though some designs seem to be intended more for high street than hill use while others are aimed at Himalayan mountaineers. Most will perform adequately for hillwalking. Many are very expensive but it is not necessary to spend a small fortune to get a good quality garment.

Both design and materials matter so both should be considered when selecting rainwear. The first is useless if the latter fails so the right material is crucial.

Materials

Luckily making fabrics waterproof is not difficult and there are many waterproof materials. The most basic and least expensive are made from polyurethane coated nylon. The biggest problem with such fabrics is that body moisture cannot escape and therefore condenses on the inside of the garment and then soaks back into your inner layers. You can get very wet inside a basic polyurethane garment but it is a warm wetness, at least while you are moving, and therefore preferable to the cold wet of rain.

These days most waterproofs are made from 'breathable' fabrics. These are materials that keep rain out but allow moisture vapour to escape. There are two main ways they can do this. In microporous fabrics there are millions of tiny holes that are too small for rain drops to enter but that allow vapour to pass through. Hydrophilic fabrics are a bit more complex. In these, chains of moisture loving molecules are built into the fabric and vapour is conducted along these to the outside of the fabric. Because the material is solid rain cannot penetrate it. Both types can let only vapour through, not liquids such as sweat. The waterproof layer itself may be in the form of a thin membrane that is laminated (glued) onto a fabric or a coating that is painted on as a liquid and then dries. Gore-Tex, Sympatex, Permatex and Aquatex are membranes. Entrant, Cyclone, Triplepoint Ceramic and many more are coatings. Membranes used to be greatly superior to coatings but now the best of each are hard to distinguish from each other. Design and construction are just as important in determining performance.

Construction and condensation

Coatings are usually applied to the inside of the outer fabric and a separate

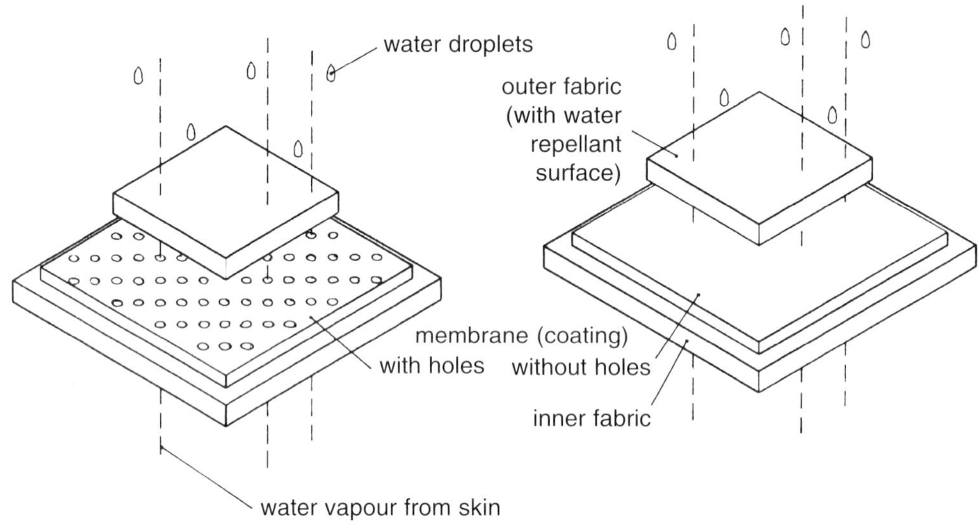

How microporous and hydrophilic fabrics work.

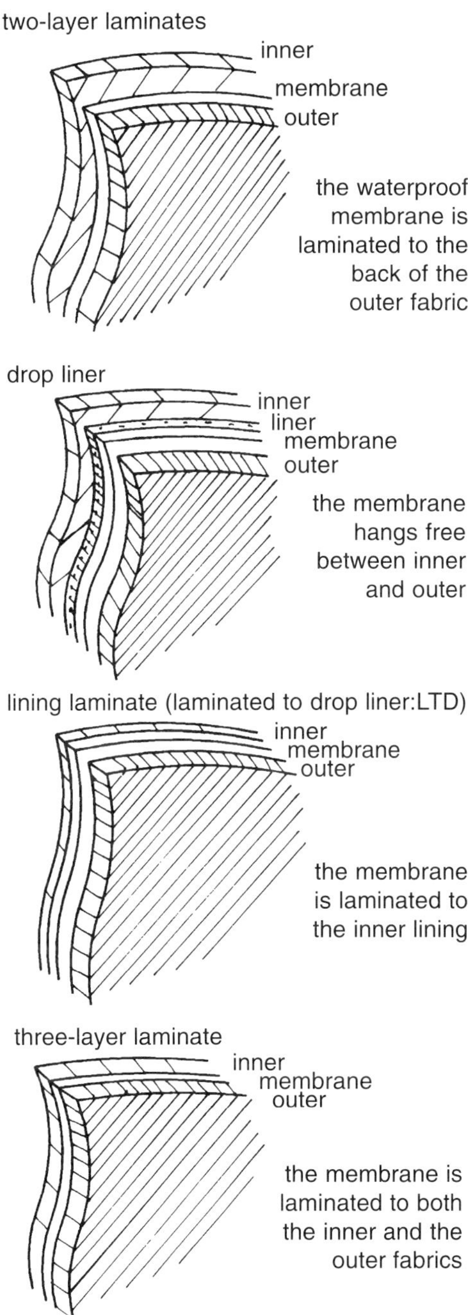

Construction methods for laminated waterproof fabrics.

lining, often of mesh, is hung inside. This method is also used for garments with membranes. It is known as two-layer construction. In three-layer construction the membrane is sandwiched between the inner and outer fabrics, confusingly producing a single layer of material. In lining laminates the membrane is stuck to the lining rather than the outer. In some garments, usually designed for more casual use, the membrane hangs free between the inner and outer. This is known as a drop liner. These details of the construction are important as they affect the breathability, durability and comfort of the garments.

In laboratory tests two-layer laminated garments are more breathable than three-layer ones. In the field I have not found this to be so. This is because the linings are not present when the tests are done as makers are free to choose their own lining materials. Whatever they are made of, linings always impede breathability to some extent. This is particularly so with solid linings. Mesh linings are better.

The construction I have found enhances breathability most is the lining laminate. I think this is because the membrane or coating is kept warmer than if it was attached to the outer layer. Condensation is more likely the colder the fabric. Another factor is that the membrane or coating is protected from rain and wind and so never becomes saturated. Concerns are sometimes expressed about the durability of this system but I think this is only a problem with microporous membranes, which is why they rarely appear in lining laminate garments. I have used lining laminate garments with hydrophilic membranes for summer long walks with heavy loads and several seasons of Nordic ski touring and found them very durable indeed.

Just how well these fabrics work is a controversial subject and many walkers are disappointed with the performance of waterproof or breathable garments. In particular, condensation is a frequent problem despite the claims made by makers – how much of a problem may well depend on the level of activity. Those who push themselves hard will often produce more moisture than can pass through the fabric.

No material or construction method will keep you totally dry in all conditions. At times I have been damp in every breathable waterproof garment I have ever used. And while all breathable garments keep you drier inside than non-breathable garments none are as breathable as a simple uncoated, unlaminated windproof, which is what I prefer to wear when it is not raining.

Working hard in warm humid weather will make you damp regardless of what you are wearing, which is why breathable waterproofs are less effective in summer than winter. If you do start overheating there are three options. The first is to ease off to reduce heat output. Second you can ventilate your garments by loosening drawcords and opening zips. Thirdly you can remove inner layers. None of these are always possible or guaranteed to work. If you are slogging uphill in warm but torrential rain with just a thin shirt under your waterproof you just have to accept you are going to get wet.

Durability

Durability is another hotly debated subject. There is no simple answer to the question of how long a breathable waterproof top will last as a number of factors are involved. First, the less you wear it the longer it will last! This may seem obvious but if you want your expensive jacket to keep you dry for years in the hills then wearing it when you go shopping or to the pub is not the best way to achieve this. Keeping your jacket for wearing only when the weather is really bad and using a light windproof layer most of the time when you are out walking will also make it last much longer.

As for fabrics there is, as always, a trade off between weight and durability. Tougher, heavier fabrics will protect the membrane or coating better than thin lightweight ones. Nylons are generally more durable than polyesters too. Backpackers need to take special care in choosing fabrics as carrying heavy packs is a main cause of wear.

The construction matters too. Generally, the more protection the better. With microporous membranes such as Gore-Tex, three-layer laminates are recommended if heavy packs will be regularly carried, as in two-layer laminates the membrane is exposed to abrasion from the lining fabric.

Over the years I have found hydrophilic membranes and coatings to be more durable than microporous ones and therefore better for two-layer and lining laminate constructions. This is not surprising when you think about it – solid materials ought to be tougher than materials that are full of holes.

Ventile and NBA garments (see below under 'Alternative waterproofs') can be re-proofed and should be far longer lasting than any coating or membrane.

Designs

To perform well a garment must be well designed, whatever material it is made from. With regard to condensation the more opportunities there are for ventilation the less problems there will be so all closures and fastenings should be adjustable. Openings can leak so how they are protected is also important. No design is perfect, and heavy wind-driven rain will find its way into any garment somewhere given time.

The length of a garment is really a matter of personal choice. My preference is for fairly short, hip length garments as these allow the legs greater freedom of movement. Longer tops give more protection to the upper legs, enabling you to wear overtrousers less often.

Seams are a weak point in any garment and all seams must be sealed or they will leak. The most effective way of making seams watertight is to seal them with tape, something done on most garments these days. Rarely this tape may peel off. Returning it to the maker for repair is the best solution as the tapes are hot-air bonded to the seams with a special machine and you cannot do this yourself. A less effective alternative is to apply a seam sealing agent to the seams. This will work for a while but will require retouching every so often. Most outdoor shops sell seam sealing products or you can use a flexible adhesive. Garments should be sealed outdoors or somewhere with good ventilation and the coating left to dry before they are packed away. A matchstick or very fine brush can be used to work the glue into the stitch holes along the seams.

Once taped or sealed, seams will not allow moisture vapour through so if they cover a high percentage of the garment the breathability can be affected. It is not uncommon to find lines of condensation along the seams when you take a garment off. Overall, garments with fewer seams are better as far as both waterproofing and breathability are concerned – but the most complex designs usually involve a high number of seams. Another advantage of the lining laminate construction is that the breathable waterproof lining only has the minimum number of seams as pockets and other features are part of the outer.

Most garments have full length zips, though some are pullover designs with short neck zips. The latter are more awkward to put on and take off and less easy to ventilate but also less likely to leak and less susceptible to zip failure. They also usually have large kangaroo style chest pockets. Pullover designs usually have a gusset behind the zip. Zips are not waterproof and full length zips need to be protected by a stud or Velcro closed flap. Double flaps are best, especially those where the inner flap folds over on itself to form a gutter down which water runs as this just about ensures rain cannot reach the zip. However secure the closure, after facing into driving rain for any length of time you may find a damp patch inside the zip where water has found its way in, often at the collar. The end of the zip can rub painfully on the chin on garments with high collars. A flap of material sewn inside the top of the zip and known as a chinguard will prevent this.

Hoods are often a weak point on waterproof jackets. The best hoods give good protection from driving rain, move with you when you turn your head sideways and have room for wearing a hat underneath. Protection and good visibility do not go well together and the hoods that give the best protection often limit severely what you can see. Good designers have solved this and there are some hoods suitable for keeping off blizzards while letting you see. Even more protection can be gained if you wear a peaked cap under your hood, something I often do in winter

A waterproof jacket should have a good hood that can be adjusted to fit over a warm hat. Note the wrap-around collar and the adjustable, stiffened peak.

can be very difficult and there is always the danger that the hood could be blown away. And while you are struggling to get it into place the rain is running down your neck. A wide overlap between the collar and a detachable hood is needed too or wind-blown rain will penetrate the gap between them. Hoods that fold or roll into the collar are a compromise that can work if they are well designed Again I would leave them out when in the hills if rain seems likely.

A hood should be roomy enough for you to wear a thick hat underneath but not so big that it flops in your eyes when you do not have a hat on. One way to achieve this is to have a volume adjuster, usually a Velcro closed flap at the back of the hood or sometimes a drawcord that runs round the hood, that will close the hood down around your head. These work well. There are some hoods whose design is such that they fit properly whether or not you have a hat on. Never buy a waterproof jacket without trying on the hood first, with and without a hat on.

All hoods need drawcords for pulling them in close around the face. These should have self-locking toggles so you do not need to fumble around trying to tie or untie iced-up knots under your chin with frozen fingers. Some jackets have separate collar drawcords so you can tighten the collar to prevent rain or snow running down your neck. Most jackets also have waist and hem drawcords. I use the former only when I am not carrying a rucksack as the hip belt or waist strap will prevent rain or wind entering up the skirt of a jacket. I usually remove hem drawcords as I can see no use for them.

Sleeves need to be cut full for freedom of movement and to stop them riding up when you lift your arms. Some

weather. This is also a good way to improve the performance of a hood.

Peaks on hoods are a good idea anyway as they help keep rain off your face. People who wear spectacles will probably find them essential. Some form of stiffening in the peak is needed or it will flap about maddeningly in high winds.

Hoods fix to jackets in three ways. The simplest are sewn on and cannot be folded or rolled away. These are also generally the easiest to use and as far as function goes the best. They are not that smart, and so less popular with people who want to use their jackets around town or on the alpine ski slopes. Detachable hoods can be left at home on such occasions. For hillwalking they are best left in place. Trying to fasten a set of studs with cold fingers in a strong wind garments now feature articulated sleeves, with a built in curve at the elbow. These work quite well but are not essential. Cuffs need to be adjustable as they are an important ventilation point. I like really wide cuffs that allow a good airflow up the sleeves when fully open and that let you roll the sleeves up if you need to. Simple Velcro closures are best as these can be fully tightened when required without restricting ventilation at other times. Half-elasticated closures with Velcro tabs are closer fitting and not quite so good for ventilation. Cuffs that cannot be adjusted lead to hot, sweaty arms.

Some garments come with underarm or 'pit' zips for better ventilation. These do work but can be difficult to open or close when you have a rucksack on. They also need flaps over them or they can leak.

Most waterproofs come with a plethora of pockets. For hill use most of these are unnecessary and I prefer just two map-size chest pockets as these can be reached when you have the rucksack belt fastened. Map pockets that lie under the flap but outside the zip are also useful. It is worth checking that map pockets will take a map as many will not. And some women find that carrying maps in a chest pocket is not particularly comfortable. Hem pockets are often covered by hip belts and also have an annoying habit of slapping you on the thighs if there is anything in them. However, hem pockets are standard on most garments and may be the only pockets provided.

Whatever pockets your jacket has it is unlikely they will be fully waterproof. Even if they do keep most rain out moisture can condense on non-permeable items like maps so do not expect to keep things dry in pockets.

Alternative Waterproofs

Most waterproofs are made from coated or laminated fabrics. These work well most of the time but do have a number of drawbacks, the main one being the relatively poor durability and short lifespan as once worn or damaged the coating or membrane cannot be repaired.

There are two alternatives to these fabrics. One is the original waterproof or breathable fabric, the other is the very latest material. Ventile cotton has been around since the 1940s, when it was developed for immersion suits for pilots ditching into the sea. When I began hillwalking in the late 1960s it had a reputation as a very expensive, luxury fabric. Then, most waterproofs were very cheap, very basic and not very waterproof. Gore-Tex changed all that, and high-priced waterproofs are now the norm. Ventile is no more costly than other breathable waterproof fabrics, less so over the years as it is very durable and can be re-proofed.

Most garments come with a ten-year guarantee. This is because Ventile's water resistance is due to the construction of the cloth and there are no coatings or membranes to wear off or delaminate. Ventile works because the specially woven cotton fibres swell when wet, blocking the gaps between the yarns so that rain cannot penetrate the fabric. Ventile is a soft fabric and extremely comfortable. It is also rustle-free, a boon for bird watchers and naturalists.

I have used Ventile in the worst conditions imaginable: gale force winds, freezing temperatures and wet snow and sleet falling. It has always performed superbly, keeping me warm and dry inside with just a thin base layer and light fleece sweater on. The outer fabric does become wet but it quickly dries when hung up somewhere warm. Double layer Ventile jackets are also effectively waterproof in heavy rain, though the outer does wet out and become quite stiff after several hours. The inner remains dry. Breathability in all conditions is excellent, far better than with any laminated or coated fabric, and I have had no visible condensation appear inside a jacket at all (though the inner layer has sometimes been damp where pack shoulder straps and a hip belt have pressed on it).

All these advantages might make you wonder why Ventile does not dominate the shell garment market. There are a number of reasons for this. One is weight. A double Ventile jacket will weigh 2lb (900g) or more. This is not a problem when you are wearing the jacket but if you are carrying it in a pack it is, especially as it is quite bulky as well.

Another difficulty for some users is that when wet Ventile garments need to be hung up to dry. They should not be stored wet in confined areas, which rather rules them out for backpacking. I suspect that fashion plays a part too, and brightly coloured synthetic garments are heavily promoted. However, for day walking and tours where accommodation with drying facilities is used every night Ventile is an excellent choice.

Like Ventile, Nikwax Biological Analogy (NBA) materials do not use coatings or membranes, require two layers of fabric to be waterproof and can be re-proofed. There the resemblance ends, for NBA garments are synthetic, not cotton, and will keep you dry day after day without needing to be dried out overnight.

The reason for the strange name is that NBA clothing mimics animal fur. Fur keeps animals dry as well as warm.

Because the individual hairs are very close together at the skin but move apart towards the outside of the fur rain droplets that penetrate deep into the fur are forced into long, thin shapes. Water droplets naturally form spheres so the moisture moves away from the skin to where it can do this. As it does so it connects with other droplets to form larger drops that need even more space to form spheres. The fur acts like a one-way pump, pushing moisture outwards. Rain cannot be absorbed by the fur as it is water repellent due to the oils secreted by the animal.

To make clothing that works like animal fur Nikwax developed a very thin polyester fleece, called Parameta, with a smooth side and a brushed, fluffy side. Like fur Parameta has fibres on the raised side that are tightly packed on the inside but further apart on the outside. It looks a bit like very fine corduroy. Like fur, Parameta pumps moisture one way only, away from the smooth inner side of the garment. This is known as directional breathability.

By itself Parameta would need to be very thick to be wind or waterproof, like animal fur. This would make it too warm for most uses, so Parameta is very thin and NBA garments have a separate outer of smooth tightly woven nylon or polyester to break the wind and absorb and deflect heavy rain. Finally, all the components of NBA garments from the fabrics to the zips are treated with Nikwax's waterproofing treatment TX.10, which makes them non-absorbent and water repellent.

NBA garments will keep out rain and also pass more moisture than any membrane or coating. They will also transmit liquids – such as sweat – unlike conventional waterproofs, which only transmit vapour. The latter depend on a temperature and humidity differential between the inside and the outside of the garment. The less this differential the less well they work. As they are not directional, vapour can in theory pass through in either direction.

I have used a number of Paramo NBA garments over the years and they have kept me warm and dry in a wide variety of conditions without any problems with condensation. NBA trousers and salopettes are now my standard winter hillwear as I find them just as comfortable as any non-waterproof trousers and it means I need not carry overtrousers. In summer they are a bit warm, however. The jackets can be worn year round as long as you do not wear too much underneath them. In warm wet weather I wear them next to the skin. They are heavier and bulkier than other garments, so I mostly keep them for three season use: autumn, winter and spring.

NBA garments can be re-proofed with TX.Direct if they start to leak. By washing them as recommended and not using detergents you should not need to do this often. Unlike garments with coatings or membranes NBA garments can be damaged without losing their waterproof properties. Paramo provided me with a 'second' that had pinholes in one shoulder. These made no difference to the performance. If you tear a garment you just need to patch it and it will work fine. The seams do not need sealing as the fabric and the TX.10 treatment stops them leaking.

Waterproof Legwear

Overtrousers are not popular – most walkers I know hate them and rarely wear them. Some do not even own a pair. Not so long ago my feelings were the same. Overtrousers were uncomfortable, restrictive garments that sagged at the waist, bulged at the knees and snagged at the ankles. I only ever wore them during the heaviest downpours.

Breathable fabrics made overtrousers slightly more comfortable but it was only when designers got to work on them that they really changed. In part this is due to changes in legwear in general. Traditional overtrousers were big and baggy because they were designed to fit over wool breeches, which were also big and baggy. Modern legwear is made from lighter, thinner fabrics and is much slimmer fitting. Voluminous overtrousers are simply not needed. Softer fabrics have helped too. Overtrousers need no longer feel like suits of armour.

So dramatic have been the changes that the best waterproof legwear is comfortable enough to be worn instead of normal outdoor trousers, especially in winter. As such garments are best worn either next to the skin or over long johns the description overtrousers is a bit of a misnomer: 'waterproof legwear' would be better.

There are two basic designs of waterproof legwear, simple trousers and salopettes with a high back and a chest section. For most walking trousers are best, especially if they will spend much of their time in your pack, as salopettes are heavier and bulkier. Salopettes, on the other hand, are excellent for winter wear as they are warmer than trousers, prevent gaps appearing at the waist when you stretch and minimize the chances of snow getting into your clothes. They are difficult to put on in a wind, so they are designed to be worn all day rather than carried in case of need.

Features to look for in waterproof legwear are adjustable drawcords at the waist to prevent trousers slowly slipping down your hips as you walk and knee length zips to allow you to get them on over your boots. Pockets, or slits to allow access to inner legwear pockets, are useful. If you intend wearing waterproof legwear all the time then full length side zips are advantageous as they can be opened up at the top for ventilation if you overheat. These are also useful in winter as they can be put on over crampons or skis, though handling long zips and strips of Velcro in a strong wind can be difficult. For men, trousers with flies are worth considering. Elasticated ankle hems are a feature I do not like as I find they ride up above the boot top, letting water in. Non-elasticated hems, perhaps with drawcords for adjustment, are better.

It is very difficult to make full length side zips fully waterproof but I still prefer this design. I would rather have good ventilation and suffer the occasional bit of leakage. Gussets behind knee length zips help to keep rain out here but tend to catch in the zips. Again I do not feel getting a little damp is a problem.

What you wear next to the skin affects the breathability and I have found that base layer long johns or, in really cold weather, thin fleece trousers are best. Synthetic stretch track suit type bottoms and microfibre trousers are quite good too but polycotton (or pure cotton) trousers tend to feel damp and cold.

Simply put, heavier garments will outlast lighter ones. So if you plan on wearing them all the time you should consider weight as a positive factor. If they will spend most of their time in your pack the lighter the better. Note too that heavier garments are also warmer and might be too hot in summer. Conversely, in severe winter conditions the lightest trousers do not give much protection.

Modern waterproof legwear is much more tailored than traditional designs so I recommend trying garments on before you buy, preferably over the underlayers you will wear with them. As well as general comfort you need to check that they do not bind anywhere when you move. Leg length is important too. Only one maker (Paramo) offers different leg lengths in the same waist size. Alterations are possible though zipped legs make this difficult (those where the zips start a little way above the hem are easier to shorten). It is better to find a pair that fit to begin with.

Water Repellency

All waterproof garments work best if the outers do not absorb moisture. When new you can see rain beading up and running down the fabric. But after not too many weeks of use (or days in some garments) dark patches start appearing where the water repellency has worn off. This is known as 'wetting out'. It does not mean the garment is leaking but it can inhibit breathability and lead to condensation that makes you think rain is getting in. It also slows down drying time.

To get the best out of your waterproof clothing you need to maintain the water repellency. The first way to do this is by not washing garments in detergents as these can strip away water repellent treatments. Instead pure soap powder or a specialist washing agent should be used.

Ironing can restore the water repellency by spreading out the treatment that is left. Keep the heat low and the iron moving. Tumble drying can do the same but tests have shown that this is also a good way to damage a garment as it thrashes around inside the machine. If you do tumble dry an item do up all the zips first.

Eventually, the water repellency treatment will need repeating. There are various wash-in and spray-on proofing agents for doing this.

REPLACING THE LAYER SYSTEM

The layer system is the accepted way of dealing with the wide variety of weather conditions found in the hills. Mostly it works well, but it does require constant adjustment and there are times, usually when the weather is cold and wet, when finding the right combination of layers can be difficult if not impossible. In stormy weather, the whole system depends on the outer shell layer. If the outer shell stops functioning, the wearer will soon be cold and wet regardless of what is worn underneath. Such failures do occur. I know people who have gone back to non-breathable rain gear after soaking in a breathable set, saying they would rather be wet but warm with sweat than wet and cold from the rain. I have had microporous breathable jackets cease working on three separate occasions. Even when the shell keeps out the rain or snow it will not always allow all your body moisture to escape, leading to dampness in your inner layers.

There is an alternative to wearing layers, and that is to wear a single garment. A single layer of Buffalo clothing replaces wicking underwear, warmwear, and shell. Made from Pertex nylon and pile (hence Double P), Buffalo clothing is designed to function best in the most foul conditions – heavy wind-driven rain in near freezing temperatures, for example – but also to be comfortable in more equable conditions. The basic Buffalo system consists of three garments: trousers or salopettes, shirt, and jacket. There are design variations for various planned uses (different styles of shirt, for instance).

The premise behind Buffalo clothing is that, in order to stay comfortable, it is more important to remove sweat than to keep out rain. Keeping completely dry is virtually impossible – all shell garments leak at the cuffs or neck eventually or cause undergarments to become sweat-sodden. Buffalo clothing is designed to be totally condensation-free, warm, windproof, and highly rain-proof, which means that a single Buffalo layer will keep out rain falling at a rate of half an inch per hour, which is most rainfall except a cloud-burst. The polyester pile inner provides warmth and wicks away perspiration, while the Pertex shell keeps out the wind and allows moisture from within to spread over its surface and quickly evaporate. The two fabrics in combination keep out most rain, and two layers of Buffalo clothing should deflect the heaviest downpour. If the clothing does become saturated, say from a fall in a river, it quickly dries and keeps the wearer warm. Other advantages include a lighter pack – no spare clothing except socks is needed – and fewer stops because less clothing adjustments are needed.

Can these claims be substantiated? Much to my astonishment, the answer is yes. I and others, including Arctic explorers and Himalayan mountaineers, have tested this system and come to this same conclusion. For extremes of wet and cold, Buffalo clothing is well proven.

The standard garment is the Mountain Shirt. This pullover top has a short neck zipper, side zippers running from armpit to hem for ventilation, Velcro-adjusted cuffs, lower hand-warmer pockets, a large chest pocket and an optional Velcro-attached hood. The shirt is designed to be worn next to the skin and without a shell garment on top. Indeed, according to the manufacturer, if you wear other garments, you will overheat and then chill when you stop and your sweat evaporates.

I first used the shirt on the Karrimor International Mountain Marathon, a two-day mountain orienteering event held that year in the Galloway Hills of south-west Scotland. The weather was some of the worst I have ever been out in, with lashing rain, winds that knocked me off my feet, and bitter cold. After an hour or so of fighting uphill, wearing a synthetic thermal inner layer, a thin wool shirt, and a microporous, breathable jacket, I was soaked to the skin and starting to shiver. In the nominal shelter of a large boulder I stripped off all my layers, donned the Buffalo shirt, and – because I had no hood for the shirt – my shell garment, and continued. I stayed warm for the next eight hours of the storm's battering, even though the Pertex outer of the shirt was soaked by the time I reached the overnight camp. Once in the tent I removed the shell jacket. The shirt then dried very quickly and I stayed warm. At no time did the pile next to my skin feel damp. The next day in cold, windy, but dry weather, I wore the shirt on its own and found that, by using the side and neck zippers, I could prevent overheating and stay comfortable. I met only one person who also stayed dry during the first day of the event – he also had worn a Buffalo shirt, but his had a hood.

Further use has convinced me that the shirt is effectively waterproof and also breathable. Any sweat I have worked up, such as on my back and under pack shoulders straps, has disappeared rapidly when I have stopped,

the pile wicking it away at an amazing rate. Neither does the shirt ice up when I wear it skiing in temperatures well below freezing. The salopettes are too warm for me, though, even in the coldest weather. I sweat profusely when I move in them, though they do dry quickly when I stop. I also do not like the hot clammy feeling they produce while I am moving. In winter, the Mountain Trousers (16oz or 450g), which I have not tried, might prove more suitable, but I suspect these too would be hot in temperatures above freezing.

The Mountain Jacket is designed to be worn over the shirt at stops and in extreme cold. I have not used one, preferring a down top, which is lighter and less bulky and probably warmer, as I need an extra layer only when the temperature is below freezing, and then it is not raining. I can imagine situations, such as days of continuous rain with the temperature hovering around freezing point, when the jacket might prove useful. A very recent addition to the line is a shorter top, the Belay Jacket, which is the same weight as the Mountain Shirt but has a full-length zipper. There are also several other ranges of clothing clearly modelled on Buffalo and using similar fabrics and designs.

For places with guaranteed wet, cold, stormy weather, such as many arctic and sub-arctic regions and northerly destinations swept by wet, ocean winds such as Scotland in winter, the Buffalo shirt is an excellent garment. I would happily rely on it, the trousers, and the jacket as long as the forecast was bad enough. I have yet to try this full system, however. In mixed weather, worries about overheating cause me to carry other garments in addition to the Mountain Shirt. On long winter trips with a variety of weather conditions I have combined the shirt with a thin base layer, a lightweight waterproof jacket and a down top and found this system very good, though I suspect the waterproof layer is unnecessary. A thin windproof would probably be better, being lighter, less bulky and more breathable. The possibilities of the Buffalo Double P System go beyond just clothing to wear during the day too. In conjunction with Pertex or pile sleeping bags, the clothing can be used for bivouacking and camping.

WINDPROOFS

Waterproof clothing can be worn in all conditions, not just when it is raining, but if you do so you will shorten its life. You will also be less comfortable than if you wear a separate windproof top when it's not raining heavily as no waterproof is as breathable or as light-weight and non-restrictive as a simple single layer windproof. If you are going to wear a waterproof all the time I would suggest NBA or Ventile because of the better breathability and durability of these fabrics. But even these can feel restrictive and, in summer, a little too warm.

In dry windy weather or light showers I find a simple pullover-style wind-shirt made from a synthetic fabric like Pertex ideal. The lightest weigh around ½lb (225g) and take up little room in the rucksack. I use mine instead of a shirt in summer, wearing it over a thin base layer. If it starts to rain I often pull my waterproof over the top while if I feel chilly at rest stops I put on my warmwear over the windshirt.

Designs should be simple to keep weight and bulk down. I look for adjustable cuffs and hem, a high collar, a hood (on some garments these are optional extras) and a large map pocket.

GAITERS

Gaiters are tubes of material, usually waterproof, that fit round the lower legs

A windshirt may be welcome on a breezy summit even in warm weather.

and cover part or all of your boots. They were originally designed to keep snow out of boots, but most people also use them to repel mud, bits of heather, grass seeds and other detritus. Keeping water out is not what they are for, although they will keep your feet drier in rain than if you do not wear them. As anyone who has relied on gaiters to keep their feet dry when fording a stream knows, most are not fully waterproof. Gaiters also add appreciably to the warmth of your footwear as they seal the gap at the ankle where hot air and moisture can escape. This is welcome in cold conditions and when walking in snow but not so good in warmer weather. I do not use gaiters in the summer as I find them far too hot. I would rather have wet feet. When there is deep snow on the ground I always wear them. I also carry them in cold weather to wear when crossing particularly muddy terrain.

Gaiters are not my favourite garments. Too often using them means struggling with jammed iced-up zips and frozen underfoot cords in bitter weather when your fingers are screaming with cold. Gaiter design has improved in recent years and some models are relatively easy to get on and off even in bad weather while others can be left on your boots most of the time.

Gaiters are available in cotton mixes, breathable waterproof fabrics and non-breathable polyurethane coated nylons. Canvas gaiters, whether 100 per cent cotton or mixed with polyester, are hard-wearing, water resistant and breathable and can be re-proofed. They are also easy to repair if ripped, something that often happens to gaiters. At the same time they are relatively heavy and stiff and there is not a great choice of models.

Breathable waterproof gaiters are lightweight and comfortable and there is a wide selection available. They are generally not as hard-wearing as canvas gaiters, cannot be adequately re-proofed and are hard to repair. They are also expensive. Coated nylon gaiters are waterproof, lightweight and inexpensive. But the coating soon abrades and the lack of breathability makes condensation a problem and also makes them hotter than gaiters made from the other fabrics. Avoid coated nylon unless you rarely wear gaiters or are on a tight budget.

There are two basic styles. Standard gaiters, which can be used with any boot, cover the top part of the boot only, fastening to the laces with a hook and having a cord or strap that runs under the instep to stop the gaiter riding up. The lower edge and ankle are usually elasticated to ensure a close fit. Fastening is usually by a rear, side or front zip though sometimes Velcro is used. The most basic models are simply tubes that have to be slid on before you put on boots. Avoid these. Front zips are the easiest to use and allow boot laces to be adjusted without having to take the gaiters off. They are also the least prone to getting jammed with mud or ice. Most models unfortunately come with harder to use rear zips. Underfoot fastenings may be laces, shockcord, nylon webbing or wire. Whatever the material, sooner or later it will snap so gaiters should always have loops on the lower edges through which replacement cord can be threaded.

The second type, supergaiters, cover the whole boot and have a thick rubber rand that grips tightly round the lower edge of the boots and a wide band that passes under the instep. Supergaiters have front zips, protected by Velcro flaps, and they can be left on the boots when you take the boots off, a good thing as they are hard to put on. They will not fit lightweight bendy boots, and the rands can be damaged if worn over rocks and rough ground. For snow they are excellent as they are warmer than standard gaiters and keep your boots drier longer. I find them ideal for Nordic ski touring and also for wearing with winter mountain walking boots when the hills are snow covered. In my experience the rands will last for several seasons if the gaiters are used mostly in snow but only a few weeks if used regularly on snow-free ground. The rands are replaceable but you have to send the gaiters away for this to be done and it is not cheap.

Supergaiters usually come in four sizes. If your boots lie between sizes go for the smaller one to ensure a close fit. As properly fitted supergaiters grip your boots tightly they can make the toes curl up so it is best to flip them off the toes when you take the boots off. Otherwise they can be left on for weeks at a time as they protect the boots so well that cleaning them is not necessary. Because I keep supergaiters on my Nordic ski boots all season I need to wax the boots just once a year.

HATS

'If your feet are cold put on a hat.' This adage was one of the first pieces of gear lore I ever learnt. It is also one of the most accurate. When you start to get cold your body protects its core by first slowing down the blood supply to the extremities – fingers, toes and nose. But your brain requires a constant supply of blood in order to function properly so the circulation to your head is maintained. If it is unprotected in cold weather you can lose masses of heat through your head. A warm hat stops this heat

Even in summer a warm hat like this fleece balaclava may be needed on chilly summits.

loss, helping restore warmth to your fingers and toes as well as your ears.

Not so long ago the choice of hats was simple. The only material was wool and the only styles bob hats and balaclavas. Then came synthetic fabrics – nylon, polyester, acrylic though designs did not change until fleece became the main material for warmwear during the 1980s and outdoor companies began employing designers to make their clothing more stylish. Now outdoor hats come in a wild variety of colours and styles and every sort of fleece as well as wool, knitted synthetics and base layer fabrics.

Whatever the style warm hats can be divided into two categories: those that are windproof and those, the majority, that are not. Windproof hats are either made from windproof fleece or have an outer made from a waterproof breathable or microfibre material. Most fleece hats are not windproof and in cold windy weather a jacket hood will be needed. They are more breathable and better for milder weather use than windproof hats.

The warmth of a hat is mainly due to the thickness of the material. The style matters too – in particular whether it can be pulled down over the ears. As with other clothing the warmest hat is not always the best. One that will keep your ears warm in a blizzard will be a bit hot for fending off a cool summer breeze. How much you feel the cold matters too. Some of my hill companions are happy bareheaded when I need a thick hat while others wear balaclavas pulled down in what feels like warm weather to me.

There are four main styles of hat, all available in windproof and non-windproof fabrics. The basic bob hat or ski hat (tea cosy style) is still with us, though it may have Andean type ear flaps. The balaclava still survives too. A newer design consists of a tube of fleece with a drawcord at one end. This style can be worn as a hat when the drawcord is tightened and as a neck warmer or gaiter with both ends opened. Some can also be worn as balaclavas. In the simpler form of a tube open at both ends it is known as a headover. The final style is the peaked cap with ear flaps and a fleece lining. This is the most weatherproof design, protecting the head and face from rain, snow and sun, and can be used in place of a jacket hood.

Some hats come in several sizes, many do not. As most fleece does not stretch in the way that knitted wool or acrylic does it is important to get a good fit if you go for a fleece hat. While a loose rather than a tight fit is preferable, if the fit is too slack the hat will blow off in every breeze. Chin straps are useful to prevent this.

In cold, wet weather a fleece lined, waterproof hat will keep your head warm and dry without you having to put up your hood

I carry a warm hat most of the year, only leaving it at home on hot summer days. My standard hat is a basic bob hat. I have collected several over the years in knitted acrylic, fleece and wool. The last I find a bit itchy so I do not wear it often. The other two are very comfortable. Neither are windproof, both will resist showers and both provide about the same warmth. Acrylic hats are well under half the cost of fleece hats. They may not look as stylish but they work just as well.

Any hat can blow off if you are not careful. Many years ago I lost a wool hat on Helvellyn on a bitterly cold winter day. My ears were burning by the time I got down to the valley. I have never gone out in winter without two hats since. My second hat is a peaked one with fleece lining and waterproof or breathable outer. Because it is waterproof I rarely need to wear my jacket hood when I have it on, which gives better visibility and a less restricted feeling, while the peak keeps blown rain and snow and, at times, the sun out of my eyes. There are several makes of these hats available.

In winter I also usually carry a headover made from polypropylene. I have tried thicker versions made from wool and fleece but find these too warm. Although I do so rarely in extreme cold I can wear the headover and the peaked hat together, which gives the same protection as a balaclava without the feeling of restriction. The headover can also be rolled up and worn as a bob hat if you lose yours as I did once in the Canadian Rockies when I had foolishly stuck it through my pack hip belt from where it was plucked away by the bushes I was walking through. The headover did until I reached a town a week later and could buy another bob hat.

A hat can ward off heat as well as cold. In bright sun a hat with a peak or a brim can keep your head cool and keep the sun off your face and neck (see 'Sunshine' in Chapter 6).

GLOVES

However warm the rest of you may be, if your hands are cold it is hard to enjoy yourself. Yet keeping your hands warm is surprisingly difficult. This is especially so when doing tasks that need the use of your fingers and that cannot be done when wearing thick mitts. Re-warming your hands after you have removed your mitts to get something out of your rucksack or a jacket pocket can take a long time and be quite painful. Fingers cool down very quickly. One way to warm up cold hands is to wave your arms round and round like the sails of a windmill, until you feel the warmth seeping back into your fingers.

When you take thick mitts or gloves off for any length of time, at a lunch stop say, stuffing them inside your clothing will keep them warm and perhaps dry them out a little if they are damp. Putting them on the ground or on your rucksack means they will be very cold when you put them back on.

Warm hands are so important that in cold weather I carry a spare pair of thick gloves or mitts in case those I am wearing get wet or, even worse, are blown away by the wind, something that happens surprisingly often. I once had a thick wool mitt blow away on a cold winter day in the Peak District after I had tucked it under my arm while I got something out of the rucksack. By the time I reached the valley below my hand, clad only in a liner glove, was very cold. As well as carrying spares you can also add wrist loops to your mitts or even tie them together with a long length of cord that goes over your shoulder and down each sleeve. Spare socks can also be used as extra mitts if your hands are really cold.

The layer system works well for hands. Thin liner gloves, made from base layer fabrics, silk, wool or lightweight fleece, can be worn all the time with thicker fleece or wool mitts or gloves worn over the top in colder conditions and then waterproof breathable shells donned in storms. Not all gloves and mitts fit well over each so it is best to try layers together before buying. If the layers all come from one maker they should work well together but this is not always the case. There are a number of systems on the market that combine a fleece or pile inner with a breathable waterproof outer. These are usually quite expensive but they do work.

Thin liner gloves make up the first part of a hand layering system. Much of the time I find these adequate on their own and in spring and autumn they are often all I carry. In colder weather I wear them under thicker pairs, both for added warmth and so I can keep my hands a bit warm when I have to remove my mitts to adjust zips, check the map or take photographs. Liner gloves are not very durable and I usually get through at least one pair a year. There are models available with reinforced palms and fingers, which might be tougher.

As far as warmth is concerned thickness is the most important factor. Mitts are warmer than gloves of the same thickness because they keep your fingers together but the thickest gloves are still very warm and allow better dexterity. The warmest gloves or mitts I have ever worn are Black Diamond gloves, which have thick pile inners and a waterproof or breathable shell. I usually carry these as spares. I wear them only in extreme cold but when I do I really need them. Because they are very bulky

they do not allow much dexterity but you can still do more with them than with thick mitts. There are other waterproof shell and thick fleece combinations available but most seem to have the furry side of the inner glove away from the skin instead of next to it, unlike the Black Diamond ones.

Most of the time I wear Pertex-covered pile mitts. These are lightweight, hard-wearing, warm and inexpensive. They are not at all waterproof but they do dry quickly and are quite warm when wet. The flexibility of the Pertex shell means you can do a bit more when wearing them than with most mitts. Alternatives are thick shrunken Dachstein wool mitts or gloves, insulated ski gloves and thick fleece mitts or gloves. The last are not usually windproof and so have to be worn with a shell most of the time.

Windproof fleece gloves and mitts are available and these work well though they are not as warm as thicker types. Unlined shell mitts made from breathable waterproof fabrics make up the final part of a layer system for the hands. It is surprising how much extra warmth they provide.

CLOTHING IN USE

Your clothing will keep you warm and dry – or cool when it is hot – only if you use it properly. The layer system must be adjusted regularly to take account of conditions. This means dressing for what you are doing and what the weather is at the time not for what you expect. If you are walking up a steep hill in a light breeze and you are dressed for the cold wind you expect on the summit you will get hot and sweaty and then cool down and feel chilly when you reach the top. If you can see the wind whipping sheets of rain or snow across

the ridge above you could stop just below it and put on extra clothing so you are prepared for the colder conditions and do not have to try and struggle into your jacket as your fingers go numb in the bitter wind.

Taking off and putting on layers is the way to adapt to very different conditions. When the changes are less dramatic you can adjust clothing by opening and shutting closures. Your head is very important here, putting on a hat can warm you up immediately while taking it off makes you feel instantly cooler. Because of this I always have a hat close to hand, often in a jacket pocket. The neck is also important. Zipping up the collar of your jacket can make a huge difference to how warm you feel. I am astonished at how often I meet people complaining of the cold on a windy summit with the top twelve inches of the zip of their outer jacket undone and their inner garments folded back to show their bare necks. A lot of heat escapes through that gap. Side or underarm ventilation zips do let some heat out but can be awkward to use. Front zips are better as these are easy to use. Loosening wrist cuffs or rolling your sleeves up are ways to cool down sweaty arms. Rucksack waist straps prevent a flow of air through your garments, leading to overheating and condensation at times. If you can leave your waist strap undone some of the time this will keep your clothes drier.

Except on the hottest days the clothing that keeps you comfortable while walking will not be warm enough at rest or lunch stops. Rather than wait until you feel cold it is best to put on warm clothes as soon as you stop so you can retain the heat you have already generated. When it is very cold I keep my warm clothing on when I set off after a stop, removing it after ten or fifteen minutes when I start to feel too warm. Similarly I often start off in the morning with several layers on and then stop and remove some of them once I have warmed up, usually after half an hour or so.

All this can be summed up by saying that you should never be too hot or too cold and that you should be constantly adjusting your clothing to allow for the many variations in the weather that occur during a day on the hills. This does not mean you have to think about your clothes all the time. After a while adjusting closures becomes almost automatic while changing clothes should be necessary only once or twice a day.

3 Rucksacks and Other Equipment

Early in the morning I tied my notebook and some bread to my belt, and strode away full of eager hope. (John Muir, My First Summer in the Sierra)

RUCKSACKS

Rucksacks come in a surprising variety of shapes and sizes. The first thing to consider when selecting one is the size. For three season hillwalking one with a capacity of 20 to 30 litres (1220 to 1830 cubic inches) should be fine. Rucksacks smaller than 20 litres (1220 cubic inches) are really only for summer strolls or for people who venture out with very little gear. If you intend walking the hills in winter a larger rucksack of 30 to 50 litres (1830 to 3050 cubic inches) will be needed for extra clothing and safety items. Such a rucksack can be used in summer, of course.

Only those intending camping in the hills or hut to hut touring or trekking abroad need consider rucksacks larger than 50 litres (3050 cubic inches) in capacity. These are discussed in Chapter 8.

Design

Even small rucksacks come in many different designs. Many have foam padded backs to stop hard objects poking into you. It also means you can sit on them at rest stops (though makers do not recommend this). Removable foam pads are better for this, but they can be difficult to slot back into place when the rucksack is full. Sitmats (see below) can be used in packs that do not have padded backs. The length of the back matters, especially if you are tall, as short rucksacks are uncomfortable and can feel as if you have a football stuck between your shoulder blades. Waist and chest straps are useful to stop the pack swaying. On the larger sacks – say above 35 litres (2135 cubic inches) – a padded waist belt is useful as it can support some of the weight of a heavy winter load. Shoulder straps should be padded and easily adjusted to take account of different thicknesses of clothing. The angle at which they leave the rucksack at the top is important too. People of a small build might find some too wide here, so that the straps slide off the shoulders. As with clothing trying on a rucksack is a good idea. Put a bit of weight in it too – any rucksack can feel comfortable when empty.

Comfort is provided by the back length, shoulder straps and waist belt. The actual bag matters less. The most basic designs are just a simple compartment with a drawcord at the top and perhaps a pocket in the lid. Most rucksacks have a few more features than this though. Some, designed for climbing, have side tension straps that can be pulled tight to keep the load in balance and also used for strapping on extra gear such as skis, trekking poles or even detachable pockets. These rucksacks are quite slim and suited to scrambling as there are no pockets sticking out at the side to catch on rocks.

Side and back pockets are useful for holding those small odds and ends that otherwise always seem to migrate to the bottom of the pack. Some packs have mesh pockets on the sides and lid, sometimes with elasticated edges rather than zips or flaps. These are useful in dry weather or for items unaffected by rain. Open-topped pockets known as wand pockets and made from mesh or solid material are occasionally found at the base of each side on rucksacks without side pockets. They are designed for holding wands for marking routes on glaciers or the ends of skis but walkers can use them for holding maps. I find this particularly useful when walking alone in good weather as I can get the map without having to remove my pack when I am not wearing clothes with a map pocket. Whether they have any pockets or not rucksacks that will be used for winter hillwalking should have ice axe attachment straps and perhaps straps or attachment points for fixing crampons to the outside.

Most rucksacks have a top opening with a drawcord closure and perhaps an extension to cover large loads and help keep out rain and snow. Over this goes a flap that fastens with a single or, more usually, twin straps and buckles. This lid generally contains one or two zipped pockets.

The only problem with this design is that it can be difficult to gain access to items in the bottom of the rucksack, especially if it is a long, narrow model. A way round this is to have a long zip curving round the top half of the sack instead of a lid. Rucksacks with such zipped openings are usually tear-drop shaped – wider at the bottom than the

A small daysack with side and back pockets suitable for summer walking. Notice how high it sits on the back. This could make it uncomfortable for tall walkers or those with long backs.

top. They follow the shape of the back well and are very stable but do have the problem that you cannot tighten the lid down when the rucksack is not full. Side tension straps are an answer to this. Top pockets can still be found on some of these designs while others have back pockets or large flaps here with adjustable straps behind which you can keep anything from crampons and snow shovels to wet waterproofs.

Materials and Quality

Most rucksacks are made from various weights of nylon or polyester though

A standard 25 litre daysack with lid and side pockets and ice axe loops for occasional winter use.

The back of the rucksack showing curved shoulder straps, short padded back and webbing waist strap.

some polycotton (or pure cotton) rucksacks are available. Texturized nylons like Cordura are the most common as these are very durable. Ultralight packs, designed for fast movers such as fell runners, may be made from thin ripstop nylon. These need greater care but they do save weight.

The quality of rucksacks varies enormously. The cheaper makes will not last long – I have seen one start to fall apart on the first day of use. It is not the fabrics but how they are made that matters here. Before buying a rucksack I would check for untidy stitching with unfinished ends and fraying edges of material. Check also that seams are double or triple sewn and bar-tacked at the ends. How the shoulder straps are attached is particularly important. Buckles can slip, even when new, so these should be tried out too. A quality brand name does not ensure you will have no problems with a rucksack, but it helps. You should get good after-sales service from the best companies.

Water Resistance

Rucksacks always leak, however expensive they are. This is because even when the fabrics are waterproof, as they usually are, the seams are not. Seams oversewn with a separate strip of material are more water resistant than simple seams but still let in rain after a time. Proofing seams requires coating them with seam sealant, a long and tedious job that is very difficult to do properly. And even if you bother doing it the coating will probably wear off fairly quickly.

Some rucksacks are more waterproof than others – the best I have used come from New Zealand company Macpac and are made from a heavily proofed polycotton fabric. This gives them a curiously old fashioned look but they certainly keep out the rain even at the seams. I used one on a 1,300 mile

A 30 litre rucksack with lid pocket, compression straps and ice axe loops for year round use.

A typical winter rucksack with long padded back, padded shoulder straps, webbing waist strap and sternum strap.

(2100km) walk through the mountains of Norway and Sweden in what turned out to be an exceptionally wet summer and it never leaked, except slightly at the lower compartment zip. The most recent idea for waterproofing rucksacks is welded seams, said to be a 100 per cent waterproof construction.

The simplest way to keep your gear dry is to use a waterproof liner inside your rucksack. Rucksack makers offer suitable plastic bags but heavy duty rubbish bags work just as well. Plastic liners do not last long, however. Better are the neoprene coated nylon liners, available from Field & Trek, with taped seams, which can be found with capacities of 30, 50 and 70 litres (1830, 3050 and 4270 cubic inches); there are smaller liners for side and lid pockets. I use these and they last a long time. I also keep water sensi-

tive items like paper maps and down clothing inside individual plastic bags or waterproof stuffsacks.

TREKKING POLES

It is rare to see hillwalkers in the UK using trekking poles yet as well as preventing injury and damage to your joints such poles increase safety and speed, especially on rough terrain. The safety comes from having three or four points of contact on steep descents and traverses and when crossing streams, the speed from having extra support. In both cases I have found that two poles are better than one and I now use a pair most of the time. The benefits are greater when carrying a heavy pack too. No longer do you feel that your unwieldy burden will tip you over on

A 35 litre rucksack with top, side and back pockets. This can be used for year round daywalking and is also just big enough for Himalayan trekking and hut-to-hut touring.

A 50 litre rucksack wtih a padded hipbelt for winter daywalking, Himalayan trekking, hut-to-hut touring and lightweight summer backpacking.

steep slopes or throw you into the stream you need to ford.

Using Trekking Poles

To gain the most from trekking poles they need to be used properly. Skiers will already know how to do this. For those who are not skiers note that gripping the handles tightly is not necessary, indeed it is a good way to make your arms ache. Instead, use the straps for support. By doing this you can flick the poles back and forth without having to jerk your arms around.

When descending steep ground you can lengthen a pole by placing your hand over the top of the grip and place it further down the slope for greater support. When traversing steep slopes you can also slip your hand out of the strap on the upper pole and grasp it lower down the shaft so it does not push you away from the slope.

Designs

Most trekking poles are based on ski sticks (indeed, with some the only change is in the name) but there are differences. Those designed to be used in pairs generally have alpine ski pole type handles and baskets while those designed to be used singly have either curved walking stick style handles or wood or foam grips topped by wood knobs. They may or may not have baskets. The latter are useful in soft snow and mud but are not essential. Except when the hills are snow covered

An ultralight ripstop nylon 30 litre rucksack, ideal for fast movers and minimalist backpackers to whom every ounce counts.

small baskets are best as larger baskets can catch on rocks and bushes.

Virtually all trekking poles are telescopic. This makes it easy to find the right length – which is when you can hold the pole with the tip on the ground and your arm bent at right angles at the elbow. Different poles have different maximum lengths so if you are tall check poles are long enough before you buy. Telescopic poles are also useful when travelling as they can be packed away easily and for scrambling when they can be strapped to your pack. Three-part poles generally have the shortest packed lengths.

Tips may be alloy, tungsten carbide or steel and may come with rubber or plastic covers. For general use the tip material does not matter but if you are venturing onto hard ice or greasy rocks then carbide tips are best as they are far less likely to slip.

ACCESSORIES

A few items should always be carried in the rucksack for safety reasons. Those needed year round are a map, compass, whistle, torch and bivvy bag. In summer insect repellent and sunscreen may be needed too. The latter is also useful on sunny days in winter and spring when snow lies on the hills. Sunglasses can help keep off the glare from the snow then too. A sitmat adds comfort to rest stops but is not essential. Even less needed is a knife, though many walkers carry one. The specialist gear needed for safety on snow and ice and for wild camping is covered in Chapters 8 and 9.

Map and Compass

You should never be without a map and compass. As navigation is the essential hillwalking skill it is covered in detail in Chapter 5, along with all the equipment involved.

Bivvy Bags

There are two sorts of bivvy bag: those you would only use when you had to and those you enjoy using. The first are just large plastic bags, the second are made from waterproof breathable fabrics and much more comfortable to use. Both sorts provide basic protection against the elements, keeping out wind and rain. While you will probably never need a bivvy bag it is wise always to carry one, in case you need to stay out overnight or have an immobilizing injury.

If you only carry a bivvy bag in case of an emergency and you hope never to

A trekking pole is useful for balance on icy paths and other difficult terrain.

How to hold a trekking pole.

use it except perhaps as a seat on wet ground then the standard plastic variety will do fine. All outdoor shops sell these, sometimes under the name survival bags and usually in bright orange so you can be seen from a distance if you are awaiting rescue. They often have the mountain safety code or survival information printed on them. Weights are around 10 to 15oz (280 to 420g) and the cost is very low. This is for the single size, measuring about 36 × 72in (0.9 × 1.8m). There are also double bags available at about 50 × 100in (1.3 × 2.5m) and around half as

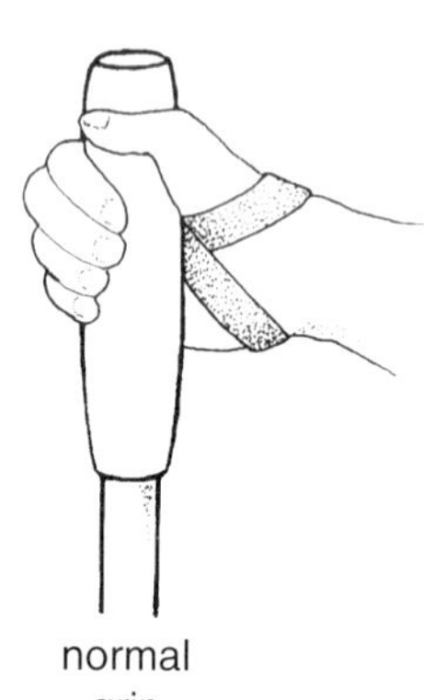

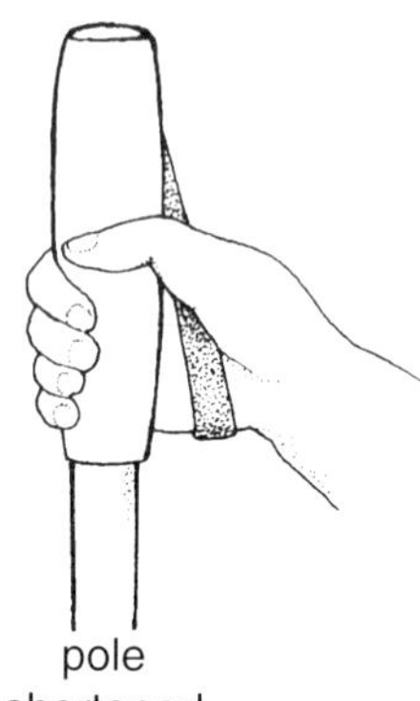

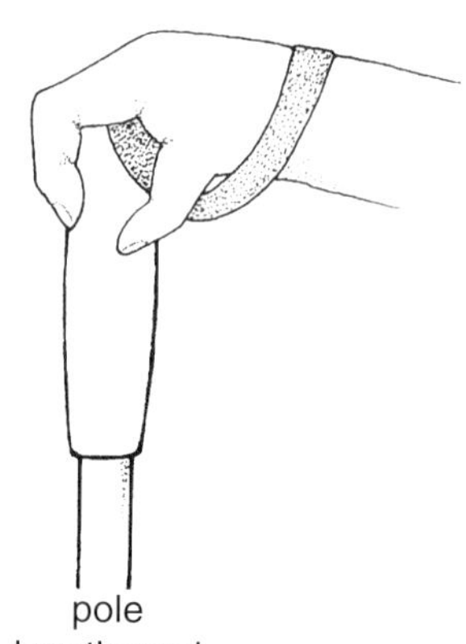

How to hold a trekking pole.

much again in weight and price. These bags are made from 500-gauge plastic. There are a few 120-gauge bags available too but these are very flimsy and not recommended for general use.

In an emergency the best way to use an ordinary plastic bivvy bag is to cut a hole to breathe through near the closed end, which also cuts down on condensation, and then pull it over your head while you sit on your sitmat, pack or spare clothing for insulation. This is so you do not get cold from lying on the ground. If the ground is warm or you have a full length foam pad you can lie down in a bivvy bag but make sure there is ventilation for your head if you do. Plastic does not let air in.

A plastic bivvy bag will keep rain out but body moisture in as I found out the first time I used one, in the early 1970s. Two of us decided to bivvy out in a forest in the Peak District in what appeared reasonable weather. In the evening rain began, however, forcing us into our bivvy bags. An extremely damp and uncomfortable night ensued. Despite propping open the mouths of the bags with small sticks it was impossible to prevent copious condensation from forming and soaking back into our down sleeping bags. Rain came in through the gaping openings too. I have never used a plastic bivvy bag to sleep in since.

If you regularly go out in a group of two or more it could be worth considering a survival shelter. These are giant bivvy bags in which a group can sit for extra warmth and better morale. They are typically made from lightweight proofed nylon and have a drawcord closed hem plus a drawcord closed ventilation and window panel.

The silver foil sheets sometimes sold as 'emergency blankets' are to be avoided. These may be fine for

wrapping round the shoulders of marathon runners but they are useless for serious mountain use. First, they tear very easily. Second, trying to wrap a blanket round someone is much harder than putting them in a bag, especially in a high wind.

The soggy experience described above kept me from trying bivouacking again until breathable waterproof fabric bivvy bags appeared. In the early 1980s I bought a Gore-Tex bivvy bag, which I still have and use, and was delighted to discover that it was fairly condensation-free. I have used it during several nights of heavy rain and stayed dry inside. It also adds several degrees of warmth to a bag, cuts the wind and keeps off dew. I also use it inside tents in below freezing temperatures and in snow-holes, in both cases to protect my sleeping bag from drips. In winter I carry it on day trips instead of a plastic one as a night out then would be far more serious than in summer and keeping dry far more important.

Since I bought my bag a large number of different designs have appeared. The original simple style is still best for most purposes though. This is tapered with a large hood and a horizontal zip, protect-ed by a flap. Other designs have long diagonal and vertical zips for easier access. Although I have never used one of these I suspect that they might allow easier ingress to rain and snow as well. Keep the entrance small. I prefer all Gore-tex bivvy bags too rather than those with non-breathable polyurethane coated nylon bases as I often turn over with the bag during the night and hav-ing the non-breathable section on top could result in condensation.

I always use an insulating mat under the bag because the type of Gore-tex that bivvy bags are made from needs to be kept clean as it can leak if dirty. For

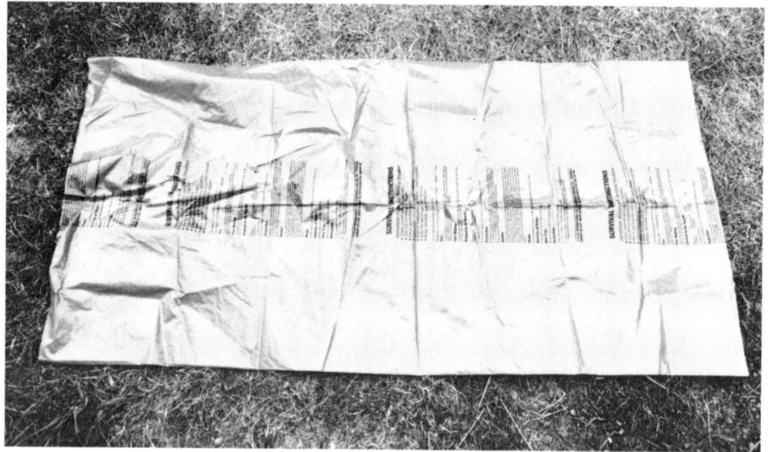

A plastic survival bag like this should be carried in case of emergencies or benightment.

A waterproof breathable bivvy bag. This is excellent for bivouacs as it allows most of your body moisture to escape and is useful in winter in case of emergency or benightment.

the same reason I also wash the bag occasionally. This type of Gore-tex is used because it is more breathable than that used for clothing so you can safely seal yourself in the bag. Weights of Gore-tex bags are around 1 to 1½lb (450 to 680g). Colours are usually olive, useful if you are intending to bivvy where you would rather not be seen – not of course that I am suggesting you would dream of spending a night out somewhere you should not.

There are now a growing number of alternatives to Gore-tex, usually made from nylon coated with breathable polyurethane. Many are half the weight and half the cost of Gore-tex. My brief usage of such bags suggests they work acceptably. I have also used a Sympatex bivvy bag and found this good too.

Whatever the material, condensation can occur in any waterproof or breathable bivvy bag and I would not want to use one for days on end. They are excellent for the occasional night out.

Despite the efficiency of breathable fabric bivvy bags, if I am intending to bivouac I now use a Buffalo Pertex and pile sleeping bag instead as I do not have to worry about getting it wet. Even if you sleep warm and dry breakfasting and packing up in the rain can be a very damp experience, so generally if I sleep out it is in fair weather and with a tent to hand. I still use my Gore-tex bivvy bag then though, to keep off wind and dew if nothing else. I have also occasionally used it at rest stops when the wind is really bitter.

Sitmats

Small squares of closed cell foam are useful as seats at rest stops. These can be bought or you can use a piece cut from a worn-out camping mat. They can also be used as padding for the back of the rucksack, particularly if you have one without padding built in.

I do not bother with a sitmat in summer, sitting directly on the ground if its dry or using my plastic bivvy bag if it is wet. I carry one in winter, when insula-

tion against the cold ground is welcome.

Torch or Headlamp

A small torch should be carried just in case you are out longer than intended. On a cold wet November night many years ago I fumbled my way down Kinder Scout in the dark without one, falling over boulders and into wet holes. I have never been on the hills without a torch since even in midsummer when some people do not bother. With a torch walking at night can be surprisingly easy, without one it can be impossible. Any lightweight torch will do, though a headlamp is better as it leaves your hands free to read the map or check the compass.

The best torches or headlamps have recessed switches or bulb housings that are twisted to turn them on, as these types are unlikely to be accidentally switched on in the rucksack. If your light is easily turned on it could be worth removing or reversing the batteries to prevent this. Some people do this with any type of lamp.

A small torch or headlamp with spare batteries should be carried year round in case you are out longer than expected.

Whether you carry a torch or a headlamp a spare bulb and batteries should always be carried. I use alkaline batteries as these last far longer than zinc carbon batteries and work better in the cold. For a really bright light you can get krypton and other high-powered bulbs but these eat up batteries and are not needed for most uses. I have walked all night in winter using a standard headlamp bulb and found it fine.

A torch can also be used for signalling for help. Six long flashes followed by a pause – repeated as often as necessary – is the accepted international distress signal.

Whistle

Attracting attention in an emergency is much more easily done with a whistle than by shouting. Orange plastic whistles are a standard item of safety gear. Six long blasts followed by a pause and then repeated is the standard distress signal but any repeated blowing of a whistle should bring assistance. For that reason whistles should never be blown except in an emergency. It is wise to keep whistles easily accessible, in a jacket pocket say or even hung round your neck, perhaps on the same cord as your compass.

First Aid Kit

Hillwalking is generally a safe pursuit. Serious accidents are rare, but those that do occur often attract so much media attention that a greatly exaggerated impression of the dangers is given. Minor injuries occur to most regular walkers at some time or other and it is wise to be prepared for these. This means both carrying a small first aid kit and knowing how to use the contents.

Learning how to deal with serious injuries is best done on a course. Many outdoor centres run special mountain first aid courses. Those run by the British Association of Ski Patrollers (see Useful Addresses section) are very good as is their Outdoor First Aid and Safety

Essential items laid out on a closed cell foam sitmat. Top: two types of insect repellent and two types of sunscreen. Bottom: dark glasses, whistle and compass.

Manual. People who lead walks, whether formally or informally, should seriously consider taking one of these courses. Most walkers probably will not do so. Instead they could study one of the excellent books on the subject or at least the instruction leaflet that comes with most pre-packaged first aid kits. (One can be bought separately if you make up your own kit.)

What should be in a first aid kit depends on where and when you walk. For short summer strolls on popular, well-marked footpaths where you are never far from a road or village a few plasters may be more than enough. For longer walks in more remote areas where help could be several hours or more away a much more comprehensive first aid kit should be carried. Solo walkers in particular need to be as self-sufficient as possible. It could be a long time before anyone finds you after an accident even if, as you should, you have left details of your route and when you are expected back with somebody. If no one expects to hear from you for a week a minor injury on your second day out could be serious. In a group only one comprehensive first aid kit is needed though everyone should carry items for dealing with blisters, and any personal medication.

A good first aid kit can be assembled by browsing along the shelves of your local chemist. That way you get exactly those items you want. Nylon pouches, tough plastic bags or snap-lid plastic boxes all make suitable containers. Whatever container you use it is a good idea to mark it clearly with the words First Aid in large bright letters so it can be found quickly in an emergency, perhaps by somebody who does not know what it looks like if the injury has happened to you.

Ready made kits are available from outdoor shops. There are many of these, most adequate, a few very good, a few very poor. When you look at what is available note the container, whether a first aid advice leaflet is included and what the contents are. You may find you could put a similar kit together yourself at a lower cost. Suggested contents are shown on page 65.

On long backpacking trips in remote places and when leading ski tours I also carry wide-ranging antibiotic pills and powerful painkillers, both prescription drugs, just in case of serious illness or injury a long way from anywhere.

Blisters

By far the most common injury to hillwalkers is a blister (or more often several blisters). More walks have probably been ruined by blisters than by all other causes combined. Ignoring the first signs of a blister is a sure way to have problems later. Any feeling of irritation or soreness on a foot should be checked immediately. It could be due to a bit of grit in your boots or socks or it could be the footwear itself rubbing.

Sometimes changing socks from foot to foot or adjusting laces can be enough to solve the problem. If there is any sign of reddening of the skin you should put a piece of tape or plaster over it and the surrounding area to minimize further aggravation. Sometimes a big plump fluid-filled blister appears before you notice any pain. There are many ways to deal with this; do not ignore a blister as it will not go away and will eventually burst. If not then kept clean it can become infected too.

Ideally you should expose the blister to the air and not put pressure on it so it can slowly dry out and the skin below heal. This is not practical on a walk, so other measures have to be taken. The

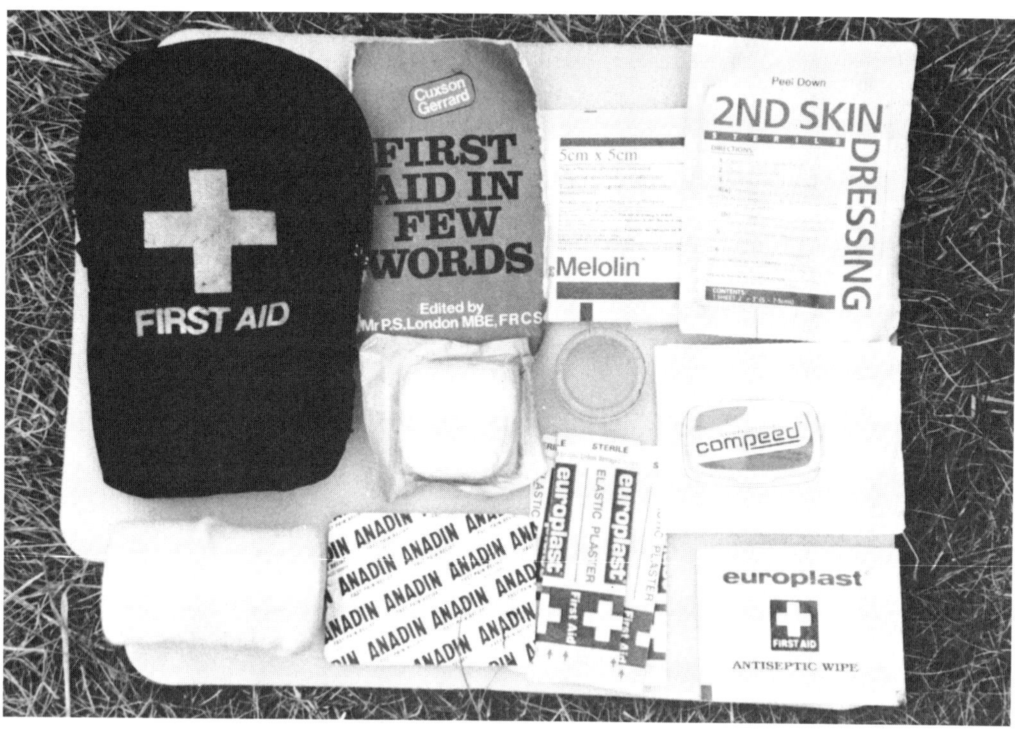

A small personal first aid kit including pouch, advice leaflet, blister dressings, burn dressing, tape, small wound bandage, plasters, painkillers and crepe bandage.

aim is to stop the pain so you can walk in comfort. Because this usually involves bursting the blister you also need to keep the blister clean to avoid infection. Waiting for a blister to burst itself can mean hours or even days of painful walking followed by a sticky, sometimes bloody, mess where the fluid has oozed into your sock. This makes infection much more likely. Very small blisters can be simply covered with a blister covering if they are not too painful.

Bursting the blister requires a sharp, thin needle or the point of a small safety pin. If possible this should be sterilized in the flame of a match or lighter. The needle should be inserted at the edge of the blister and the fluid squeezed out, onto a tissue if you have one. The blister must be fully emptied or it will be very painful. I find rolling the needle over the blister is a good way to achieve this. With large blisters several holes may be necessary to get out all the fluid. Care should be taken not to tear the skin over the blister as leaving this in place speeds up healing and makes infection less likely. Once the blister is empty the area can be cleaned with an antiseptic wipe and then a dressing put on it.

Which dressing is best is a matter of debate. Moleskin is the traditional one and still popular with many people. However, I prefer gels that absorb shock and help with healing. Second Skin comes in sheets of various sizes, covered with thin cellophane on both sides. I find it easiest to remove one of these coverings, apply the gel to the blister and then remove the second covering. Some form of tape is needed to hold the gel in place. In theory the

I have two first aid kits, one for day trips in less remote areas and one for longer trips that take me farther into the wilds. The contents of both vary over time but the basics stay the same. Neither kit contains scissors as I have a pair on my Swiss Army Knife. Both contain a small first aid instruction leaflet. The basic lightweight kit contains:

- Small wound bandage
- Crepe or elastic bandage
- Zinc oxide or micropore tape
- A few assorted plasters
- 1 small burn dressing
- Second Skin or Compeed
- A few antiseptic wipes
- 2 safety pins
- 12 foil wrapped painkillers
- Paper and pencil (for writing down information to give to the resue team if someone has to go for help)

The larger kit, suitable for long trips and several people, contains:

- 6 × 4in (15 × 10cm) wound dressing
- 12 or more assorted plasters or a roll of plaster
- Elastic head net
- 6 antiseptic wipes
- Triangular bandage
- 4 safety pins
- Crepe or elastic bandage
- 3 or 4 assorted burn dressings
- Zinc oxide or micropore tape
- 24 foil wrapped painkillers, paracetamol and aspirin
- Paper and pencil

Table 1

dressing should be replaced every day but I find that the same dressing will ease the pain for several days. Compeed is already backed by a piece of sticky plaster, which makes it much easier to apply, but there is no choice of size.

If you regularly suffer from blisters it is likely that your boots or shoes do not fit properly or are too stiff and heavy. Another possibility is that the footbeds are the cause. I have twice been on trips where people who suffered blisters discovered their footbeds were responsible. Trimming these with a knife provided instant relief.

Sunscreen and Sunglasses

These are discussed in Chapter 6 in the section on sunburn.

Insect Repellent

In areas such as the Scottish Highlands where biting midges are a problem you can be driven crazy if you do not have any insect repellent. Long-sleeved shirts and long trousers made from tightly woven fabric can help and you can use a head net and even netting mitts for your face and hands.

Repellent will still be needed though. (Have you tried eating sandwiches or drinking coffee through a head net?) The standard ingredient for repellents is diethylmethyltoluamide (DEET). This is very effective but also not very good for you if used for long periods. Children should not use it at all. This powerful substance will melt the plastic of a camera, watch strap or knife handle. To minimize the harm it might do to you I would suggest using repellents with low quantities of DEET, say 5–20 per cent, rather than 75 to 100 per cent. They can be just as effective as those with higher amounts. DEET can also be applied to the cuffs and bottoms of your shirts and trousers rather than to your skin. It also helps keep midges off your face when put on a hat. Because of concerns over the use of DEET there are an increasing number of non-toxic repellents available. Most are based on the pre-DEET repellent citronella. Unfortunately I've not found this as effective as DEET. A new product is Myrica, made from an extract of myrtle and developed after it was noticed that midges avoided the small shrub called bog myrtle. This I've found works pretty well and it's now my first choice repellent. Even newer is Mosiguard Natural, made from a blend of eucalyptus oils, which comes recommended by the London School of Tropical Medicine. I've not used it but intend doing so.

Water Bottles and Vacuum Flasks

A small water container is useful all year round. See Chapter 4 for more details.

Knives

Whipping out a long shining knife from a sheath on his belt the rugged backwoodsman slashes down a few small trees, deftly slices them into poles and within minutes has a secure shelter built. A movement catches his eye, the knife flashes through the air and skewered on the end is a rabbit for dinner, cooked of course on the wood fire already blazing in front of the shelter.

So the myth goes. Romantic perhaps but also environmentally destructive and redolent of a view that says nature is an enemy to be conquered and overcome and that the reason for going out into the wilds is to prove yourself by fighting nature and winning. Sadly, this macho approach still recurs periodically under the guise of 'survival' techniques. The knife is central to this backwoods image and it must be a big knife. Magazines and books covering the 'survival' approach recommend huge knives 12 to 20in (30 to 50cm) long. Presumably some people feel the need for such implements but for modern camping and outdoor pursuits where minimum impact on the environment is the aim they have no practical use.

Most walkers need knives only for mundane food chores like slicing open dehydrated food packets, spreading margarine and cutting cheese. Sometimes I need to cut some cord for bootlaces. Very occasionally, usually on trips in remote wildernesses abroad, I have used a knife for making 'feather' sticks for lighting a fire. All these tasks can be done easily with a small, lightweight, short-bladed folding knife.

Running through the purposes for which I carry a knife I find that many of them do not involve the actual blade at all. Also often used are screwdrivers, can opener and scissors. For that reason, like many if not most other outdoor people, I have for years carried a stainless steel, red plastic handled Swiss Army Knife.

There are plenty of simple folding knives for those who do not want other features; Opinel ones are very light and inexpensive and are available with either stainless steel or carbon steel blades in lengths from 2½ to 4in (6 to 10cm). Costs are low, the amount depending on blade length and material. Mine, with a 3in (8cm) blade, weighs just 2oz (50g). It has a wooden handle and a simple but effective locking device.

One knife you do not need is an ordinary kitchen knife. I acquired a camper's version early in my walking career as part of a knife, fork and spoon set. I think I used it once. These knives are not sharp enough to cut anything and for eating all you need is a spoon.

Sharp knives are more efficient and less likely to tear or damage things (including yourself) so keeping knives sharp is a good idea. Whatever sharpener you have in your kitchen will work fine. On a long trip knives can be sharpened on smooth stones. If you do this the stone should be slightly damp.

Knives need cleaning too, especially if used for food preparation. Folding knives, particularly those with many blades, can get quite filthy if not washed regularly as food and dirt particles collect in the blade recesses.

Mobile Phones

The carrying of mobile phones in the hills has become controversial in recent years, mostly because of misuse. There are stories of people phoning the mountain rescue to ask for water to be brought to them or for directions because they have got lost. I have never carried a mobile phone but I can see that one could be useful in an emergency for contacting the rescue services or letting those awaiting your return know you will be late.

That said, many people go to the hills to escape from such things as telephones. More practically, any electronic instrument can fail or break and batteries can run down and so should not be relied on. Mobile phones will not work everywhere either. In some areas, including much of the Scottish Highlands, there is no coverage at all – though this situation is improving – while even in areas where coverage exists phones may not work down in a valley or deep corrie. A mobile phone is also yet another item to carry, adding weight to your rucksack.

If you do carry a phone it should be thought of as an emergency backup only, not something that increases your safety. You still need good navigational and mountain skills. A phone should only be used in an emergency where self-help is impossible.

Equipment List

It is easy to forget to pack items of gear. I have embarrassing memories of the times I forgot the map or compass and I have also left my lunch, my water bottle, torch, trekking poles, cameras and more at home on occasion. One hillwalker I know has left her boots behind several times!

The solution to this is to have a list of gear and tick off items as you pack them and only then. Ticking off your gaiters because you remember they are hanging up in the back porch just about ensures you will leave them at home. Table 2 shows a basic list from which you can compile your own.

The Basic Equipment List

- Rucksack
- Boots
- Waterproof jacket and trousers
- T-shirt, shirt or base layer
- Warm top
- Insulated top (winter)
- Windproof top
- Shorts
- Long trousers
- Long johns
- Gloves or mitts (two pairs in winter)
- Warm hat (two in winter)
- Sun hat
- First aid kit
- Head lamp or torch with spare bulb and batteries
- Bivvy bag
- Sunscreen
- Dark glasses
- Insect repellent
- Sitmat
- Water bottle or flask
- Lunch
- Ice axe (winter)
- Crampons (winter)
- Trekking poles

For backpacking trips the following will also be needed:

- Tent with poles and pegs
- Sleeping bag
- Insulating mat
- Stove and fuel
- Pans and cutlery
- Extra food

Table 2.

4 Food and Drink: the Walker's Fuel

You think you get tired at the end of the day? You are wrong. Actually, you have n't had enough to eat. (Ronald Turnbull, *Across Scotland On Foot*)

EATING

Hillwalking is an energetic pursuit. The energy required comes from food in the form of calories so eating well is important for the hillwalker. Running out of energy is unpleasant and potentially dangerous.

If you are very fit and the weather is benign you can walk all day without eating and not run out of energy. I once walked for several days on less than I normally eat at one meal during a long walk through the Canadian Rockies when I ran out of food far from the nearest supply point. I was very hungry by the time I emerged from the woods and had lost a fair bit of weight. The walking, on steep slopes in dense undergrowth, was very strenuous and I was carrying a heavy load, yet I did not suffer any ill-effects. The weather was warm and sunny, however, and I was extremely fit – having been walking all day every day for two months.

I would not suggest going out without food; I am just pointing out that it is not absolutely essential, at least in dry summer conditions. In cold wet weather I would not want to be without food as it helps keep you warm as well as providing energy. Also, tiredness during a walk is as likely to be due to a lack of food as a need for a rest. On long fell runs I have several times felt exhausted and had my legs turn to jelly, yet been able to go on for a significant distance once I had stopped and eaten.

What I learnt from these experiences was to eat little and often to ensure a constant supply of energy rather than to eat large amounts infrequently. A succession of snacks is better than one long lunch stop. Apart from the irregular energy flow if you eat a large amount of food at one go your body will take longer to digest it and you

Frequent snacks are good for morale as well as energy, especially in cold, windy weather.

should really rest for a while afterwards – fine when you are relaxing on a summit in the sunshine, not so attractive when you are huddled behind a boulder in the rain.

Quantities, Calories and Content

How much food is needed depends on personal metabolism and body size as well as energy output so no definite daily figure can be given. But approximately 2500 to 3500 calories for women and 3500 to 4000 calories for men should be adequate for three season walking. In winter more may be needed.

Food should not be chosen purely on its calorie content. Fats contain twice as many calories per unit weight as protein or carbohydrates but are hard to digest and slow to release their energy and so not a good idea to eat in any quantity while walking. Protein you need not worry about as any balanced diet will contain enough. Indeed, many people eat more protein than necessary. This leaves carbohydrates, the component of food that most directly and quickly supplies energy and therefore the one that should make up the bulk of the hillwalker's diet.

Carbohydrate comes in two forms: simple and complex. Simple carbohydrates are digested so quickly that they can lead to a rush of energy. Unfortunately this may be followed by a slump soon afterwards. Sugar is a simple carbohydrate and while it is worth having a few sugar based snacks along in case quick energy is required it should not make up most of your food. The energy provided by complex carbohydrates is released more slowly and steadily, making these the best for walking. Cereals are largely made up of complex carbohydrates so bread,

biscuits, cake, oatcakes, crispbread, flapjack and grain bars are all excellent for keeping you walking. Also good for snacking on are dried fruits as the fructose contained in these takes a little longer to be processed than refined sugars.

Perhaps the best food for nibbling is trail mix as an open bag can be carried in a pocket and dipped into whenever you feel like it, a good ploy on days when the weather is so nasty you really do not want to stop to eat. What goes into trail mix is completely up to you. The original is just raisins and peanuts. This can get a bit dull so other dried fruit such as glacé cherries, banana chips, apple flakes, papaya and pineapple chunks plus different sorts of nuts can be added. Smarties and M&Ms are tasty extras too as are yoghurt and chocolate coated raisins and peanuts. Shredded coconut adds a savoury taste as do sunflower and other seeds. Granola can be added too – and anything else you can think of. I know one walker who chops up chocolate bars to add to his never empty bag of trail mix.

Eating is more than just a way of supplying energy. It should also be enjoyable. My own choices for lunch are cheese and jam sandwiches, trailmix, flapjacks, grain bars and the occasional chocolate bar. Whatever your choice, if your food is at all fragile it is probably best to carry it in a plastic box. Otherwise wrap it in plastic bags to keep it dry – there is nothing worse than soggy, disintegrating sandwiches!

Breakfast

While the amount you eat on a hillwalk is important so is the food you eat beforehand. Breakfast is an important meal as it provides the energy for at least the first few hours of walking and probably more. What you eat for breakfast is unimportant, what matters is that you eat enough. Many people do not bother with more than a cup of tea or coffee first thing in their everyday lives. This is not a good idea before a hillwalk so even if you do not usually eat breakfast you should then. If you really cannot face food when you have just got up you could pack some sandwiches or other snacks and eat them immediately before you start walking. It is better to eat earlier than that, so that the energy from your breakfast is available as soon as you set off.

When breakfasting at home I usually just have a larger helping of muesli than usual, but when staying in a mountain lodge or other place where breakfast is provided I eat whatever is going. In Scandinavia where large buffet breakfasts are the norm I eat far more than just a bowl of cereal but less during the day.

Emergency Supplies

Carrying extra food in case of a longer day than planned or even an unintended night out is a good idea. Many people suggest carrying food you do not like so that you will not eat it until you have to! I do not like this idea as I think the morale boost from food you enjoy could be important in a difficult situation or emergency. If emergency food is to be carried on several walks it must last well and not be easily crushed. I usually carry ½lb (225g) of sun-dried bananas, which are compact and high in calories.

Winter

In winter more food is needed than in summer and it is good to have something hot. Usually this means a drink rather than food, though a flask will hold soup as easily as tea or coffee. Wide-mouthed flasks will hold thick stews as well. An alternative is to carry a lightweight stove and small pot with you plus some instant soups or other quickly cooked snacks. If you melt snow or draw water from a stream the weight of the stove need be no more than that of a full flask. And of course you can have a hot drink whenever you want or need one as long as there is water nearby.

Extra time is needed with a stove but the hot food produced can be very welcome. I can remember lunching on coffee and sandwiches on the summit of Lochnagar on a bitterly cold winter's day and feeling very envious of a nearby couple as the smell emanating from their stove was delicious. For a discussion of the types of stove and fuel available see the section on 'The Backpacker's Kitchen' in Chapter 8.

DRINKING

Plenty of liquid is needed even more than plenty of food, especially in hot weather. Even slight dehydration can lead to a loss of energy and an inability to think clearly, while getting really dehydrated is very serious. Drinking often is a good idea when out walking. You should not wait until you feel thirsty, as that is a sign you are already a little dehydrated. On extremely hot days you may feel thirsty all the time. In that case keep drinking.

What you drink does not really matter as long as it is not alcohol, which dehydrates you as well as having other effects not conducive to competent hillwalking. Many walkers like to carry cartons of fruit juice or cans of soft drinks. Water is a good choice, especially as in most hill areas there is

In hot weather drink often.

When you cross a stream it's worth stopping for a drink.

plenty of it so none needs to be carried. Once you are above farms and other habitations water is generally safe to drink, though it is always wise to check there is not a dead deer or sheep just upstream. Avoid streams just below bothies or alpine huts as those using these shelters may not site their toilets far enough away from the water. You can check for water sources on the map and in guide books before you set off on an unknown walk too as some walks, especially along ridges, have little or no water on them.

Is the Water Clean?

If you are dubious about the water there are various ways of purifying it. The simplest is to add iodine or chlorine tablets and wait the required time. These tend to add a rather unpleasant taste to the water but there are tablets that neutralize this. Adding dehydrated fruit drink crystals is an alternative. Water filters are heavily promoted these days but in my view are unnecessary, expensive and heavy. If you have a stove with you bringing water to the boil will kill all dangerous bugs. You do not have to boil it for any length of time as any bugs will be dead before the water boils. Boiled water tastes a bit flat, but shaking the bottle or tipping it from one container to another several times will liven it up a bit.

Drinks Containers

For cold drinks a plastic or aluminium water bottle is needed. You can just re-use a soft drinks or mineral water bottle. These are lightweight and fairly durable. Purpose-made bottles are slightly heavier but will last longer. Wide-mouthed bottles are easier to fill from trickles and shallow pools. If the lid is attached to the bottle it is less likely to get dropped in the stream as you are filling the bottle, something that has happened to me a couple of times.

Except in winter I find cold stream water perfectly refreshing but some people do like a hot drink year round. If you do carry a flask I recommend a stainless steel one, as glass flasks are easily broken. I carry a ½-litre flask in winter and find this adequate but some people prefer the 1-litre size. You can top up the contents with cold water from a stream or even snow, though this reduces the temperature (fine with fruit juice, not so pleasant with tea or coffee).

Foam padded jackets are available for water bottles as an alternative to a flask. You could easily make one yourself with bits of closed cell foam and sticky tape. I have one for my 1-litre water bottle that has a nylon outer and a zipped lid. Liquids stay warm inside all day but only really hot for a few hours so I carry fruit juice rather than coffee when I use this cover. The advantage is that my bottle plus cover weighs just 9oz (250g) but holds 1 litre

A selection of drinks containers. Clockwise from top left: a ½-litre size stainless steel vacuum flask, a litre size polythene bottle with attached lid, a litre size anodized aluminium bottle, a soft drinks bottle with screw-on cap, a mineral water bottle with screw-on cap, a ¾-litre size anodized aluminium bottle with attached lid.

while my stainless steel flask weighs twice as much and only holds half the liquid. I use the flask in midwinter when daylight hours are shortest so I am not out for so long and do not need so much to drink but when temperatures are also lowest and a really hot drink is welcome. The insulated water bottle I use in spring when days are longer and I want more to drink but it is still cold enough for a warm one to be pleasant. Both containers can be refilled from streams and pools, though high up in the hills during a big freeze these may all be solid ice.

5 Finding the Way

There is a charm, rarely attainable in these ordered days, of travelling blindly, in profound ignorance of the country ahead. (H.W. Tilman, Snow on the Equator)

Being able to navigate correctly over featureless or mist-shrouded terrain is essential for safe hillwalking. While skill with map and compass is required, navigation is not just about techniques. It is also about developing a feel for terrain, an ability to quickly pick out important features, both on the map and in the hills, so a good route can be selected. It should be fun too. Planning a route from a map then going out and successfully walking it can be very satisfying.

A competent hillwalker should be able to select a safe and enjoyable route from the map, follow that route on the ground (making any necessary devia- tions when the terrain is not exactly as expected) and be able to use the compass in poor visibility. Walkers who cannot do all of these should stick to well marked paths or only venture out with more able companions. The latter is still risky, however. People have become separated in bad weather, leading to some of the group becoming lost. No one can really describe themselves as a fully fledged hillwalker until they can find their way in dense mist on pathless terrain. It does not matter how much hillwalking you have done – if you cannot navigate properly you are still a novice.

Hillwalkers heading into complex mountain country. Good route finding skills are needed even in good weather.

Wide open plateaus can be very difficult to navigate across if the mist comes down as there are few features.

MAPS AND MAP READING

Learning to read a map is not difficult. All maps contain keys explaining the symbols – known as conventional signs – used. You do not need to learn all of these but some, like those showing cliffs, are important. A good way to pick up the basics is to study a map of an area you know well, learning to relate what is on the map to the actual landscape. Once you are in the habit of reading maps hours can be spent on imaginary journeys as you trace possible routes over them, all the time improving your skills.

The map is your basic navigational tool. You should be able to use it for most of your route-finding, only turning to the compass in difficult situations such as dense mist or when crossing flat, featureless moorland. Using the map properly means studying the route before a walk and knowing what to expect so

Good maps are available for many mountain ranges.

that in good weather you only need to glance at the map occasionally while walking. You should never put off looking at the map if you are at all unsure of your whereabouts.

Scales

The scale of a map is important. This is the relation between a distance on the ground and the same distance on the map. Maps come in many different scales. The larger the scale the greater the distance on the map that corresponds to the same distance on the ground. Large scale maps thus show more detail than small scale ones making them more useful for hillwalking. For example, on a 1:250,000 scale map a centimetre on the map equals 250,000 centimetres or 2½ kilometres on the ground, but on a 1:25,000 map a centimetre on the map equals 25,000cm or a quarter of a kilometer on the ground. Obviously the 1:25,000cm scale map will show far more detail. The most common scales on maps suitable for hillwalking in the UK and many other countries are 1:50,000 (2cm to 1km) and 1:25,000 (4cm to 1km). These correspond roughly to 1¼ and 2½ inches to the mile. The Ordnance Survey Landranger series maps have a scale of 1:50,000, their Pathfinder, Explorer and Outdoor Leisure series are 1:25,000.

There are maps specially designed for hillwalkers available from Harveys in

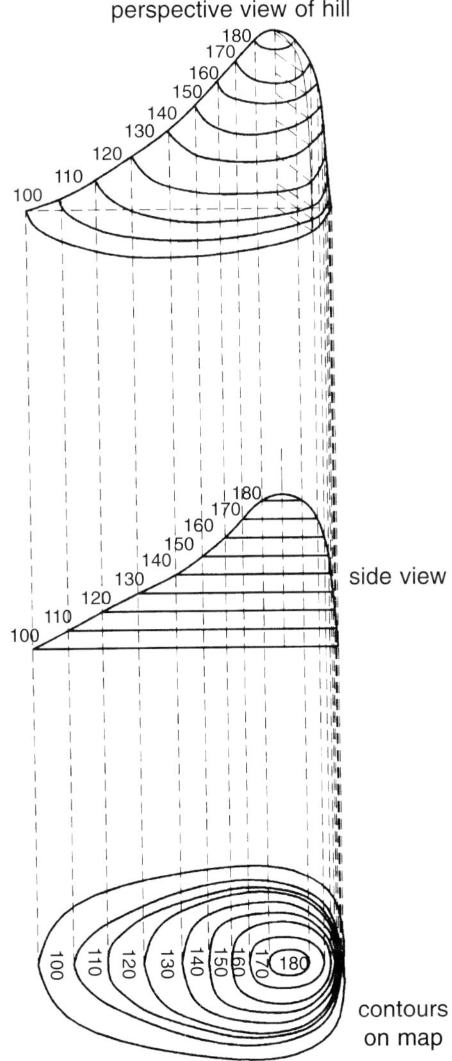

Contour lines showing derivation from landscape.

two scales – Walker Maps at 1:40,000 and Superwalker maps at 1:25,000. Smaller scale maps such as 1:100,000 are useful for planning long walks but not out on the hill. In some countries they may be all that is available.

Contours

There are two sorts of maps: planimetric and topographic. The first are simple, flat plans such as street maps and of no use to hillwalkers. Topographic maps show the shape of the land. They do this with contour lines, which join points of the same height. The closer contour lines are together the steeper the slope. Contour lines reveal the shape of hills so you can gain a good idea of what to expect. They tell you where ridges, cirques and plateaus are and whether summits are small and pointed or flat and spacious.

A common problem with reading contours is distinguishing between spurs and valleys. The quickest way to do this is to look for a stream as if one runs down the middle of the contours it is clearly a valley. The absence of a stream does not mean it is a spur though, as not all valleys have streams in them. However, contour lines are always marked with the elevation above sea level at certain intervals. Ordnance Survey maps are marked every 50m – more often in places on Outdoor Leisure maps – and Harveys every 75m. Some of these heights are printed the right way up on the map, some upside down or sideways. This is because they always read upwards so if they are the right way up then the ground slopes up towards the top of the map, if they are upside down the low ground is towards the top. These contours are also drawn with a thicker line. By following them until you find the

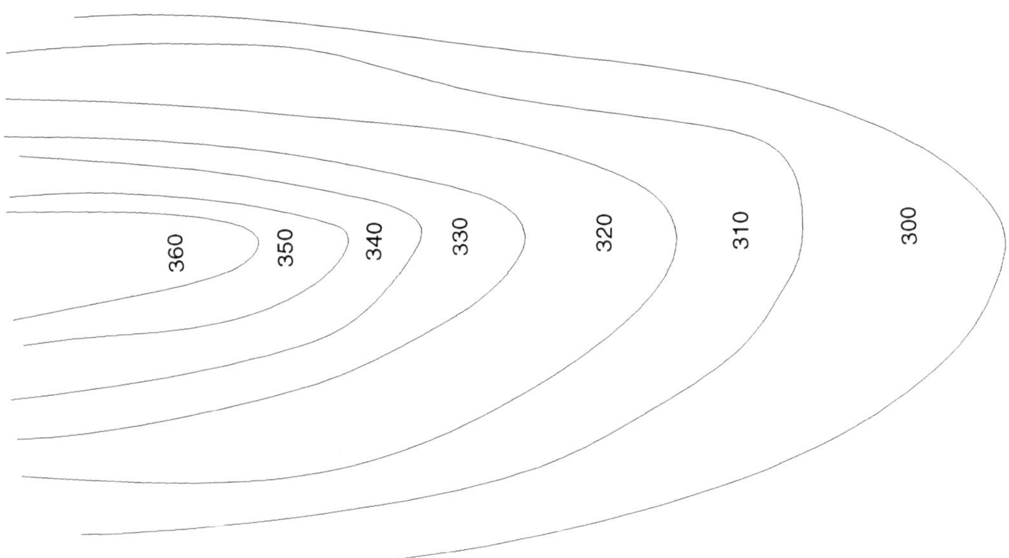

Contour lines showing a spur.

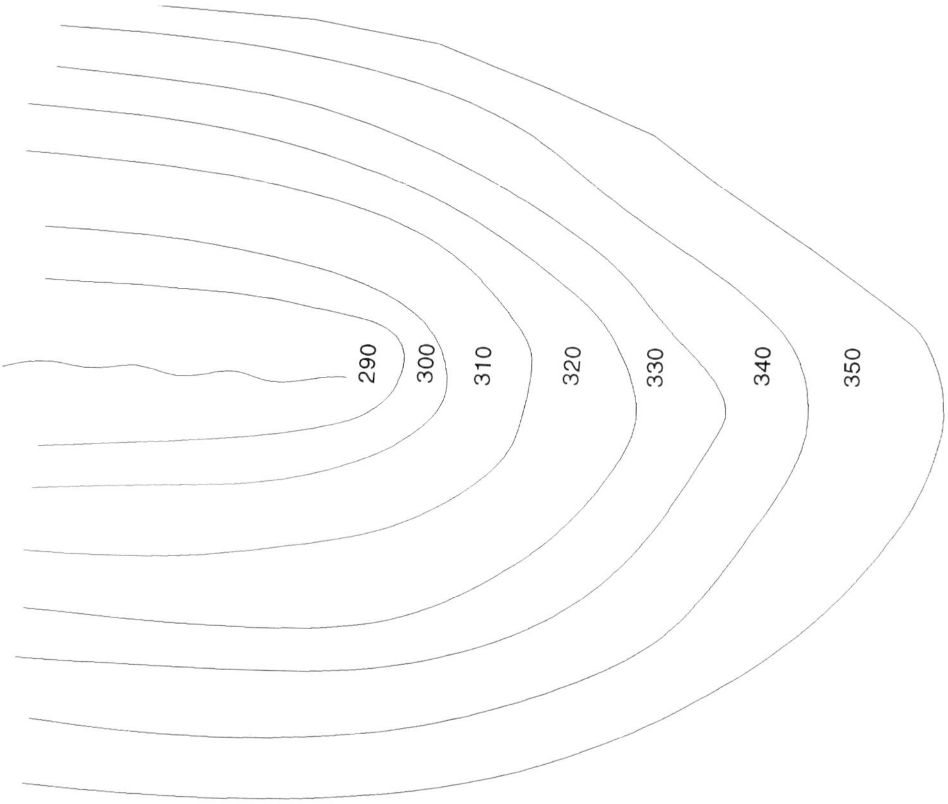

Contour lines showing a valley.

heights you can work out whether a feature is a ridge or a valley.

Contours are also drawn at regular intervals, every 10m on Ordnance Survey maps or every 15m on Harveys. Knowing the interval is important as features shorter than the interval, such as sheer drops, may not be marked – 8m is still a long way to fall. Where maps of different scales have the same contour interval the contour lines will be closer together on the smaller scale map so a slope will look steeper than on a larger scale map. Becoming familiar with the contours on different maps is important for accurate reading of the terrain.

Grid References

Ordnance Survey and Harveys maps, plus many maps covering other countries, have a grid imprinted over them. The sides of the squares of the grid run north–south and east–west. Each square covers one square kilometre and each line on the grid is numbered. By combining the numbers of the east–west line at the bottom of a square with the north–south one on the left edge you get a four-figure grid reference that identifies that square. By dividing each line into tenths you can get a six-figure reference. This can be done by eye, or more accurately with the ruler – or the romer, if it has one – on your compass.

The number of the line to the left of the square is always given first. (The standard way of remembering this is that you go along the corridor and then up the stairs.) The Ordnance Survey grid is unique to the British Isles. Other countries use the Universal Transverse Mercator (UTM) grid, which covers the whole world. As grid numbers are repeated from map sheet to map sheet it is important to add the name or number of your map if giving a grid reference

to someone else, especially in an emergency.

Grid references are used to give positions in the hills and are often found in guide books. Knowing how to give and read them is a useful skill as it means you can quickly give your position or the position of an important feature if you need to, whether for meeting someone or because of an emergency.

Carrying Maps

Your map must be easy to consult. If it is in your pack there is always the temptation not to bother getting it out. 'Oh, it must be this way' is the first step to getting lost. (I know. I have done it.) Maps also need to be protected from the rain unless they are made from a waterproof material like those from Harveys.

There are a number of ways maps can be carried that give easy access. Map cases that can be hung round the neck or over the shoulder are favoured by some walkers. The map can be kept folded so that the side you need is visible and they are waterproof. Despite that I hate them. I cannot stand having a map case dangling in front of me and flapping about in the wind. I prefer to use one that is flexible enough to be folded and stored in a pocket.

Many waterproof and windproof jackets and some fleeces come with map pockets at chest level. These may or may not be big enough to hold a map. They can be useful but condensation can build up behind the map, which is not breathable of course, and may dampen a paper one considerably unless it is in a map case or plastic bag. The large pockets found on the thighs of some walking trousers can also be used for maps, though unless the pocket is very roomy this can be uncomfortable.

My favourite place for carrying a

One way to have quick access to the map is to carry it in the wand pocket of a rucksack.

map is in a wand pocket of a rucksack. Here it does not affect the comfort or breathability of my clothing and it is still available when I am only wearing shorts and a T-shirt. Not all rucksacks have such open pockets and care does need to be taken to put the map back properly. I have occasionally dropped it.

Care is also needed when handling maps, especially in high winds. People have become lost because their maps have blown away. It is best to carry the map folded to the side you want so you do not have to unfold it every time you use it. On high ground with a good view opening up the map gives a general overview of your surroundings. You do not want to have to do this though. In a group everybody should have a map both in case one blows away or becomes so wet as to be useless and so that everyone can be following the route.

THE COMPASS

When visibility is poor or you are crossing featureless terrain such as flat moorland a compass is needed. One should always be carried on a hillwalk, whatever the weather when you set off, as conditions can change rapidly. In thick mist, at night, even perhaps in dense forest, it is only by using a compass that you can ensure you keep to your route and do not wander round in circles or onto dangerous ground.

A difficult situation is not the place to learn compass techniques. Practise in clear weather and in a place where an error will not lead you onto hazardous terrain. Somewhere you already know well is ideal.

The basis of a compass is its magnetic needle. This aligns itself with the Earth's magnetic field, which runs north–south, and points to magnetic

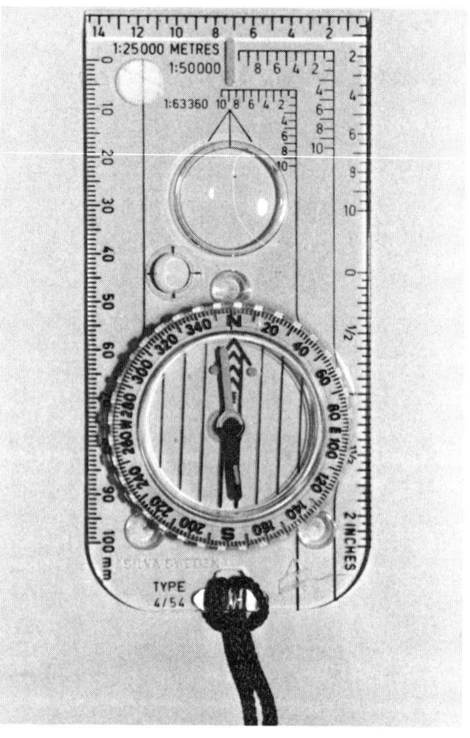

An orienteering compass with magnifier and romers.

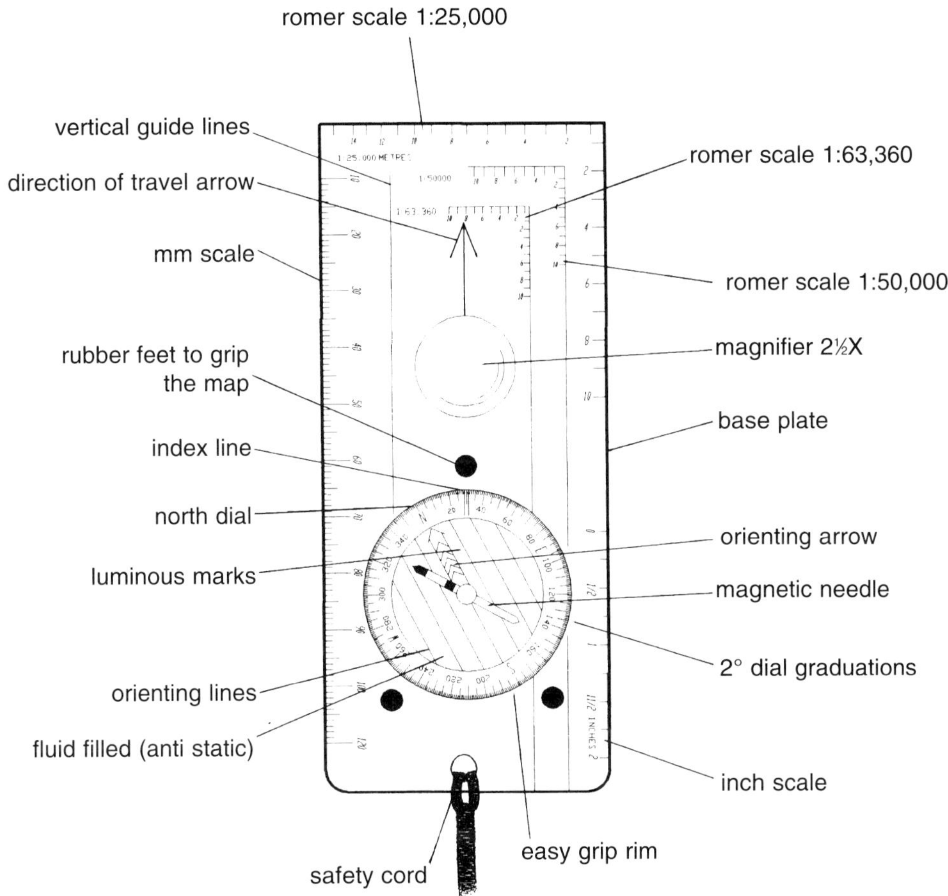

The parts of an orienteering compass.

north, which lies in the far north of Canada. However, it is not necessarily of much use just knowing where north is. Much more important is to be able to work out from the map the direction in which you want to go. This is known as a bearing.

Types of Compass

There are many types of compass available but only one that is really useful for hillwalking. This is the protractor or orienteering compass, which combines the compass with a protractor so that angles relative to north can be measured.

Sighting compasses have mirrors, prisms or lenses for precise navigation. These are extremely accurate when used properly but are heavier and much more expensive than orienteering compasses. They are also harder to take bearings with. People who venture into remote mountain ranges, especially when snow-covered, often use them but for ordinary hillwalking they are not as useful as simpler designs.

On an orienteering compass the housing dial contains the familiar points of the compass – north, south, east and west – plus the 360 degrees of a circle, usually marked every 2 degrees. Inside the housing is the needle, floating in oil to dampen its movement. The magnetic end, which points north, is usually coloured red, the other end white. Some specialist compasses have the magnetic part of the needle, often in the form of a separate magnet, placed near the centre rather than at the end. This means the needle hardly swings at all when you use it while moving, an advantage for orienteers or fell runners but not of major importance to hillwalkers. The base of the housing has parallel lines known as orienting lines on it plus an arrow called the orienting arrow. On some compasses the latter may be in the form of two coloured parallel lines rather than an actual arrow.

The housing sits on a base plate but is free to turn through a complete circle. The base plate contains several lines parallel to the sides, rulers along the edges and a central arrow parallel to the sides called the direction of travel arrow. Many also contain a magnifying glass for reading detail on a map in poor light and romer scales for different scales of map, usually 1:50,000, 1:25,000 and 1:63,360 (the latter for one inch to the mile Ordnance Survey maps, discontinued in the 1970s). Romer scales are divided into tenths on the same basis as grid squares and can be used for calculating accurate grid references and measuring distances on the map.

Setting the Map

A basic use of the compass is to assist in setting the map, which means aligning the map with features on the ground by turning the top of the map so it points north. It should then be easy to identify features on the ground on the map. If there are plenty of features around you that you can identify on the map you can set the map without using the compass. If you are not sure just which ridge on the map is the one you can see to your right or which of several pools the one in front of you might be then you need to use your compass.

First ensure that the housing is turned to a bearing of 0 degrees (due north) so that the orienting lines are parallel to the edges of the base plate and the orienting and direction of travel arrows are in line with each other. Then place the compass flat on the map with the sides parallel to the north–south grid lines and with north towards the top of the map. Next turn the map and compass together until the red end of the magnetic needle lines up with north on the dial. The map is now set and features on the ground should correspond with the map. If you are facing south the map will be upside down now but you should be able to identify the ridge and the pool. If the former is to your right, it should be to the right of your position on the map. If you are still not sure you can point the direction of travel arrow at the feature, turn the dial until the magnetic needle and the orienting arrow are aligned, and then read off the figure in line with the direction of travel arrow to get a bearing. Put the compass on the map and set the map. The same bearing on the map should point to the feature.

Taking a Map Bearing

The compass is a complex and versatile instrument and books on navigation cover large numbers of compass techniques. But a few simple techniques are all that most walkers ever need. The main purpose of the compass is to help you find your way in poor visibility or across featureless country. To do this you need to take a bearing from your

Align the compass with your objective on the map ...

then rotate the housing to line up the orienting with the N–S grid lines.

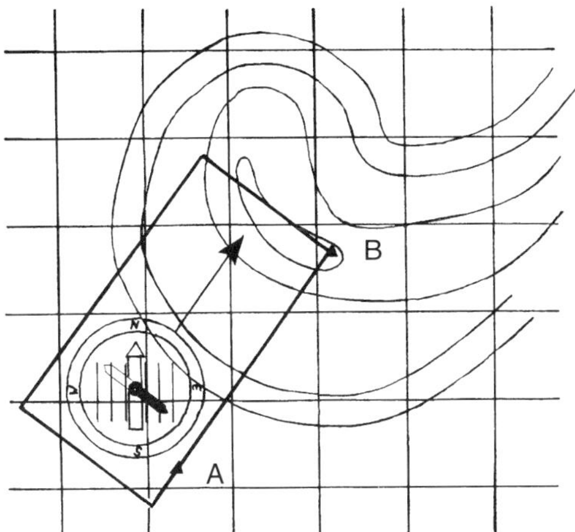

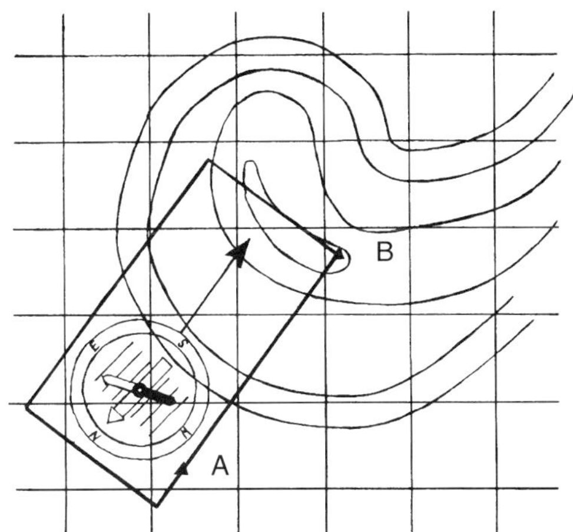

Taking a bearing from the map.

map. This is done by lying the compass on the map with the upper edge running between your position and your destination so that the direction of travel arrow points where you want to go. The magnetic needle can be ignored for now.

Next twist the housing until the orienting lines on the base are parallel with the grid lines on the map and north is towards the top of the map. The bearing is the number on the compass housing that lines up with the direction of travel arrow. If you now remove the compass from the map and turn it, without moving the housing, until the red end of the needle is lined up with the orienting arrow the direction of travel arrow will point in the direction you want to walk.

It is worth noting the number of the bearing as it is possible for the housing to be moved when the compass is in your pocket. It is also worth checking that the red end of the magnetic needle is pointing north. People have been known to get this wrong and head off in the opposite direction to the one they want.

Magnetic Variation

Unfortunately taking a bearing is not quite as simple as described above because there are three different north directions: true north, grid north and magnetic north. The first is where the North Pole is and, unless you are going there, is not important for hillwalking. Grid north is where the grid lines on a map point while magnetic north is where your compass needle points. The variation between these two is called the magnetic variation or declination. To make matters more confusing magnetic north moves about from year to year. All Ordnance Survey and Harveys maps give the variation at the date of publication and the rate of change per year. In the British Isles in the mid 1990s magnetic north is about 5 degrees to the west of grid north. For accurate navigation magnetic variation must be taken into account. When you transfer a bearing from the map to the compass, as described above, the variation must be added. So if the bearing from the map is

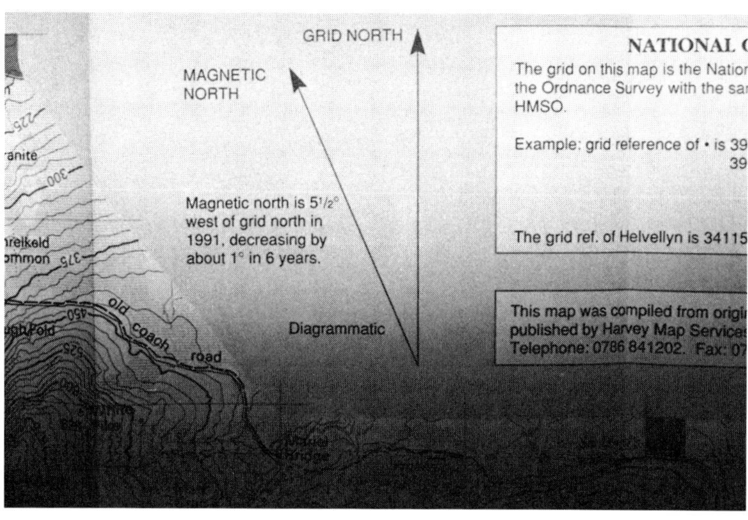

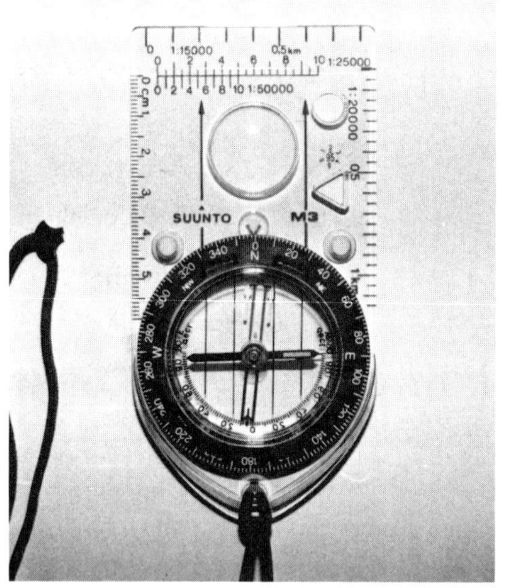

This compass can be corrected for declination.

230 degrees and the variation is 5 degrees then the correct compass bearing is 235 degrees. (There are various mnemonics for remembering this. The one that stuck in my mind decades ago is 'empty sea, add water' – MTC, map to compass, add.)

If you go to a region such as the western United States where magnetic north is east of grid north you have to subtract the variation. In any area you should always check the variation on the map. Some compasses can be corrected for magnetic variation, which is very convenient though you must remember to alter the setting if you go to an area where the magnetic variation is different.

Following a Bearing

Once you have a compass bearing you can head off towards your destination. Even so, walking in a straight line while looking at a compass for any distance is difficult, especially over rough terrain. Also, obstacles such as cliffs and lakes may mean you cannot stay on your bearing. Rather than take a bearing on your ultimate objective it is better to take one on a much nearer point, ideally one that is visible and certainly one that you can see from the map you should be able to walk to directly. Once you reach that point take another bearing to another point. By connecting up these 'legs', as they are called, you can reach your destination.

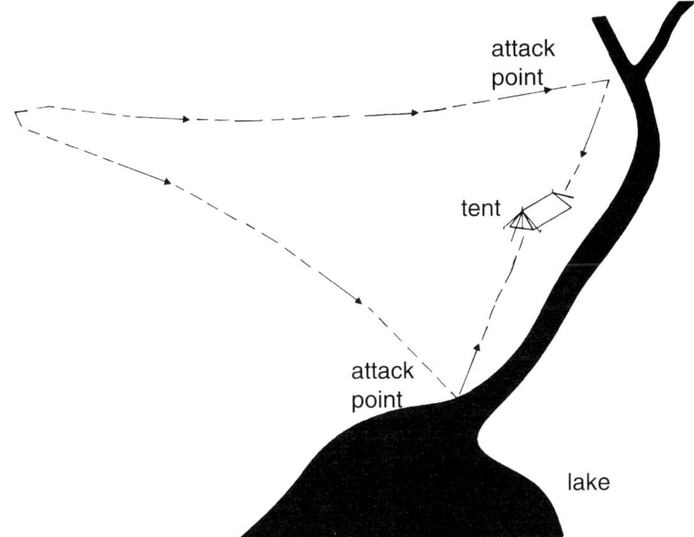

Attack points.

Attack Points

It is unlikely that all your legs will be on the same bearing; in hill country being able to walk in a straight line to your destination is unusual. Normally you walk on several bearings between your start point and your destination, linking different points along the way. These are known to orienteering enthusiasts as attack points.

The best are small, easily identifiable features such as cliffs, minor summits or tarns. In really poor visibility it can be better to head for such features even if they lie well off your route rather than

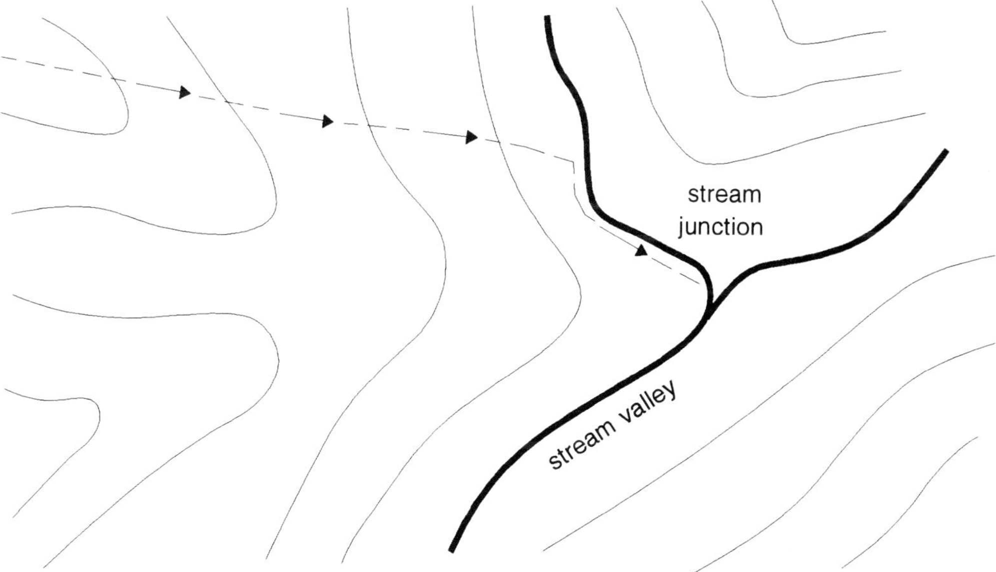

Aiming off.

do a long leg with no identifiable points along the way. Using a series of attack points makes it much less likely that you will get lost than if you aim directly for a distant feature.

Aiming Off

If your next objective, whether your final destination or a point on the way, lies on a linear feature such as a stream, ridge, path or road and you take a bearing directly on it you have a problem if you reach the feature and cannot see your destination. Which way do you go? To avoid this happening you can 'aim off', another orienteering term. This means deliberately taking a bearing to one side or other of your objective. Then when you reach the feature you know which way to turn to get where you want to be.

Compass Problems

I was originally taught always to trust the compass. Then I found myself descending the wrong side of a mountain (Ben More on the island of Mull) in thick mist despite following the compass. The reason, I found out later, was that the summit rocks of Ben More are magnetic, causing the compass to give an incorrect bearing. There are a very few other places where this is so, such as the Cuillin hills on the Isle of Skye.

Mostly, though, the advice to trust the compass is sensible. Do observe the land around too, so if you are going wrong you will notice as quickly as possible. Places where the compass will not work are usually very small so taking a few bearings and averaging them out may give you at least a rough idea as to the direction to go. Checking the compass regularly is worthwhile too. If I had looked at it a short while after leav-

ing the top of Ben More I would have seen I was going the wrong way. Guide books usually give information about problem areas. Metal objects can also cause the compass needle to deviate from magnetic north so it is wise to take bearings away from watches, ice axes and anything else metallic.

Air bubbles sometimes form in compasses due to changes in atmospheric pressure. This occurs most commonly at heights above 2000ft (600m). It is not a problem and the bubbles usually soon disappear. If they do not and start to get bigger it could be that the housing has sprung a leak. This can be repaired by the maker but it is probably only worth doing this if you have an expensive model. Otherwise it is cheaper to buy a new compass.

If you travel widely you may find that in some countries your compass needle dips and presses against the housing so it cannot be used. This is called inclination. The earth has five magnetic zones running roughly parallel to the equator and compasses are balanced for one of these. The further you go from the zone for which your compass is balanced the more likely you are to have problems. Compasses balanced for the zone in which the British Isles lie will work fine in Alaska and Siberia but not in Australia or New Zealand where a differently balanced compass will be needed.

There is much more you can do with a compass. For further information consult one of the books devoted to mountain navigation (see Further Reading section).

ALTIMETERS

The map and, in poor visibility, the compass are all you need for navigation. However, there are other tools that can help at times. The altimeter is one of these. This is a barometer and measures air pressure. As pressure drops with elevation, measuring it can be used to give the altitude.

Altimeters used to be bulky, expensive instruments used by Himalayan mountaineers rather than hillwalkers. But now there are many wrist-watch style altimeters available that are easy to use, reasonably priced and quite durable.

For most hillwalking an altimeter is unnecessary though using one can be fun, especially if it is the type that measures how far you have climbed and at what speed. Once you leave footpaths or venture onto snow-covered hills an altimeter can be quite useful as knowing your exact height can aid and speed up navigation. Although you may know which slope you are on it can take time to work out exactly just where on the slope you are with a map and compass. An altimeter tells you this. Is this important? It can be if, for example, you need to change your bearing at a certain height in order to circumvent some crags that lie below you but that you cannot see in the mist.

Altimeters need care in use. As pressure changes will alter the reading as well as differences in height an altimeter must be reset to known heights frequently. If you cannot do this for several hours the elevation given may well be inaccurate, especially if there is been a change in the weather.

Altimeters can also be used for weather forecasting, especially when you are camping or using huts or hostels in the hills. If your tent or hut appears to have risen during the night then the pressure has fallen, suggesting the weather might deteriorate, while if you appear to have sunk the pressure is rising and good weather could be on the way. The speed and amount of the change matters too. A big, rapid change implies a quick change in the weather. Although this is not a foolproof forecasting method, I have several times changed my plans for the day on the basis of rapid pressure changes – and been glad I have done so when a big storm has blown in and I am down in the valley rather than high on a summit as intended. It is even more pleasing when you set off up in poor conditions and, as you predicted from a steep rise

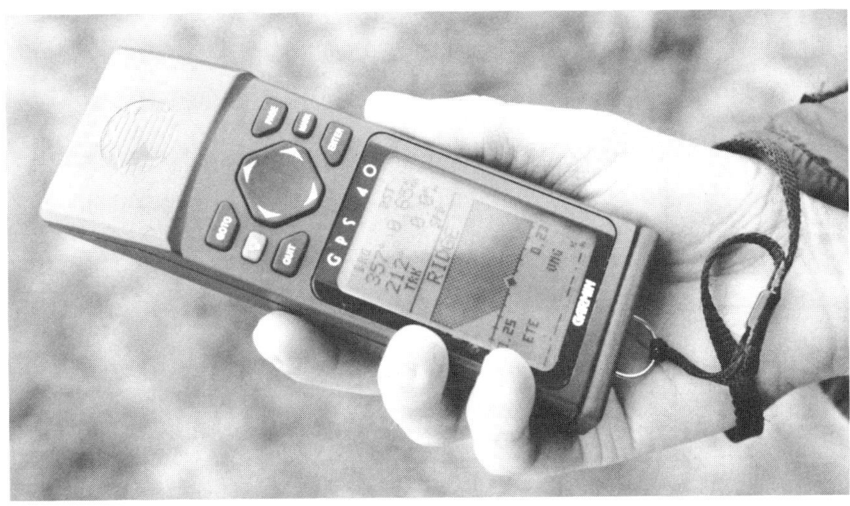

A global positioning system (GPS) receiver.

in the pressure, the skies clear and the day turns out fine.

SATELLITE NAVIGATION

The latest devices for navigation are electronic Global Positioning System (GPS) receivers, which work with 24 satellites put into space by the United States Department of Defense. These orbit the Earth twice every day and send out continuous radio signals. By locking onto at least three of these signals a GPS receiver can work out its position by triangulation. The position can be given as latitude and longitude or a grid reference.

GPS receivers will do far more than just tell you where you are. You can put a series of grid references, known as waypoints, into a receiver and it can then guide you to them. It can also record grid references during a walk so you can reverse your route in thick mist using the receiver as a guide. Other information provided usually includes the distance to your next waypoint and your ultimate destination, the speed you are travelling and the time it will take to get to the next waypoint. Displays often include a moving map or roadway that show where you are in relation to your objective and whether you are heading in the right direction.

It would seem that a GPS receiver could solve all navigational problems but this is not so and there are many disadvantages. To begin with, the receivers are complex electronic instruments and time is needed to learn how they work. If you have problems programming a video recorder then a GPS receiver will probably have you tearing your hair out. But if you use computers regularly much of the way the software works will be familiar. There are also great differences between the models

available and some are much easier to use than others. Carefully compare several models before buying one; the technology is changing rapidly.

For hill use, you also need to consider how easy a receiver would be to use in bad weather. Could the controls be operated when you have thick mitts or gloves on? How easy is the display to read? How comfortable is it to hold in your hand? Is it small enough to be carried on your rucksack hip belt or in a pocket?

To use a GPS receiver properly you need to be a good navigator and very competent with grid references, as these are what the receiver gives you and what you programme into it. If you cannot read them accurately then the receiver is useless. Your route planning needs to be good too. The GPS receiver knows nothing about terrain. If you plot a route that goes over a cliff that is where it will lead you.

GPS receivers are expensive, but prices are dropping. Even so at the time of writing the least expensive model is still twenty times the price of a basic orienteering compass. Then there is the weight to consider. The lightest models weigh ½lb (225g) or so, many are much heavier. As they require four to six AA size batteries and go through them fairly quickly, spares should be carried so the actual weight in your rucksack is more than this.

Although very accurate much of the time GPS receivers cannot be relied on. There is a built in random margin of error called 'selective availability' and positions are within 100m (330ft) 95 per cent of the time or 300m (980ft) the remaining 5 per cent. This is fine for crossing featureless moorland but nowhere near accurate enough in places where very precise navigation is needed such as getting safely off the summit of

Ben Nevis in winter. There that level of inaccuracy could lead you onto dangerous cornices or into the notorious trap of Five Finger Gully where there have been many accidents, some fatal. I have usually found receivers accurate to a few metres but obviously you cannot assume this. Unfortunately there is no way of knowing when the error is in operation. Differential GPS, due to be introduced during 1996, should give an accuracy within 10m (33ft). At the same time it appears that both the US Department of Defense and the Royal Air Force are experimenting with ways of electronically jamming the system so it could be that at times and in certain places it will not work at all.

A constant problem for hillwalking is that GPS receivers depend on line of sight. If you are in a steep-sided valley, below a cliff or in a dense forest you may not be able to pick up enough satellites for the receiver to work. The better receivers show you where satellites are and which are being picked up. If it is safe and possible to do so you can then walk away from the obstacle to where you can pick up more satellites. Some receivers also warn you if the signals are not strong enough. Even so, at times I have been unable to get a position even in fairly open terrain. When the mist has been thick I have been glad I was using a map and compass as well.

Receivers also give your height, but as the margin of error can be 150m (500ft) or more this function is useless for hillwalking. Some receivers tell you the degree of error in altitude readings.

Despite all this I do think GPS receivers are useful in some circumstances. For footpath walking they are unnecessary but when going cross-country, especially in featureless terrain and on snow-covered ground, they are a useful backup to map and compass. I have found I can travel faster using a GPS in dense mist than when using a compass. You do need to bear in mind the limitations though.

I am sure that GPS receivers will play an increasingly large part in hill navigation, especially as lighter, less expensive models appear. It is likely too that we shall soon see receivers that have moving topographic map displays built in. Eventually there will be GPS guide books available so that Pennine Way walkers will simply programme the route into their GPS and set off. Some people abhor the idea of walking in the hills guided by an electronic device, spending your time staring at a screen. But is this really that much different to walking along with a guide book in your hand as so many people do?

GUIDE BOOKS

There are now few walking areas not covered by at least one guide book. In popular areas like the Lake District there are masses of guides with new titles published every year. Guide books can be split into two types; those designed for the bookshelf and coffee table and those designed for the rucksack. The former are generally packed with colour photographs. The best can be read for inspiration and to gain an idea of what an area is like rather than for route information. Some are an odd mixture of detailed route information and photographs. I say odd because you would never carry one of these books on the hill. I have seen plenty of photocopied pages about though! Even so the best of these books are for daydreaming over in your armchair at home rather than taking on the hill.

The more practical sort of guide book is the footpath guide. These are small and lightweight and generally have only a few illustrations, often just drawings. The route descriptions are functional and often allied to sketch maps. Such guides are useful, especially for areas you have never visited before, but they do have a tendency to push people onto certain routes – particularly in open hill country where you can wander where you like. For finding the rights of way through cultivated land in valleys in order to reach the hills such books are very useful. They are also good for information on facilities such as bridges and shelter huts. They are not a substitute for a map, nor for good navigation skills.

SIGNPOSTS AND WAYMARKS

The places where hill paths leave roads or car parks are often signposted and in

A signpost showing the way through the lower fields towards the summit.

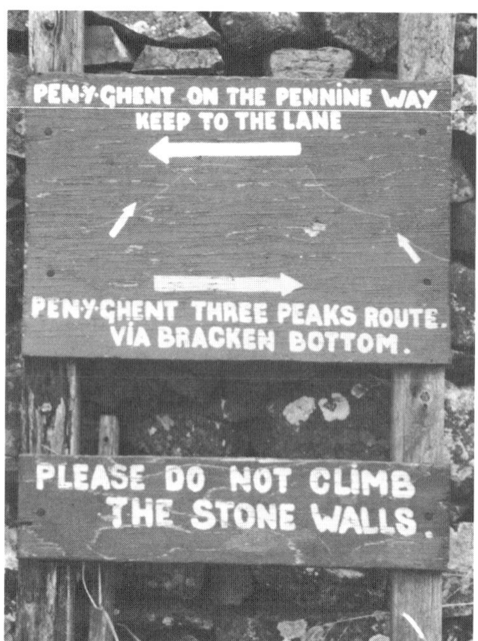

Often the hardest navigation can be escaping from the confines of the valley. Signs like these help.

Public footpath signs indicating routes through the hills.

places you may find signposts in the hills, often marking rights of ways or popular routes. More common are way-marks of some sort that show where the route goes. In the UK piles of stones known as cairns are used to mark routes. While these can be useful in most areas there are far too many of them, often lining very distinct, wide paths. Worse are those that appear in places where there are no paths as these can lead to a path developing. I knock such cairns down as I do others I consider unnecessary and I would urge others to do the same. If you do build a cairn – to mark the point where you need to leave a ridge on your return from a summit for example – do please dismantle it when it is no longer needed.

Abroad, other methods are often used for marking paths. In much of Europe from Lapland to Spain red paint splashes on rocks are used, while in forested areas of North America blazes cut into tree trunks may be found.

It is never sensible to rely on waymarks or signposts. They can easily disappear just at the point you need them most. Sometimes there may be a gap between waymarks on an otherwise well marked route. In my experience this is usually where the route makes an abrupt turn. If you know where you are on the map this should not be a problem.

PLANNING AND FOLLOWING A ROUTE

A walk can be worked out from a map or simply selected from a guide book. In both cases you need to know the length of the route, the time you expect to take, your fitness and that of any companions and the weather forecast. The time of year matters too: in winter days are short and snow and ice may slow you down. A good guide book should give information about the state of paths, the nature of the terrain and any problems you may encounter. If you plan a walk from the map you will not necessarily know about these unless it is an area you are familiar with. If the route is one that could be difficult in bad weather escape routes where you can drop down to easier terrain should be noted and a shorter, lower level alternative planned in case the day dawns stormier than expected.

When going out in a group remember that you will progress at the speed of the slowest member. If you are the leader or the person who has planned the route, make sure everyone knows how far the walk is and how long you expect it to take. If you are a group member and you do not feel happy with the distance or time say so. It is better to amend timings or distance before you start than have to do so on the hill when someone becomes tired.

Working out distances on the map can be done in a number of ways. A little wheel known as a milometer that measures the distance can be run along the route or you can place a piece of cotton, wool or thin string along it. You can also use the scales on your compass base plate. I usually just count the number of grid squares crossed, including those crossed at corners only. Each square crossed is a kilometre. The result seems as accurate as any other method. The amount of ascent can be more accurately found by counting the contour lines then multiplying this by the contour interval. To speed this up you can just count every fifth contour.

Timing

A key skill is knowing how long it should take to walk a route. You should be able to break this down to cover each

Stony ground like this can make for slow walking even in good weather. Allow time for crossing such terrain.

leg of the walk too so that when the mist is down you have a good idea of when you should reach certain features. The accepted formula for estimating time is that worked out by Scottish mountaineer W. Naismith in the nineteenth century, and hence called Naismith's Rule. This allows for an hour for every 3 miles (5km) plus an extra half hour for every 1000ft (300m) of ascent. Rest stops are not included and allowances have to be made for difficult terrain and weather conditions.

Dry firm footpaths make for the fastest walking, deep mud or snow the slowest. Steep rocky terrain where great care is needed can slow you down too, whether descending or ascending. When planning a walk do not just look at the distance and the amount of ascent, also consider the terrain and whether you will be following paths or not. I reckon on walking 20 to 25 miles (32 to 40km) a day on good paths but only 12 to 15 miles (20 to 24km) when

A steep path cutting up the back wall of a cirque. These slopes would be much harder to climb without the path.

High on the path in the picture on page 92 showing it is quite wide and easy to follow.

The top of the path shown in the picture above. There isn't a notice like this at the bottom!

going cross-country.

Weather can have odd effects on walking speed. In wet weather I find I walk faster and stop less often and for less time than in dry conditions. Overall, though, only extremes of wind, snow or heat have any great effect on walking speed.

Naismith's Rule can be broken down for more precise timing over short sections to the following imperial and metric equivalents:

- 20 minutes per mile or 12 minutes per km
- 10 minutes per ½ mile or 6 minutes per 500m
- 5 minutes per ¼ mile or 1.2 minutes per 100m
- 1000ft (300m) per 30 minutes
- 500ft (150m) per 15 minutes
- 33ft (10m) per minute – 10m is the contour interval on Ordnance Survey Landranger and Outdoor Leisure maps

Once you have done a fair amount of walking you will know the rate at which you walk, which may vary a great deal from Naismith, and be able to plan walks on that basis and use it for short legs where good navigation is needed.

When precise navigation is needed, for finding the start of a path down a steep, rocky slope in mist for example, pace counting can be very accurate. To do this you need to know the length of your stride, which can be found by walking a measured distance (such as 100m) at a sports stadium. I have never measured my pace like this. Instead I used a tape measure to measure a number of steps. The average came out at 76cm (about 2½ft), which would mean 131 paces per 100m (330ft). When walking a leg of, say, 300m (1000ft) you can

count every pace, or more easily every two paces, knowing that you should be there after about 393 paces. This sounds a very good way of navigating precisely but I have never done it. I prefer to use timings instead but knowing my pace does mean I could use pace counting if necessary.

Following a Route

Walking a clear footpath is easy, even high in the hills. Once you leave paths behind and plan cross country routes there are a number of factors to take into account. First, unless the area is one you are familiar with, you cannot know exactly what you will encounter. The best maps do not tell you everything, in particular how rough the terrain may be. For this reason you should allow more time for a cross country walk than you would for a footpath walk of similar length and have alternative routes in mind in case it proves impassable at some point or takes too long. Flexibility is needed too. If it is apparent on the ground that it would be easier and safer to contour across the hillside above the boggy bottom of the valley you had intended walking up, or descend the broad buttress rather than the back wall of the bowl you had planned going down because the latter is rockier than it looked from the map, then do so. Sticking rigidly to a route is not sensible if it leads you into dangerous terrain or takes longer than an easier alternative. A different route may look more fun or more scenic too.

There are few rules for cross country travel. Even those you commonly hear have many exceptions. 'Do not gain unnecessary height' is one that appears to make sense, though there are plenty of places where minor summits lie between two hills you want to climb.

Mountain lakes often lie below steep cliffs up which there may be no routes for walkers.

Following a stream may provide a good way up or down a hill though you do need to watch out for crags and waterfalls.

Too often I have heeded that advice and contoured round these tops only to spend far too long on a difficult clamber across steep, rocky or thickly vegetated slopes. It is often much easier to go over the top.

'Do not follow streams downhill' is another dictum that is not quite as sensible as it sounds. While it is true that water always takes the quickest way down this does not mean that there will be waterfalls on every stream. I follow streams frequently as this is often a far more enjoyable way to descend than slogging down a steep, featureless hillside. Obviously, care is required. If the slopes start getting too steep I traverse out to the side. I never descend anything I cannot easily get back up again if I have to and if the stream enters a narrow, steep-sided gully I stick to the banks high above.

GETTING LOST

Being lost is a state of mind. You may be temporarily unsure of your whereabouts but you are not lost unless you think you are. If you can read a map well and use your compass properly and you check your map regularly you should always know where you are. However everyone makes an error at some time and finds they are unclear as to exactly where they are, especially in poor visibility. If this happens the first thing to do is stay calm. It is all too easy to rush off in a panic searching for a path or a cairn. People have even been known to abandon their rucksacks so they can move faster. The result is all too often an accident or hypothermia. If you are properly equipped you should have the means to survive an unplanned night out if absolutely necessary.

Once you have recovered from the initial shock of discovering you do not know where you are stop and think about what you are going to do. Have a snack and a drink while you do so. The important thing is to stay calm. If it is possible you should consider backtracking to your last known position. How long is it since you last knew exactly where you were? If it was not long ago you cannot have strayed too far. You are unlikely to be walking at more than 2½ to 3mph (4 to 5 km per hour) so if you knew where you were an hour or so before you must be within 3 miles (5km) of that spot. Using your compass baseplate you can check the area within that distance on the map, looking for terrain that resembles where you are. If you know in which direction you left your last known point it should be even easier to work out roughly where you are. Have you been following a compass bearing? If so, you must be somewhere along it or at least not too far away.

If it is several hours since you knew where you were it probably is not worth trying to retrace your steps. This should not happen if you consult your map often (unless your map reading is very poor).

If you cannot retrace your steps to somewhere you recognize it is best to work out how to reach the place you want to be at the end of the day rather than bothering with any intermediate destinations. If your car or camp or accommodation is to the north then descending into a valley to the south is not a good idea. A compass bearing should ensure you do not do that.

If there is an obvious large feature not too far away, such as a lake or forest, heading for that would be sensible as then you would know your rough location. Be wary of man-made features as these can disappear and may not be marked accurately on the map.

On rolling moorland terrain you can

Be wary of descending steep slopes when you can't see what lies below.

usually make a direct descent quite safely, though you should always watch out for small crags and deep stream gullies. In rockier, more mountainous terrain more care is needed and you should study the map to see where any difficult or dangerous ground lies and descend by a safe route even if it lands you some distance from where you want to be.

While walking you should always be on the lookout for features you might be able to identify from the map. The chances are that within a short time you will come across a feature that enables you to find out where you are. Sometimes an obvious feature that should be visible may not appear for unexpected reasons. When I was walking the Pacific Crest Trail in the United States a companion and I took a very unwise short-cut in the northern Sierra Nevada mountains. It was unwise because for a short section we were not on the maps we were carrying nor on a path. Unsurprisingly we became a little mislaid. In fact we camped that night with no real idea of where we were. We knew the general direction in which we should be heading in, so the next day we continued that way. An obvious feature we expected to see clearly was a pointed hill called The Nipple. Despite trying very hard we could not convince ourselves that the only prominent summit we could see really corresponded with the topography on the map, though we headed for it anyway. Eventually we came on a path, which we followed as it ran in approximately the right direction and walking along it was a lot easier and quicker than going cross country. After a while a sign appeared. It read 'Pacific

Crest Trail' – although we had not realized it we were back on our route. It was still some time before we knew exactly where we had rejoined it. When we did work it out we realized why we could not see The Nipple. We were contouring below the summit!

Overall it is best to view being lost as an adventure and an experience to learn from rather than as a disaster. By doing so it will be far more enjoyable and you will probably find out where you are more quickly too.

LEAVING WORD

Whether you travel solo or in a group you should always tell somebody where you are going and when you will be back. And do not forget to let them know once your trip is over. Mountain rescue teams spend too many hours looking for walkers who are back home or sitting in a café. On trips longer than a weekend you should arrange to contact somebody at points where you have access to a telephone.

6 Skills and Hazards

Body-swerving through peat hags is a wonderful way to improve suppleness. (Ralph Storer, The Joy of Hillwalking)

Other than the ability to navigate, hillwalking does not involve any technical skills, though there are ways to walk that make it easier and safer, especially on steep terrain. Neither is hillwalking particularly dangerous, especially if you keep to paths. There are potential hazards you should know about, however, just in case you encounter them.

HOW FAR AND HOW FAST?

How far can you walk in a day? This is a common question but not one with an easy answer as there are many factors involved including fitness, the length of your stride, the weight carried and the nature and gradient of the terrain. In Chapter 5 I detailed Naismith's Rule. Using this formula a 15 mile (24km) walk with 3000ft (900m) of ascent should take 6½ hours. This does not allow for any stops so at least an hour, more likely an hour and a half, could be added on for time taken looking at the view, eating lunch, consulting the map, adjusting clothing, taking photographs and more.

Hillwalking is not about moving as far and as fast as possible, even though some people like to do this. If you want truly to appreciate wild land then you need the time to see what is around you. Finishing each day tired out is not a good idea either. For safety you need to have something in reserve.

REST STOPS

Exhaustion is dangerous, it can lead to slips and stumbles, errors of judgement in route finding, even having to stay out overnight. It is also not much fun being over-tired. To avoid this, allow for several rest and snack stops in your planning. In wet or cold weather stops may be only a few minutes long, just enough to allow you to regain some energy. On hot days the danger can be in stopping for too long. I have more than once fallen asleep on a sunny hillside! Overall, short stops are better than long stops so that your leg muscles do not stiffen too much.

Where you stop depends on the weather. Summits are wonderful viewpoints in fine weather but not places to linger in a storm. It is always worth seeking shelter, even if it is only behind a boulder, in cold windy weather. Unless it is warm you should put on extra clothing or even get into a bivvy bag if you stop for more than a few minutes. A snack at every rest stop is a good idea too.

GROUPS

Most walkers go out in small informal groups, often just two or three people. Three or more is the safest number as in the unlikely event of an emergency help can be sought without the casualty being left on their own. If there are four or more of you no one has to go for help alone either.

In any group, whether organized or informal, everyone should know the plans for the day and be individually equipped so they could continue alone if necessary. Everyone should be able to navigate too. It is not safe to have a group totally dependent on the abilities of one member. What if it is that person who falls over a cliff?

Good group leaders should take into account the strength and fitness of all members. If someone wants to turn back or shorten the route because of tiredness they should do this. Pushing on could lead to serious problems. If the group becomes strung out, as can easily happen with more than three or four people, the leader should make sure everyone has proper rest stops. Otherwise those at the back can arrive at a resting place to hear the rest of the group saying 'thank goodness you are here, now we can move on'. All too often they will not say they need a rest and something to eat and drink, but will simply push on getting more and more tired.

Many areas have local walking groups, often branches of the Ramblers' Association or the Long Distance Walkers' Association (see Useful Addresses section), which organize regular walks at both low and high levels. If you are a beginner or seeking companions to walk with joining a group is a good idea. When on a group walk remember that the leader has

Organized walks can be fun and a challenge. This is a checkpoint and snack stop on a Long Distance Walkers' Association event.

responsibility for the whole group and the right to make decisions they feel are in the best interests of everybody. If you find yourself chafing at the leader's decisions or frustrated at the lack of challenge on the routes walked then it is time either to take up walk leading yourself or to plan and undertake your own walks.

SOLO WALKING

The usual advice given in books like this is not to walk alone as it is too dangerous. But I like solo walking and go out alone a great deal, sometimes on summer-long walks in remote mountain areas, so I can hardly condemn it. Some of my most memorable times in the hills have been when by myself. Solo walking puts you more in touch with the natural world and leaves you free to make decisions about where or how far to walk on the spur of the moment.

I would not advise anyone to do the same until they have a fair amount of experience and feel confident in their abilities. Those new to solo walking would also be wise to start off in summer on popular hills with good footpaths. Solo walking in winter is obviously a serious activity and should only be undertaken by those who really know what they are doing.

SCRAMBLING

Once a route leads onto steep rocky terrain and you have to use your hands it becomes a scramble, that grey area where hillwalking merges with rock climbing. Some walkers love scrambles and seek them out, others avoid them at all costs. Scrambling is much more dangerous than walking because a slip can often result in a serious fall. A head for

Easy scrambling on granite slabs.

heights and a good sense of balance are essential requirements. Scrambles vary greatly in difficulty. The easiest can be hard to distinguish from steep walks while the hardest are really easy rock climbs and require some of the techniques and equipment of that pursuit.

Many popular hillwalks, such as Striding Edge on Helvellyn and Crib Goch on Snowdon, are easy scrambles that do not require any technical equipment or expertise.

Harder scrambles may require the use of ropes and some rock climbing ability. Rope handling, protecting climbs and climbing techniques are best

A steep scramble. Confidence and skill are needed before this sort of easy climbing is attempted. Carrying a rope is sensible in case of problems.

learnt on a course at an outdoor centre or from an experienced climber. Scrambling guides are available to popular areas, most of them published by Cicerone Press, who grade scrambles so you can soon get an idea of what to expect.

Scrambles are easiest when the rock is warm and dry and the air is still. Rain can make rock slippery while strong winds can blow you off narrow ridges. In winter conditions most scrambles become serious mountaineering routes.

When scrambling one cardinal rule is never to ascend anything you do not think you can climb back down as you may have to do this if you reach an impassable barrier higher up. This is where having a rope in the party makes sense as it can be used to get someone out of trouble if they become stuck. I can remember being very glad of one on a scramble in Snowdonia when I fell off a greasy gully wall into a pool and found myself unable to ascend or descend.

In general you should always be prepared to retreat when scrambling and find a safer route. If you start to feel unhappy with the terrain do not go on. You are not trying to prove anything, you are there to have fun.

THE WEATHER

If the weather was always sunny and warm hillwalking would lose much of its variety and its challenge. Knowing the sun will always shine is fine for a while but the predictability can become tedious, something worth trying to remember the next time you are floundering around trying to find a summit cairn in driving rain and dense mist! Actually, continuous sunny weather is very welcome, but in the UK it is not that common so we have to learn to cope and enjoy our cool, wet and windy climate. Stormy weather can be exhilarating as well as infuriating. Taking a positive attitude always helps. If you view a storm as an exciting challenge rather than a reason to complain and head back down or stay inside you will enjoy more days out. In the words of mountaineer and conservationist John Muir as he set out to climb a peak in Alaska in threatening weather, 'Storms of any kind are well worth while'.

One important feature of mountain weather the world over is how fast it can change. Just how quickly this can happen I learnt many years ago on a walk round the Mosedale Horseshoe in the Lake District on a summer's day. The sky was clear and the sun hot as my companion and I descended from Red Pike towards Scoat Fell when out to the west I noticed a distant thin dark line of cloud rushing towards us. We barely had time to struggle into our waterproofs before the rain hit us. The rest of the day was cold, windy and very wet with minimal visibility as thick cloud blanketed the tops. As walking became difficult in the rising wind we cut our trip short and descended to the comforts of the Wasdale Hotel bar in the valley below.

Weather Patterns

Much of the weather in the British Isles begins out in the Atlantic where cold air from the arctic meets warm air from the tropics to create the areas of low pressure known as depressions. These rush in from the south-west, bringing wet and windy weather. Unsurprisingly the highest rainfall is in the west with the hills there having almost twice the average rainfall of eastern hills.

Rainfall also increases with altitude. The town of Fort William in the west of Scotland has less than half the rain that falls on top of Ben Nevis a little under 5 miles (8km) away. This is because Fort William is at sea level while Ben Nevis is 4400ft (1340m) higher.

Wind speeds increase with elevation too because the mountains force air to rise and flow over them, which squeezes the air and makes it speed up. This compression of the air is also the reason passes and mountain valleys can be very windy as the air is funnelled through them.

As well as being wetter and windier hills are colder than lower areas. The rate at which they cool is roughly by 2°C (3.6°F) for every 300m (1000ft) gain in altitude. This is known as the lapse rate and is why a warm day in the valley can be a cold one on the tops, especially if a wind is blowing.

Sometimes a temperature inversion may occur. Then the lapse rate works the other way and it is the cloud-filled valleys that are cold and the hill tops that are warm.

Precipitation may fall as snow rather than rain. This can happen on the summits at any time of the year, especially in the Scottish Highlands. However, significant snowfall usually only occurs between October and April. In some years there may be little snow, especially on lower hills and in southern England. Heavy snowfall can also be followed by big thaws that virtually clear the hills of snow. This can occur several times during the winter. In higher mountains such as the Alps there is snow cover year round with permanent glaciers. Here in winter the lower levels are covered too, which means many walkers' routes are impassable then. In other areas such as Scandinavia where the hills are higher than in the UK but lower than the Alps many hills are free of snow in summer but covered for most of the winter.

Spring and autumn are often the best times of year for settled summer weather, though in higher mountains outside the UK melting snow may make spring unsuitable for hillwalking. The summer months, July and August, are often the warmest but can be very hazy. They are also the most popular, both with walkers and climbers and with biting insects such as midges and mosquitoes.

Sunshine

The skies are blue, the clouds white and fluffy, the sun high. A cool breeze drifts down from the tops – perfect weather for a day in the hills. These are perfect conditions too for returning home sunburnt. Anyone can get sunburn even if their skin is black; there are plenty of people with skin cancer who thought they were 'immune'. If the burning is very severe it can lead to blistering, chills, fever and headaches, though not everyone suffers to the same extent.

The cold and the wet are generally regarded as the main threats from the weather in the hills but the sun can be a problem too, especially at high altitudes in places like the Alps but also in the UK, particularly during long hot summers like that of 1995. While those visiting hot countries are obviously most in danger, walkers who do not venture abroad should not feel they are not at risk from sunburn. I have seen several people with bad sunburn, including two cases that led to severe blistering, after days out hillwalking in the UK.

Sunburn is caused by exposure to ultraviolet (UV) radiation. So, unfortunately, is skin cancer. It is now known that various man made pollutants in the upper atmosphere, CFCs being the most notorious, are damaging the layer of ozone that protects the earth from much of the UV radiation. The problem is expected to worsen, leading to an increasing number of skin cancer cases. Protecting your skin against the sun is now very important whether you burn easily or not. It should also be noted that UV radiation can still be a danger on overcast days, especially those with high, thin cirrus clouds. The middle four hours see two-thirds of the day's UV radiation occurring, making that a critical time to protect yourself. This can be done with sunscreen, dark glasses and clothing.

To minimize the chances of suffering sunburn, sunscreen should be used on exposed skin whenever you are in sunlight for any length of time, even if you think burning is unlikely. The best sunscreens for walkers are water resistant creams as these will not run off with your sweat as you slog uphill. Try outdoor stores rather than chemists for these. I have found those from Outdoor Cosmetics very good. All sunscreens have a Sun Protection Factor (SPF) number. This tells you how much longer it will take skin coated in the sunscreen to burn than unprotected skin. The higher the SPF, the more protection given. SPFs of 15 and above give virtually total protection and are recommended for people whose skin burns easily and for high altitudes where UV radiation is stronger (it increases by 4 per cent in intensity for every 300m or 1000ft of altitude). Creams with SPFs of 8 to 12 applied at least twice a day are probably adequate for most people at low levels in the UK. Good sunscreens should also filter out both UVA and

UVB rays, as each can damage the skin. When using a sunscreen all exposed skin should be covered.

Burnt lips are especially painful and may erupt into cold sores. Although sunscreen can be applied to the lips many brands leave an unpleasant taste and wash off quickly. Lipstick-like tubes of lip salve work much better.

Dark glasses are only really necessary for snow travel when they are essential to prevent snow blindness. But they can be useful in summer in order to reduce glare from the sun when crossing pale surfaces such as limestone pavements or sandy beaches that reflect the light. The main requirement of sunglasses is that they cut out UV light; many cheaper brands do not. Of the many types of lenses available grey or brown tints render colours accurately and are best for most usage. Glass lenses are the most scratch-resistant, though polycarbonate lenses are very good and weigh less. Glacier glasses with side shields, though popular, are only really needed for high altitude travel.

The face, head and neck are the parts of your anatomy most vulnerable to sunburn and to skin cancer. The best way of protecting them is with a hat. One study found that the amount of UV radiation on your upper face, head and neck can be reduced by around 85 per cent by wearing a hat with a wide, floppy brim. Peaked caps, in contrast, shade only the face but there are some available with neck protectors and neck flaps. You could tuck or pin a bandanna or large handkerchief under the rim of a baseball cap to achieve similar protection. I often wear a wide-brimmed, high-crowned cotton canvas hat, which I find very comfortable and not too hot.

The key to comfort and coolness with a hat is to ensure the fit is not too tight and that there is space between the top of your head and the crown of the hat. Close-fitting hats are sweaty and hot to wear. But loose hats can blow away in a wind so a neck cord is necessary.

As well as protecting you from UV light a hat helps you keep cool by shading your face from the sun. If you still feel hot a good way to cool down is to fill your hat with water and then put it back on! Apart from the initial instant cooling the heat lost as the water evaporates keeps you feeling comfortable for quite some time afterwards.

Wearing long trousers and long-sleeved tops is an obvious way of protecting the skin against the sun and preferred by some to plastering their skin with sunscreen. Not all clothing keeps out the sun, and it is possible to get sunburnt while fully dressed. A study at the University of Tennessee looked at the amount of UV light transmitted through different fabrics. The researchers gave each fabric an SPF factor comparable to those used for sunscreens. The study found that the SPF of a standard white cotton T-shirt is about 7 when dry and 5 when wet.

Other results from the study were that stretched fabrics gave far less protection than those hanging free. The SPF of a dry white polo shirt was about 31 when it was not stretched but only 9 when stretched across the shoulders, dropping to 7 when it was wet. Similar results were obtained from knitted materials, woven materials and cotton and polyester blends.

This does not mean that clothing is useless for sun protection. It clearly is not. Waterproofs will keep out the sun completely as will most thick insulated garments. These are hardly practical, however. The problem is to find fabrics that keep out the sun and keep you cool. In the United States much work has been done on this and there are several specialist companies offering sun-protective clothing. On testing, one such shirt had an SPF of 75 when dry and 67 when wet. Outdoor clothing companies also make sun protection clothing that is designed to be cool and quick-drying as well so it is comfortable while you are walking, though at the time of writing none of these garments are available in the UK. Companies like Lowe Alpine and Rohan do make polycotton sun clothing with mesh panels for sweat dispersal.

I find that polycotton gets very sweaty in hot weather and I prefer completely synthetic clothing. A very effective garment in hot weather is Sequel's Solar Shirt, unfortunately only available in North America. It's made from Coolmax polyester on the top half and a wicking mesh on the lower half and under the arms. I have found it superb in the heat, never feeling sticky or clammy and drying very quickly where it did get damp, usually under the rucksack hip belt and shoulder straps. Because it is made from wicking synthetics if the weather changes it works perfectly well as a base layer, something polycotton does not do.

The main features of sunblock clothing seem to be fibres that absorb some of the radiation and tight weaves that prevent light passing between the fibres. As the favourite material for such clothing is nylon, microfibre clothing, available from many companies, should work well. However, the design of such clothing means that it is likely to be rather too warm in really hot weather. I have tried microfibre shirts without mesh panels and they do get clammy quite quickly.

Check the colour of your clothing too. A Swedish study has found that dark-coloured fabrics give twice the protection of light-coloured fabrics.

According to this study tight dark-coloured clothing might feel hotter than lighter coloured garments but if the garments are loose-fitting then there should not be any noticeable difference.

Wind

Struggling on into a strong headwind is a sure way to become exhausted. Progress can even become impossible. Turning back or seeking a more sheltered route, even if much longer, is the sensible course to take. If you set off with the wind behind you think what it could be like returning into it and adapt your plans accordingly. Consider the terrain too. Narrow ridges can be dangerous in strong winds, especially with violent gusts that can knock you off balance.

When does wind speed become a problem? According to the Beaufort Scale, the accepted measure of wind speed, when it reaches 25 to 31 mph (40 to 50km per hour) an effort is required to walk and when it gets to between 32 and 38 mph (52 and 61km per hour) walking with a pack is hard. By the time the speed reaches 50mph (80km per hour) walking is impossible and crawling is difficult. Once it gets to 60mph (97km per hour) the wind will drag you along even if you are lying down. Wind speeds over 20mph (32km per hour) are not uncommon in the hills and they do sometimes exceed 100mph (160km per hour) in areas like the Cairngorms, especially in the winter. If the wind is increasing and walking becomes difficult it is unwise to continue heading upwards.

The concept of wind chill is now familiar – wind chill figures are even given out in television weather forecasts – but it is still often misunderstood. What the wind chill figure tells you is how cold it will feel on exposed skin at a given temperature and wind speed. For example when the still air temperature is 4°C (39°F) and the wind speed is 23mph (37km per hour) the wind chill is -9°C (16°F). However, this does not mean you need clothing that would keep you warm at a temperature of -9°C (16°F). If you wore that much you would quickly overheat. What is needed is windproof clothing over layers adequate to keep you warm at 4°C (39°F).

Rain

Rain can occur at any time in the hills, which is why you should never venture out without waterproof clothing in your rucksack whatever the weather. Getting wet in itself is not dangerous. Indeed, in really hot weather it can be quite refreshing. I have at times jumped into pools to cool off on sunny days. It is the combination of wet and cold that is to be avoided, especially if it is windy as well. This is because wet clothing conducts heat far faster than dry clothing while wind whips away heat quickly. I have been out in calm and dry weather when the temperature has been below -10°C (14°F) and needed no more than a thin fleece top on to keep warm while moving, yet in wet and windy weather at 2°C (36°F) I have needed a waterproof jacket and trousers on as well.

Lightning

Thunderstorms in the hills can be frightening and dangerous. If you see the dark anvil-shaped cumulonimbus clouds starting to build up and the air is hot and humid it is best to head down immediately. Often a storm will arrive so fast you have little time to act. If you are caught out in a thunderstorm the first thing to do is to get off ridge crests and summits. If the storm is really close move quickly but take care as you do so – there is no point avoiding a storm by falling over a cliff. It is quite surprising how fast you can run even with a heavy pack on your back, as I have discovered on a number of occasions.

Other dangerous places that should be avoided include cracks in rocks, shallow caves, lone trees and small stands of trees. All of these can conduct lightning. You should also get off flat open ground where you are the tallest object around and therefore a potential target for a lightning strike.

Places to head for are deep valleys, dense forest, big caves, the base of high cliffs and depressions in flat areas. If the storm breaks all around you and there is nowhere like this within easy reach move away from any metal objects such as trekking poles or ice axes – these do not attract lightning but can burn you after a nearby strike – but do not throw them away as you will probably need them later. Next crouch down, preferably on something that will act as an insulator such as a sitmat or the padded back of a rucksack. Do not lie on the ground or lean your hands on it as currents can run along it and through you. If someone is hit by lightning and stops breathing they should be given mouth-to-mouth resuscitation and, if necessary, cardiopulmonary resuscitation. This may have to be kept up for some time. First aid training is of course needed if you are to do this.

Forecasts

Up-to-date weather forecasts are vital for planning. Radio and television forecasts are more useful and up-to-date than those printed in newspapers, while recorded telephone weather lines for specific mountain regions, although expensive, are the most useful of all (see Weather Forecasts section at the back of the book). They usually give a general synopsis followed by details of the temperature and wind speed at different elevations, the freezing level and the cloud base. In winter information on snow conditions and the state of paths is often provided as well.

When conditions are particularly hazardous these forecasts often tell you in no uncertain terms. I can remember one that said 'you would be mad to go on the hills!'. We put off our trip for two days, knowing that these forecasts are as accurate as possible and not designed to discourage hillwalking as is sometimes believed. Ignoring them can be dangerous. People have died because they thought it could not really be that bad. Where these forecasts are not available national park visitor centres or tourist information offices can probably give a forecast.

Weather forecasts are only a guide and at times they are inaccurate. One common problem is the speed at which depressions travel. Quite often one that is predicted to arrive in the evening after a day of calm, clear weather can rush in at lunch time or even earlier bringing rain and wind and leaving you cursing the forecasters. Storms can pass through more quickly too, leaving fine days when bad weather was predicted. Incorrect forecasts are not always bad! Getting the latest forecast is one way to minimize being caught out. A morning forecast for the day ahead can be very different from the one given the evening before.

By observing the clouds and changes in wind speed and direction you can learn to do some crude forecasting yourself. If you notice wisps of high cirrus cloud streaking the sky from the south-west a depression is probably on the way, even though the storm may not arrive for 24 hours. An altimeter-barometer (see Chapter 5) can also help as it shows changes in pressure and rapid pressure changes probably mean rapid weather changes too. Do not expect your forecasting to be very accurate. If the Meteorological Office with all its computers and satellite information cannot always get it right you do not really have much chance.

COPING WITH TERRAIN

As long as you stick to well used paths you should have no problems with terrain except for the occasional badly eroded or very boggy section. This is where trekking poles can be a great help in keeping your balance. They are even more use if you leave popular paths for little-used tracks or go cross country.

Steep Slopes

Steep slopes can be intimidating, especially when there is no path. Descending is usually more unnerving than ascending. The key to confidence and safety is good balance – keeping your body upright and your weight over your feet. To do this do not lean back when descending or into the slope when ascending or traversing as both of these will cause your feet to slip away from you. As far as possible put the whole of your boot sole on the slope rather than just the toe, edge or heel as this will provide much greater security. This is one reason why I prefer flexible footwear.

Unfamiliar steep slopes should not be rushed. Take the time to study a slope before starting up or down and try to pick out a route that avoids crags or stream gullies. If you are not happy

Easy if steep walking up a narrow path.

When descending steep slopes watch your footing. A trekking pole can help with balance.

A steep climb up loose stony slopes.

going straight up or down zigzag back and forth across the slope, looking out for any flatter spots where you can rest. If the ground is loose or slippery, stones or bits of tough vegetation can stop your feet slipping. In descent trekking poles placed below you are a great help too.

Steep slopes should always be treated with caution. Be prepared to retreat and find another route if you feel unhappy with the angle or the ground underfoot. Pushing on could lead you into a situation you cannot easily escape from.

Grass

Grass would seem a very innocuous surface to walk on and so it usually is but when the slope is steep and the grass is wet or, even worse, coated with ice or frost it can become very slippery and keeping your feet can be impossible, especially in descent. Trekking poles or an ice axe can be a great help though care is still needed.

Ascending is easier than descending but still difficult. If the terrain is potentially dangerous with crags or steep drops below you it would be better to find an alternative route, however long. This is preferable to a fast slide into a boulder or over a cliff.

Scree

Slopes of small loose stones, known as scree and often found in and below gullies and at the base of cliffs, can be frustrating to ascend, difficult to traverse and unnerving to descend. This is because scree slides at every step and firm footing is impossible. Only climb scree when there is no alternative. This is sometimes the case as with Sgurr Alasdair, the highest peak in the Cuillins on the Isle of Skye. The only route up the peak that does not involve difficult scrambling is by a long steep scree slope called the Great Stone Chute. I have done this a few times. It is hard work!

Descending scree is easier if you allow yourself to slide with it. Again, trekking poles help with staying upright. Do not descend any steep scree slope that ends in a dangerous drop, as it is very easy to pick up speed and lose control. Running down scree is exhilarating and a fast way to descend, but it is also potentially dangerous and very damaging to the terrain. When descending scree put your weight on your heels rather than trying to keep your feet flat as this is more stable and gives you more control. Do not lean back or you will sit down – which on sharp stones can be painful – and perhaps continue sliding. If you do not have trekking poles, holding your arms out will help with balance as the scree throws you from side to side, as it inevitably will even at slow speeds.

Whether descending or ascending scree it is easy to dislodge stones and send them whizzing down the slope. This can be dangerous to any walkers lower down the slope so if you do set a stone rolling warn them by yelling 'below'. If you are beneath others and you hear someone yell this do not look up! A group should ascend or descend scree diagonally or in an arrowhead formation so that no one is ever below anyone else, at least not for long.

Boulder Fields

Large areas of boulders can be awkward to cross and care needs to be taken

Care is needed descending rocks as they can move suddenly and throw you off balance. A trekking pole is useful for support.

as you could easily break a leg if you slip into a gap between the rocks. Stepping from boulder to boulder is fine if the rock is dry and you check each boulder for movement before you put your weight on it. With wet rock you should be more cautious as it is likely to be slippery, especially if covered with moss or lichen.

Bogs

In many hill areas bogs are common. They are not a serious threat to your health though they may be to your sanity at times. Progress can be very slow as you stagger from wobbly tussock to wobbly tussock, occasionally slipping and going knee deep or more into the black sticky mud. If you do find yourself stuck and sinking deeper the best way to try to free your legs is by moving them back and forth to create air gaps. If this does not work, lean forwards to spread your weight and crawl out. You could put your rucksack on the mud in front of you and lie on that. This depends on whether you would rather keep it or your clothes free of mud! Of course, if you have companions they can pull you out. I have only been stuck once when alone, on Featherbed Moss on the Pennine Way. Crawling was the only way I could move.

In boggy terrain it is worth ensuring your footwear is tightly laced. It is not pleasant plunging your arm into cold mud trying to locate your shoe.

There are two times when bogs are easy to cross, in prolonged droughts and in freezing weather. During the first even deep bogs can turn to dry, dusty wallows with crazy paving style cracks in the surface while in the second the

Boggy ground can be difficult to cross without getting your feet wet.

surface becomes hard and crusty, though you can sometimes feel the ooze underneath shaking as you walk above it.

Fording Rivers and Streams

In remote areas rivers and streams without crossing points can be a major hazard. Most larger streams are bridged in the English and Welsh hills but this is not so in the Scottish Highlands nor in many mountain areas further afield. If there is a bridge marked on the map and the stream looks more than ankle deep and is fast flowing you should head for it even if it involves a long detour. If you have different editions of the map in the party it is wise to check them all. I once walked for half a day into a storm to a bridge marked on my map because the stream we hoped to

Bridges are the easiest ways of crossing streams.

Some rivers can't be forded. This is Granite Rapids on the Colorado River in the Grand Canyon.

cross was a raging torrent. It was only after we had slogged up to the bridge that we discovered from a companion's more up to date map that there was a bridge only a short way downstream of where we had reached the stream!

If there is no bridge think hard before attempting to cross any stream more than ankle deep. Most people severely underestimate the strength of running water and walkers are drowned every year. If you do not think you can cross safely, do not try. It is better to turn back or seek another route than be swept away.

When you come across a stream that cannot be easily forded search up and down its banks for a safe crossing place before giving up. Consult the map too. If it shows a wide area where the stream divides into several channels this suggests a potential safe ford. Wider areas are shallower and several channels are often easier to cross than a single one. If you decide to follow the stream in search of a crossing place it is usually best to head upstream as it will gradually become narrower and less powerful. However, if you can see a gorge above you or the map suggests steep-sided ravines or waterfalls it might be better to head downstream in the hope that the stream will broaden and slow where it reaches less steep ground.

Streams that are not too deep can sometimes be crossed by stepping or even hopping from boulder to boulder. This should not be done if you could be washed away if you fell in. Do not risk it with large boulders from which you could fall a fair way either. It is better to get wet feet than risk slipping off a boulder and injuring yourself.

Wading is often the only option. You

You can keep your feet dry when crossing shallow streams by stepping from rock to rock. A trekking pole will help with balance.

should study any ford carefully before plunging in though, looking for any underwater obstructions such as large boulders or tree branches and checking whether the far bank is undercut. If you decide the ford is feasible cross carefully and slowly facing upstream so the current cannot cause your knees to buckle. Feel ahead with your leading foot and do not commit your weight to it until it's securely lodged on the stream bed. A third leg such as a trekking pole or ice axe or, if you are carrying neither, a stout stick, is just about essential in rough water. This can be placed upstream and leant against while you move your feet.

If the water is fast flowing and starts to boil up around your knees and you are crossing alone turn back as the force of it could easily knock you over. Being swept down a cold, boulder-filled rushing stream is not good for the health. On any crossing where falling in could mean being washed away you should undo your rucksack waist belt and chest strap and loosen the shoulder straps so you can take it off quickly – it could hold you face down in the water. If it is closed tightly and any liners or stuffsacks are sealed a rucksack could act as a buoyancy aid, though in a typical hill stream where being bounced through boulders would result from being swept downstream this would not be much use. In desert mountains where the rivers are deep and warm walkers have used their rucksacks like this intentionally when swimming round obstacles or to the far side, sometimes with an air mattress for added buoyancy. Colin Fletcher describes swimming the Colorado River in this way on several occasions in his superb account of his pioneering walk through the Grand Canyon, *The Man Who Walked Through Time*.

If you can see that the bottom is flat and sandy rather than rocky you could cross in bare feet but generally it is safest to keep your shoes or boots on. If your socks are dry you can take them off first. Donning warm dry socks will help your feet warm up on the other side. What clothing you should wear depends in part on the weather. Shorts are ideal when it is warm. In water that is at all deep long trousers are a hazard whatever the temperature as they can drag in the water making the crossing more difficult and dangerous. They can also absorb lots of water, especially if made from cotton or wool, and take ages to dry, making it harder to warm up once across. Bare legs are better with thick garments on your top half to keep you warm. Nothing will keep your legs dry in water that comes over your boot tops and that includes gaiters and overtrousers. It is better to keep clothing dry by taking it off.

Whatever you wear, mountain streams are usually very cold and you will often reach the far side feeling quite shivery. I find the best way to deal with this is to put on extra warm clothing, gulp down some sugary food and a hot drink if I have one and then walk hard and fast until I feel warm.

If you are in a group there are several ways you can make fords safer. Three people can form a stable tripod and shuffle across together. With more people linking arms is probably better, perhaps lined up along a pole held at chest level. What you should not do, unless you are well practised and confident, is use a rope to safeguard a crossing because of the danger that it might hold you under the water if you fall in.

If you cannot find a safe crossing there is one final option before you turn back and that is to wait. Except when snow is thawing hill streams are rain fed and can go down very quickly once

Mountain streams can rise and fall rapidly.

the rain stops. A raging torrent can turn into a docile trickle in a matter of hours. The opposite happens as well, and people have found the trickle they crossed without thought at the start of the day impassable on their return. Glacier fed streams in big mountains abroad often go down overnight when the melt stops as the temperature drops below freezing. I have camped on the banks of unfordable streams in the Canadian Rockies and crossed without too much difficulty the next morning. I have also made long detours at times rather than risk a hazardous ford.

Forests

Vegetation is not often a problem in the UK, where there are not the dense bushes and thickets of small trees that can hinder walking in many mountain areas

Dense vegetation can make progress and route finding very difficult.

Even heather can impede progress when there's no path.

in other countries. I have done plenty of bushwhacking in the Canadian Rockies and the Yukon mountains and it is not a form of walking I am fond of. In the Britsh Isles deep heather and bracken can be awkward to walk through, especially on steep, boulder-covered slopes, and care needs to be taken not to fall into hidden holes.

Forests are found in mountain ranges world-wide. The best way through them is always on a trail as dense undergrowth and fallen trees can reduce progress to a crawl. Plantations, increasingly common in the UK, are possibly even worse to fight a way through than natural forests. When young, the dense trees present a spiky barrier that can make plantations impassable. When logging is taking place a deviation has to be made, while felled areas are a tangle of torn branch-

es and ripped stumps that can be a nightmare to cross. If it is a natural forest that has been destroyed it can also be very depressing. Paths can be obliterated by felling operations too.

Even mature forests can present severe navigational problems, especially if you come upon one unexpectedly. Even the most up-to-date maps may not be accurate with regard to plantations. If you do discover a forest where you were not expecting one my advice would be to go round unless you can see a track through it. However long a diversion is necessary it will almost certainly be quicker than plunging into the trees. If fighting through the forest does seem the best option look for a stream as the banks may well be free enough of trees to make for reasonable walking – and you can always slosh through the stream itself. In descent do watch out

Dense forests can be very difficult to force a way through. If there is no path it's easier to follow the edge.

Even in a mature forest like this fallen trees can make walking difficult away from footpaths and tracks.

for crags and waterfalls if you do this.

Forest roads can be a problem too as the positions of these change constantly and often bear little resemblance to those marked on the map. I have followed forest roads for ages in the wrong direction in the Canadian Rockies, the Pyrenees, the Sierra Nevada of California, the Oregon Cascades, the Scottish Highlands and the Norwegian mountains and I still do not know an easy way round this problem! The extra distance is always better than struggling through dense forest, however.

Walls and Fences

Walls marked on maps may be just traces of stones or they may be high and hard to climb. Fences are even harder to cross as they are usually higher and less stable. In Scotland it is fair to assume that forests will have high deer fences round them. If there are no stiles it is best to follow the fence round the edge of the forest rather than try to climb it.

There are times when high walls and fences just have to be climbed. Look for a corner post or buttressed area both to make it easier and safer and to avoid damage to the fence or wall.

MINIMIZING THE IMPACT ON TERRAIN

Footpaths are expensive to maintain but very easy to damage and destroy. To avoid doing the latter it is best to stick to the path even if it is muddy rather than walk along the edges as this widens it. Paths on steep slopes are particularly vulnerable to erosion so it is important not to short-cut zigzags. Many good paths have been destroyed by people doing this. In many areas paths have been repaired or rebuilt. It is important to stick to the new path rather than walk along the ground to the edges. If you come upon a work party look for sign-posted diversions as to where to walk while the path is being restored. Wooden board-walks and stone flags

Path repairs are needed in many areas.

A boardwalk high on Penyghent in the Pennines. The grossly eroded old path can be clearly seen. The small walls are to allow the soil to stabilize and vegetation to grow back.

stretching across dark peat moorland can look very artificial and out of place, particularly when they are new. Hopefully, in time they will weather into their environment and stand out no more than older paths. Even when new they are still preferable to the wide, eroded, muddy scars they usually replace.

If you leave paths behind to go cross country aim to leave no sign of your passing. This means not marking your route with cairns or other waymarks. On soft terrain where your boots leave prints groups should spread out and walk apart so that they do not create the beginnings of a path that will soon become clearer as others follow. Where possible look for hard surfaces to walk on such as gravel and sand, rock, stones or grass. When scrambling try not to disturb vegetation, especially on gully walls. As far as possible you should stay on the rock, which makes for better scrambling anyway.

OVERNIGHT STOPS

Having to spend an unintended night out in the hills is not something that ever happens to most walkers. Descending in the dark is possible on most footpaths if you have a good torch and can be done cross country if the terrain is not too steep and rocky. If you are lost you may have to spend the night out as it is unlikely you will be able to work out where you are in the dark. Other reasons for overnight stops are illness, injury or hypothermia.

In the summer the nights are short and temperatures not too low so, with a bivvy bag and extra clothing, a night out should be no more than uncomfortable. Unless one of your party is completely immobilized it is worth spending a little time searching for shelter such as a large boulder or even an overhanging stream bank for extra protection.

Winter nights are a much more serious matter, as they can be long and cold. Plenty of warm clothing is essential and if there is much snow you should dig a shelter of some sort or at least build a snow wall to keep the wind off (see Chapter 7).

If it looks as though you will have to stay out overnight, try to get as far down the hill as possible before you stop. After shivering through what may be a long, cold night you will not be in good condition for undertaking a long trek out.

MEDICAL EMERGENCIES

Hypothermia

Hypothermia, or exposure as it used to be known, occurs when the body loses heat faster than it can produce it. The prime cause is becoming wet and cold but hunger, tiredness and low morale all play a part. Symptoms to watch out for are shivering, lethargy, tiredness, irritability and unusual or irrational behaviour. Do not ignore these signs either in yourself or others in the party. People may say they are fine but if you know them well enough to know they are acting out of character, suspect hypothermia. If someone complains of the cold stop at once and do something about it and if it is you who is feeling cold do not be afraid to say so. You cannot use will-power or toughness to deal with hypothermia. Victims are often people who have been trying to keep up with others who are too fast for them and who do not want to hold the group up by admitting they are tired or cold. They arrive last at rest stops and do not have time to put on extra clothing or eat properly, again because of fear of slowing the party down. In bad weather this can easily lead to hypothermia.

It should not happen though. Hypothermia is a killer of the unprepared and the careless. If you are properly clothed, well fed and not over-tired you should be in no danger. You must use your equipment when it is needed, of course. People have died with warm clothing and bivvy bags in their rucksacks. You should never leave essential gear behind either, even in the middle of a heat wave. During the long, hot summer of 1995 a walker died in the English Lake District after he became lost because he did not have adequate clothing when a cool, damp evening mist caused a rapid drop in temperature. Most hypothermia occurs in temperatures well above freezing, probably because people go out with minimal equipment due to warm weather when they set off. Winter walkers expect cold weather and are usually well prepared.

If someone in your party shows signs of hypothermia take immediate action. If you can, the first thing is to seek nearby shelter such as a large boulder. Do not spend time searching for shelter, though, as the sufferer could be deteriorating rapidly. The aim is to minimize further heat loss and start re-warming immediately. The casualty should be put in a bivvy bag as soon as possible, with some form of insulation such as sitmats and rucksacks underneath them. If they are conscious, they should be given hot drinks and food. Ideally, wet clothing should be removed and replaced with dry warm items. Unless you have a tent or group shelter this probably cannot be done without further heat loss, which must be avoided. In that case just the wet outer layer should be taken off then dry clothing put on over the damp inner garments. The only exception I would make to this is if the casualty is wearing cotton next to the skin, which they should not be doing. Because lots of body heat is needed to dry out wet cotton I would remove this garment and replace it with a wool, silk or synthetic top even at the risk of losing some heat in the process. Putting the casualty in a sleeping bag, if you have one, will also help. Because the casualty may not be able to produce enough heat themselves it is better if someone else gets in it and warms it up first. If there is room someone could also get in the bivvy or sleeping bag with the casualty for extra warmth. While doing all this keep reassuring the casualty that all will be well. In a group everyone can huddle round the casualty for added warmth.

What you should never do is rub the casualty to warm them up as this speeds up the circulation, which slows down in hypothermia so that the core of the body containing crucial organs like the heart and lungs stays as warm as possible. Once a person starts to become seriously hypothermic circulation becomes very slow and blood near the surface of the body becomes very cold. If the circulation is speeded up this cold blood returns to the heart where it can cause serious problems. This can also happen with re-warming by skin to skin contact so having someone naked get into the bivvy bag or sleeping bag with the hypothermia victim, a standard recommendation until very recently, is not a good idea. Alcohol has the same effect too so forget the St Bernard and the brandy and save the contents of your hip flask for when you get back down and are inside in the warm.

If the casualty shows signs of recovery descend by the quickest safe route. Further exercise will help the warming process once it has begun as long as the casualty stays warm and dry. Do not make someone try to walk if they do not recover fully as this means the

hypothermia is more severe and you have a serious situation. Whether you move on or stay put send someone for help and make sure that the rest of the party keep warm.

If you do nothing for mild hypothermia it will rapidly become much more severe, leading to a lack of co-ordination soon followed by collapse, a coma and ultimately death. You should never assume that an unconscious casualty is dead, even if there is no sign of breathing or heartbeat. People have recovered from severe hypothermia so continue warming until help arrives.

Frostbite

Frostbite is the freezing of body tissue due to exposure to severe cold. The mildest form, frostnip, usually occurs in fingers, toes, ears, nose and cheeks. To others, affected areas will look dull and white so when it is very cold you should keep an eye out for these signs. The victim may not realize what is happening as frostbitten areas go numb or even feel painfully warm. If this happens after an extremity has felt very cold and there is no reason it should have warmed up, suspect frostbite.

Re-warming of parts of the face can be done by placing a hand over the affected area. Frostnipped fingers can be placed in your armpits or groin for quick (and often painful) re-warming while feet can be placed in someone else's armpits or groin or on their warm stomach. This is when you find out who are your real friends! Fingers can also be re-warmed by rotating your arms round and round like the sails of a windmill until the feeling begins to return. If frostnip is caught quickly simply covering the area with warm clothing or adding extra clothing may be enough. Feet are the biggest problem as dealing with suspected frostnip means removing boots and socks. This is necessary as continuing without doing anything could result in permanent injury. Rubbing a frostbitten area can damage the frozen tissues so this should never be done.

If warmth does not return to a frostnipped area fairly quickly then more serious frostbite is likely. Medical assistance is now required so you should descend immediately by the quickest safe route without trying to further re-warm the area. If you cannot do this because the casualty is also suffering an injury or hypothermia or you are having a forced overnight stop then keeping them (and yourself and others in the group) warm is the priority. The frostbitten area should not be exercised or have direct heat applied to it. Neither should any blisters that may appear be burst.

Frostbite should not occur if care is taken. Adequate warm and waterproof clothing is the way to prevent it. Socks and gloves that are too tight are not a good idea as these can impede circulation and make frostbite more likely. This is particularly a problem with feet as people sometimes wear extra pairs of socks in really cold weather. If these restrict foot movement they are probably doing more harm than good. Wriggling your toes and flexing your feet will help to keep the blood flowing. Because wet clothing is cold clothing gaiters and waterproof mitts are needed. In winter I carry spare socks and gloves so that if mine get wet I can change them. Hats that cover the ears are a good idea. Neck gaiters or balaclavas can be pulled up to cover the nose if this starts to feel very cold or numb. If you do not have one of these a scarf, large handkerchief or any spare piece of clothing could be used.

Snow Blindness

Snow reflects sunlight and makes it far more intense. It also means that ultraviolet rays come from below as well as above. This can lead to the very painful burning of the cornea called snow blindness. This starts as an irritating itch – sufferers typically feel they have grit in their eyes – and a sensitivity to light. If ignored it can lead to temporary blindness and the need to spend several days in the dark, preferably with cold compresses on the eyes.

Good quality sunglasses are the answer (see 'Sunshine' above) and should be worn whenever the sun is out and you are spending much time crossing snowfields. Hazy sunshine is a hazard too so even if there is some thin cloud cover you should still wear sunglasses. Snow blindness is more likely at high altitudes where the sun is stronger but can occur lower down if it is really bright. Because the brightness comes from all around rather than just above glacier glasses with protective side shields are necessary at high altitudes. At elevations below 6000ft (1800m) I have found glasses without these side shields adequate as long as the lenses are quite large.

Heat Exhaustion

Too much heat can be as dangerous as too much cold. Heat exhaustion occurs when the body cannot get rid of excess heat. Symptoms are faintness, a rapid heart beat, nausea, cramp and a cold, clammy skin. It occurs in high temperatures, especially when accompanied by high humidity and wearing too many clothes, and is caused by severe dehydration as this leads to a cessation of sweating, which is the way the body sheds heat. The best way to prevent heat exhaustion is to drink copiously and often on hot days. If symptoms of heat exhaustion still occur you should rest somewhere shady and drink lots.

MOUNTAIN RESCUE

Mountain rescue teams in the UK came out of the tradition of mountaineers, whether hillwalkers or climbers, helping each other. Rescue teams have always been made up of volunteers who give their time to help others, often at great risk to themselves. They are not state funded and rely on donations. Where there are collecting boxes please give something if you can. You might be in need of their services one day.

Today mountain rescue teams are highly organized, well trained and efficient. The civilian teams also have the backup, when necessary, of the RAF mountain rescue teams and their helicopters. This does not mean that people can blithely wander off into the mountains unprepared, expecting the rescue teams to help them if they get into any sort of difficulty, however minor. Unfortunately some people do think like this.

Being a competent hillwalker means being self-reliant and able to deal with all but the most serious incidents. Self-help can get you out of many situations yet people have sat on a hillside in the mist for days awaiting rescue because they were not sure where they were, when a sweep of the surrounding area would have quickly located a good footpath leading down to the valley.

When someone is immobilized by illness or injury it will almost certainly be necessary to call out a mountain rescue team. Moving an injured person any distance over rough terrain without a proper stretcher is not feasible and attempting it could make the injury worse.

What you do in an emergency depends on the number of people in the group and whether there are any others around who could help. Whatever the numbers involved, if an accident has happened making sure there is no danger of a second accident is the first priority. This may mean moving to a safe area to avoid further rockfall or avalanche risk or to get away from an exposed situation. However, an injured person should not be moved unless absolutely essential. Making sure everyone is safe also means ensuring people do not get cold, so you and they must put on extra clothing.

Checking the casualty comes next, though if there are enough people others could be going for help at the same time. Ideally at least one experienced person should remain with the casualty while two, at least one of them experienced, go for help. The casualty should not be left alone so if there are two others only one should go for help while if there is only one person they should stay with the casualty and try to attract the attention of others by blowing their whistle (six long blasts, pause, repeat) or flashing their torch (six long flashes, pause, repeat). If it is necessary to leave a casualty alone leave a note with them explaining what has happened and the time you left in case anyone else happens upon them. You should also leave the casualty as well protected from the weather as possible and with a torch and whistle for signalling and some food and drink, if you have any. The place should be marked with cairns or spare brightly coloured clothing or orange bivvy bag. Obvious landmarks like large boulders, crags or streams should be noted and compass bearings should be taken so the casualty can be easily located.

Whoever goes for help should get to a telephone by the quickest safe route then dial 999 and ask for the police who will then contact the mountain rescue team leader. They will require the precise location of the accident with the grid reference if possible and any relevant compass bearings, a description of any features – with map names if any – that might help find the place, the time the accident occurred, the number of casualties and their names if known, an outline of what happened, the nature of any injuries and any treatment given and details of the weather at the accident site. If this is written down before someone goes for help none of it will be forgotten.

The person who has gone for help may then be asked to wait by the telephone for the rescue team. If they have noted the route they took down and can retrace it they could speed up the rescue by leading the team back to the casualty. Once the team are there the team leader is in charge and you should do what they say.

Those left with the casualty should make sure they stay warm and also that they are as visible as possible so they can be found quickly. Watch out for the rescue team and let them know where you are as soon as you spot them.

If you are on your own and you have an accident do all you can to get down by yourself, especially if in a remote area. It could be days or even weeks before anyone comes by. This is why leaving details of your route and when you are expecting to be back is important. As long as you are on the planned route a search should find you. Your whistle and torch can be used to help them.

Helicopters are often used in mountain rescue when serious injury is involved. If a helicopter is expected or appears you should make sure that all loose equipment is weighed down with rocks to prevent it blowing away. To signal to a helicopter that you are the party sought raise your arms in a V. If you see a helicopter and you are not in trouble never wave or raise your arms as this could be taken as a call for help and divert the helicopter from the party really in need.

Finally it should be appreciated that in some conditions rescue may be impossible and team leaders may call in or even not send out teams on foot if it is considered too dangerous to do so. The better equipped you are to sit and wait the more likely you are to survive.

7 The Winter Hills

We arrived on the summit plateau, where the great snow-fields were surfaced with an icy crust, the whole awash with the fire of sunset until we seemed encompassed by seas of live flame. (W.H. Murray, Mountaineering in Scotland)

Sometimes the hills in winter are just like the hills in summer. Rain pours down from a grey sky, the summits are lost in mist, the paths sticky with mud. The wind may be a lot colder and a little snow may dot the higher tops but overall not much is different.

But it only takes a few hours of heavy snow for familiar paths and well-known landmarks to disappear under a blanket of white. In places the snowdrifts may be knee deep and more, the muddy puddles frozen into skating rinks and the rocks that usually provide good footing slick with ice. Combine such conditions with a blizzard in

which the sky and ground merge into a pale greyness and the wind is so cold it numbs bare skin and so strong it knocks you sideways and winter hillwalking becomes very different from the summer variety.

The speed with which such storms can develop means that even more than in summer it is unwise to set off ill-prepared because the weather seems benign. The sight of brown, snow free slopes from the valley does not mean there are no steep snowdrifts hidden in the gullies you intend crossing or thick ice plastering the summit rocks.

Winter conditions can occur early in

Snow fields can last well into the summer. Whenever possible it's best to walk round them.

the autumn and linger on into early summer, especially in the Scottish Highlands. In some years there can be more snow on the tops in May than January.

Winter does not just mean blizzards and storms. When the skies clear and the sun shines the snow covered hills have a stature and magnificence lacking in summer. They are wilder too and seem bigger. The scars of summer, the eroded paths, the myriad cairns, the litter, the worn-out look of over-used terrain all disappear and the mountains are new

A big summer snowfield. Take care before venturing onto one of these. You could slide a long way if you slip.

Crossing a snowfield in summer. Kick steps with the side of your boots and use a trekking pole for support.

Snow gives the mountains a sense of grandeur and wildness they often lack in summer.

again: white, shining and pristine.

ROUTE FINDING AND PLANNING

Navigation in winter can be highly challenging, requiring a degree of skill not needed for following cairned paths in even the worst summer weather. When footpaths are buried in snow and cairns become white mounds that look like every other snow-covered boulder on the hillside, good map and compass skills are essential. The winter hillwalker may have to navigate in a blizzard across totally featureless snow-covered terrain accurately enough to avoid the corniced cliffs, invisible but highly dangerous, that lie not far on either side. You should be confident navigating cross country in the mountains in sum-

mer before you try doing the same in winter.

Route planning is important too. Thought should be given to what the terrain will be like under snow and ice. Some popular summer paths, especially along narrow ridges or with bits of easy scrambling involved, become mountaineering routes in winter conditions, simple perhaps for the experienced climber but beyond the abilities of the hillwalker not well practised in the use of ice axe and crampons. Anybody venturing on to snow-covered slopes should carry these and know how to use them properly.

In midwinter the days are short and allowance needs to be made for this. A combination of seven or fewer hours of daylight, bad weather, deep snowdrifts and icy paths can limit what can be done in a day to a fraction of what is possible in summer. Having alternative plans in case you look like running out of time are a good idea. It is much better to have such an escape route worked out in advance than have to struggle with the map in a high wind, cowering from blasts of icy sleet while you try and work one out as the daylight ebbs away and you are far from the valley. Sometimes I plan to finish in the dark, knowing that the last part is on relatively easy terrain and can be walked safely with the aid of a good torch.

KEEPING WARM

The weather is far more important in winter than summer. The heaviest August downpour should not be more than inconvenient as long as you have adequate waterproofs. But a January blizzard can bring arctic conditions, leaving even the hardiest walker unable to push on into the blinding snow and storm force winds.

Keeping warm and dry in such conditions is not easy and Chapter 2 goes into detail about clothing suitable for the hills. In brief, my winter clothing outfit is: boots, gaiters, thick socks, thick windproof trousers, thick base layer top, fleece top, breathable waterproofs, warm hat, liner gloves and thick windproof mitts or gloves. That is just about enough to keep me warm while on the move in a Cairngorm blizzard. Keeping warm in the worst conditions is essential in winter.

At rest stops, even if shelter is found, you will cool down very quickly so very warm extra clothing is needed. The thin sweater carried in summer is not enough. Also, although an enforced night out is to be avoided if at all possible, especially in a blizzard, it is wise to be equipped for one. I always like to have enough equipment with me to survive a night out in relative comfort if necessary. To that end my winter day pack always contains a spare warm top (heavyweight fleece or down), dry socks, long johns, spare hat, spare gloves, bivvy bag (breathable fabric not plastic) – this can be used at rest stops if you are really cold or it is very windy – sitmat or longer foam pad, head torch with spare battery and bulb, plenty of high calorie food and a stainless steel thermos flask full of hot coffee, fruit juice or soup. If there is much snow on the hills I also carry a snow shovel, which as well as digging emergency shelters can be used for building wind shelters at rest stops. On long day trips into remote areas I often take a solid fuel stove and fuel plus matches and lighter so I can melt snow for drinks if necessary. The steel cup from my flask does as a small pot.

WINTER WEATHER

Recorded mountain weather forecasts usually carry reports on snow and ice conditions and are worth listening to in winter even if you do not bother the rest of the year. Also important are your own observations during the day as the weather can change very quickly. I have frequently cut short a winter walk, often without reaching the top of the hill, on seeing bad weather approaching. Down in the valley I have usually been glad I did so as high winds and heavy snow blast the tops. To push on in worsening conditions when there is no need is folly. Doing so kills people every year.

ICE

Even when the weather is kind and the sun shines, snow-covered hills have hazards unknown in summer. In countries like the UK with relatively mild winters a big problem is the lack of solidity of ice on pools and streams. Temperatures are not usually cold enough for long enough for thick strong layers of ice to form. At least 1in (2.5cm) of ice is needed on lakes and pools, more on rivers. Innocuous looking flat areas can hide frozen pools whose ice might not bear your weight so cross them with care: a dousing in cold water in winter could quickly lead to hypothermia. Snow-covered streams should be approached with caution too. The banks might be overhanging. Crossing them is always hazardous as they might or might not bear your weight. Prodding ahead with an ice axe or trekking pole gives some inkling of how safe the snow is. If the pole goes through so will you. Once you commit yourself move fast so if the snow cracks you have a chance of making it to the far side.

In colder countries like Norway, Sweden and Canada mountain lakes have thick enough ice on them in winter for trucks to use them as highways. Travelling on them can be a quick way to make progress, especially on skis. Rivers are always more problematic as strong underwater currents and warm springs can affect how solid the ice is even when it is extremely cold. In one area of Norway I visited at New Year a small river that was frozen solid and could be travelled on safely when the temperature remained below -20°C (-4°F) all day began to soften and become unsafe on a day when the temperature rose to -11°C (12°F).

The advice is simple: be extremely cautious about venturing onto frozen water unless you know it is safe. And if you do cross a lake or pool keep an eye out for open water or cracked ice and stay away from streams that run into or out of it.

Ice occurs elsewhere, of course, and is a major cause of slips as wet patches on footpaths turn to ribbons of ice. This is often worse when there is no snow to cover the ice and make walking easier. Moving to the side can be the answer. One of the most slippery surfaces is dew or rain covered grass that has frozen. Crampons may be needed to cross such frozen turf and great care should be taken descending it. Icy rocks are a hazard, especially as the clear ice, called verglas, that forms on them may be hard or even impossible to see. Poking rocks with a trekking pole or ice axe will usually crack or mark the ice a little, making it visible.

WHITE-OUTS

When the ground is totally snow-covered and blanketed by a thick mist or snow is falling or being blown around by the wind it can be impossible to distinguish where the ground ends and the sky begins. This is known as a white-out. Walking in one can be very disorientating and also very dangerous. The key to safety is to proceed with great caution.

Very accurate navigation is essential. As there is nothing to take bearings on one person can be sent ahead, slowly and carefully, until they are almost out of sight. Next you can direct them, by hand signals if voice communication is difficult or impossible, onto the exact line of the bearing then walk to them and repeat the process. This leap-frogging is a slow but safe way to progress through dangerous terrain you cannot see. If you are totally unsure whether the ground ahead rises or drops away a snowball can be lobbed ahead of you. If it appears to stop in mid-air there is a slope in front, if it disappears from view there is a steep drop and you should

Ice can be a problem whether snow lies on the hills or not. Here a stream has frozen solid and ice lies on the rocks, making this easy scramble more difficult than usual.

Wind-blown snow can mean poor visibility even when the sun is shining.

back off quickly as you might be on the edge of a cornice.

CORNICES

Those magnificent curls of snow that overhang the edge of cliffs and ridges are formed by wind blown snow that builds up on the leeward side of a slope. Though wonderful to look at, cornices are potentially dangerous, even if they are small and barely extend beyond the edge of the slope. Walk onto one and it may break and plummet into the depths below, taking you with it. Cornices may not be visible if you are above or on the same level as them, especially in mist. Even approaching them is dangerous as they do not break off directly above an edge. Instead the fracture line slants

Cornice fracture lines.

inward and can be well away from the edge. If in doubt, stay well back from any steep edges, and if you see cracks in the snow near an edge back off at once. In poor visibility check the map carefully so you can stay away from any edges that may be corniced.

Cornices can collapse without warning so walking below them is unwise. Apart from the risk that they might land on your head they can trigger avalanches too. If there are big cornices above you it would be best to stay on the far side of the valley.

AVALANCHES

Avalanches are a serious hazard when there is snow on the hills. Every year walkers and climbers die in avalanches in the UK, yet there are still people who think avalanches are only a danger in big mountains like the Alps and Himalayas. The destructive power of an avalanche is tremendous. Big avalanches can destroy forests and villages and even the smallest can bury people or carry them over cliffs. If you are swept away in an avalanche, as well as the danger of being crushed and asphyxiated under tons of snow there is the possibility of smashing into boulders and rocks. Every winter hillwalker should know something about avalanches and how to avoid them. Predicting avalanches is difficult and you can never be certain that a slope is safe.

Many mountain areas have regular avalanche information available. It is always worth enquiring about this. In the UK the Scottish Avalanche Information Service (SAIS) issues daily Snow and Avalanche Reports for the Lochaber, Glencoe and Cairngorm regions of the Highlands. These reports contain information on the state of the snow pack, expected conditions and avalanche hazard category warning. The last runs from low risk (category 1) through moderate (2) to considerable (3), high (4) and very high (5). If the warning is for any of the last three you should stay off potentially dangerous slopes. Of course, low risk does not mean no risk and these are only forecasts. If the weather turns out different to that predicted then the avalanche risk may be different too, especially if unexpected snow falls. You should still make your own observations while out on the hills and act accordingly.

SAIS reports are displayed in outdoor shops, at ski resorts, in other places in the areas covered and are published in newspapers. They are also broadcast on local radio and can be accessed by telephone or fax direct or via some of the commercial recorded mountain weather forecasts. They are also on the Internet and World Wide Web. The reports are compiled from fieldwork by skilled avalanche experts and should be heeded by anyone going into the areas covered. They are your first line of defence. Hopefully in the future other areas will be covered as well.

Although avalanches can occur on slopes as gentle as 15 degrees they are most common on slopes between 25 and 45 degrees. Steeper slopes tend not to hold large amounts of snow. They may be swept by avalanches from above, of course.

Most walkers only have a hazy idea of the relative angles of slopes but these can be easily measured if you have two trekking or ski poles or two ice axes of the same length. Place one pole or axe upright in the snow then hold the other at right angles to it with the tip touching the snow and slide the tip down the snow until the pole grip or axe head touches the vertical pole. If this is at the

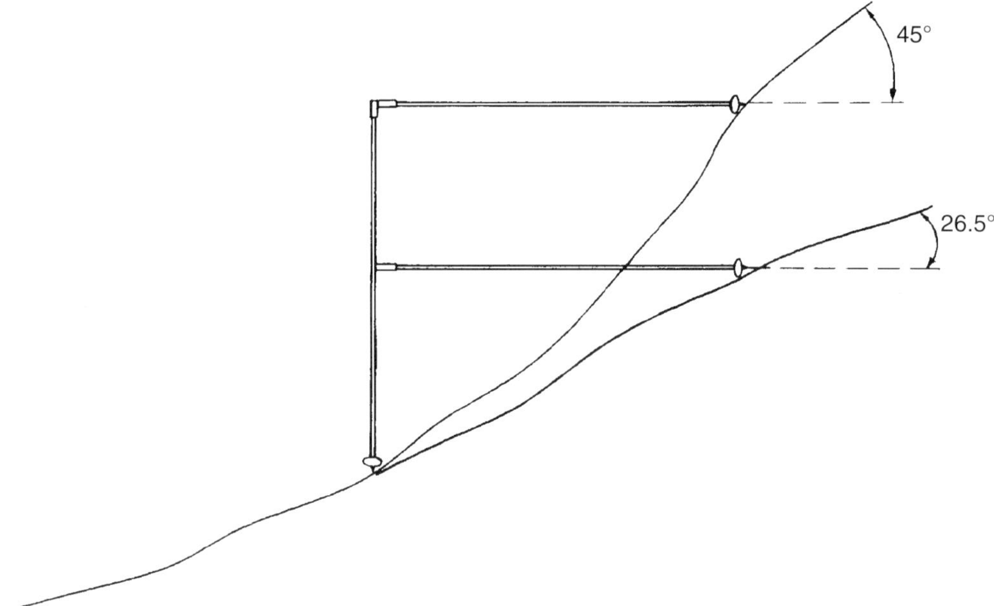

Measuring the angle of a slope with trekking poles.

top of the vertical pole or axe the slope angle is 45 degrees, halfway down is 26.5 degrees. So anywhere between halfway and the top of the vertical pole means you are on a slope steep enough to avalanche.

The type of ground under the snow and what the weather has been like are very important in assessing avalanche risk. In cold calm weather where snow has built up slowly and consolidated well the risk may be low. A freeze–thaw cycle can also lead to stable snow as layers merge into each other, though very warm temperatures can cause the snow to become unstable. Wet avalanches of thawing snow can occur in spring or during big thaws.

Convex slopes are more likely to avalanche than concave slopes as the snow is stretched over the bulge in the terrain rather than packed in tight into a hollow. The back walls of many corries often start off convex and then become concave so you need to look at what is above you as well as the slope you are on when trying to assess risk.

Recent snowfall, especially within the previous twenty-four hours, usually means a high avalanche risk, particularly if more than 8 to 10in (20 to 25cm) of snow has fallen. The higher the rate at which the snow falls the higher the risk too. Stay off steep slopes during heavy snow fall and for a day after. A storm that starts cold but finishes warm is more likely to result in avalanches than the opposite because the top layers of wet, heavy snow do not bond very well to the colder, drier snow below. Rain can turn the top layer of snow into a wet, heavy mass that is likely to avalanche.

Wind direction is very important as snow will be deposited in slabs on lee slopes. This windslab can be very dangerous. In the UK it is usually found on north and east facing slopes. Windslab can form even when the sky is clear if the wind is blowing unconsolidated

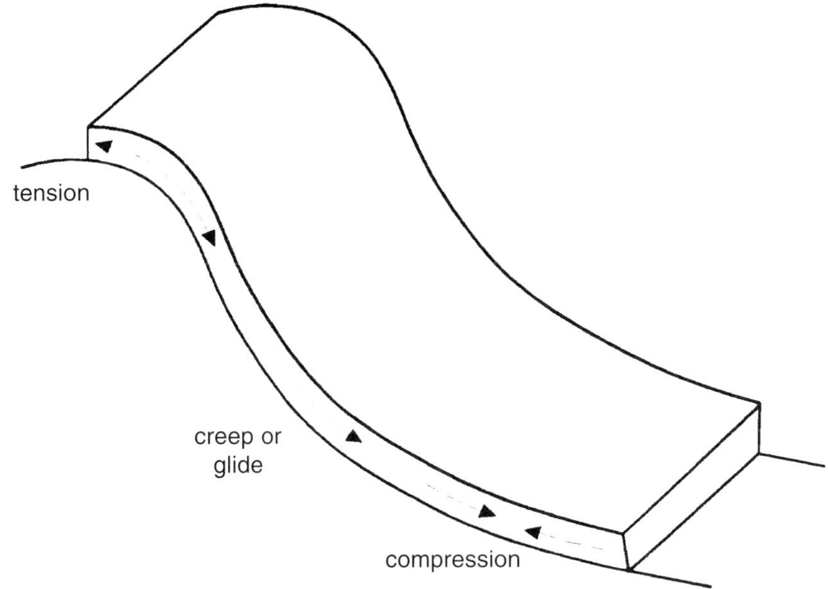

Forces within the snowpack.

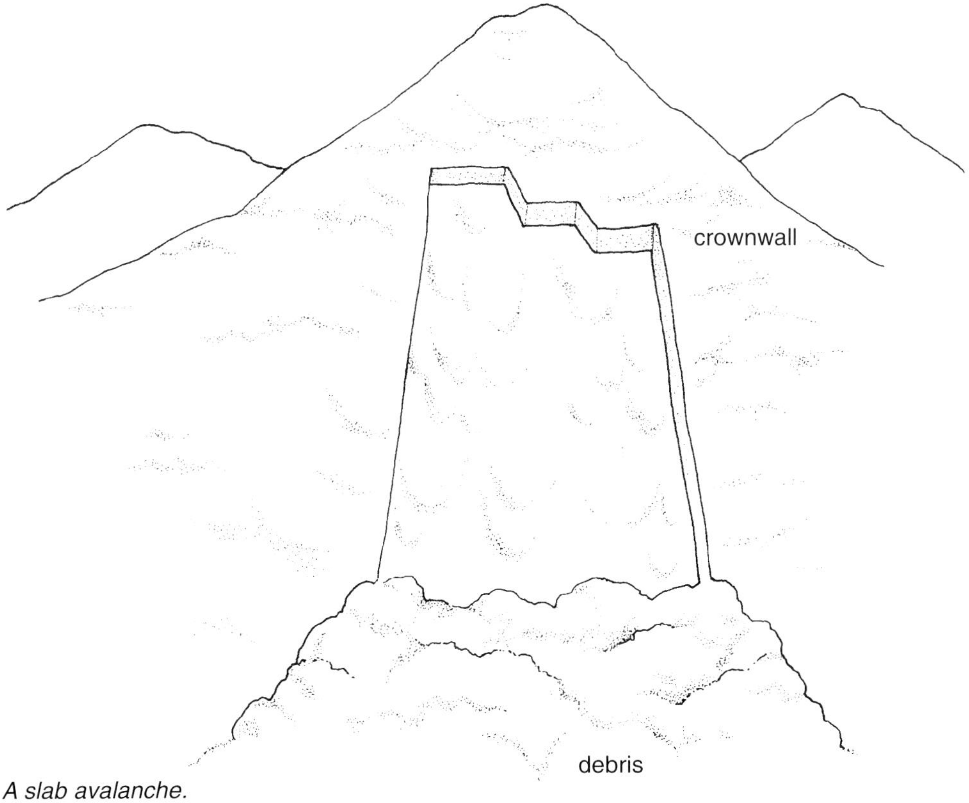

A slab avalanche.

The terrain below the snow makes a great difference to the potential avalanche hazard. Smooth easy angled slopes of rock or grass are dangerous when loaded with snow. This is the Great Slab in Coire an Lochain in the Cairngorms. Avalanches occur every winter.

snow about. Wind-blown snow plumes curving out from ridges and cliff edges are common sights.

Avalanches are more likely on smooth surfaces such as rock slabs and steep grass as the snow does not stick to these so well. Slopes of boulders or thick vegetation are safer because the snow is held more firmly. If the snow is very deep and made up of several layers that have fallen at different times and in different temperatures the layers may not have bonded well to each other so that one or more layers avalanche. In this case the underlying terrain is not so important.

Avalanches can be divided into two basic types: loose snow avalanches that start from a single point and grow in descent and slab avalanches in which a huge section of snow slides all at once leaving behind a clear fracture line known as the crown wall. The snow in both types may be wet or dry and both can vary enormously in size. Slab avalanches are more common but both can occur in all mountain ranges, including those in the British Isles.

However much information you have in advance you still need to assess the avalanche risk while you are out in the hills. This means watching for signs of instability such as cracks in the snow. These often appear during thaws and in spring as the snow begins to creep down the slope. Cracks appearing as you walk or even small slabs breaking off under your feet show instability as do balls of snow, known as sunwheels, rolling down a slope. Watch out for avalanches happening, and the tracks and debris left by previous slides. Just because a slope has avalanched does not mean it will not do so again.

If you feel a slope is potentially unstable you can check this by digging a snow pit and carrying out a number of tests. These are fairly crude but they do at least give an indication of the stability of the snow. I have turned back or changed my route a number of times after digging such pits. Practising is a good idea so you know what to look for.

To be of use a snow pit must be dug on snow of the same aspect (facing the same direction) as the slope you suspect. It should not be in a place that might itself avalanche. The aim is to see if there are any layers in the snowpack that are not well bonded and that therefore will easily slide over each other. One way to do this is to check for variations in hardness between the snow layers as big differences suggest instability. Initially you can assess this by pushing your ice axe into the slope and seeing if it hits any hard layers or suddenly slides through any very soft layers.

To find out more you need to dig a snow pit. This can be done with an ice axe but it is much quicker to use a snow shovel. The pit should be several feet across and, ideally, down to ground level or at least to a solid layer of consolidated snow. In very deep snow dig a pit at least three feet deep. Once dug the back wall can be smoothed off and a penetration test done. A finger will do or you could use the corner of a compass. By poking a line down the snow you should be able to feel any changes in hardness. Again, what you are looking for are big variations as these suggest a lack of cohesion in the snowpack. You should also notice how wet or dry the snow in each layer is as big changes in this also suggest instability.

Next you can try a shovel or shear test. An ice axe can be used for this or even a gloved hand but a snow shovel is best. First a column of snow needs to be isolated on three sides but left attached to the back of the pit. This should be about as wide as the shovel blade or no

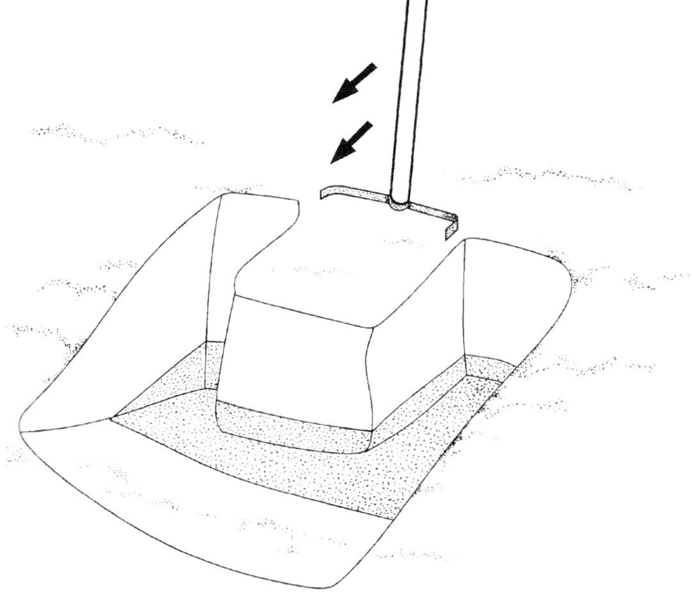

The shovel test.

more than a foot if you are using an ice axe. To do the test push the shovel down the back of the column and pull it gently towards you. If nothing happens increase the force of the pull until the top of the column slides or breaks off. The amount of pressure needed is a rough indication of the avalanche risk. The type of join should be considered too. A block that slides off smoothly, leaving two surfaces that are clearly not in any way bonded together also suggests avalanche danger. Such blocks usually come off with gentle pressure. Do not stop at just the top section though. Keep going until you reach the bottom of the column. I have known unstable snowpacks where several different layers all slid off easily.

A variation on this for skiers is the Rutschblock test. For this the column should be almost as long as the skis. A skier then approaches the column from above and applies increasing pressure to it until a layer slides. If the column fails when being dug, when approached from above or when stood on this implies great instability and a high avalanche risk. If jumping once on the column is required for it to fail caution is needed. If you can jump on it hard several times before it fails or if it will not collapse at all the avalanche risk is probably low.

These tests are fairly basic and do not apply to every slope. Digging several is the best way to check the situation but hardly practical on a day out in the hills. Any time you dig in the snow, for shelter at lunch time for example, the layers can be checked for hardness.

If you think a slope is dangerous you should not venture onto it. That is easy to say, but not always practical when out in the hills. Before you risk crossing a potential avalanche slope think hard about other options and remember that most avalanche victims trigger the slide themselves. Could you bypass the slope above or below it? Could you go straight up or down it, which is far safer than traversing? If you do cross consider where it is safest to do so. Above any convex sections would be best as these are potential start points. As high up the slope as possible is best anyway as if it avalanches you will be on or near the top and less likely to be deeply buried. The slope should be crossed one at a time with the rest of the party watching the person on the slope. Use any islands of safety such as large rocks or clumps of trees or bushes. Clothing should be closed tight but rucksack chest and waist straps undone and shoulder straps loosened so that if you are avalanched you can easily jettison it. For the same reason you should not use the wrist loops of ice axes or trekking poles. If attached to you these can cause serious injuries.

There are a number of things it is recommended you do if caught in an avalanche. The first thing to do is to stay where you are as long as possible by ramming your ice axe into the snow and hanging on. The nearer to the top of the avalanche you are the less deeply buried you should be. If you have been swept away try to stay near the surface and if possible move towards the side of the slide. Swimming motions may help keep you high in the snow. Once the avalanche starts to slow down push upwards as much as you can and try to clear an air gap round your head. Try to keep your mouth shut as you do not want to swallow snow. Once the avalanche is over and if you can move, try to reach the surface or at least thrust an arm up and perhaps out of the snow. If you are not sure which way is up try spitting to see if you are upside down or not. The chances are that you will not be able to move and will have to hope your companions can get you out quickly.

The longer a person is buried in an avalanche the less likely they are to survive. The first one to two hours are crucial so an immediate search must be made by everyone in the vicinity. There is no time to go for assistance. If the victim was being watched as they crossed the slope, as they should have been, the avalanche will have been seen. Observers should then try to keep the victim in sight and make sure they know the last spot the person was seen. Avalanches can cover large areas and finding someone can be very difficult if you have no idea where they are.

Initially the spot where the person was last seen before being buried should be marked. Then a surface search for bits of gear or any signs of someone trying to push out of the snow should be made below this point. This can be followed by probing the debris with ice axes or trekking poles. While this is being done watch out for further avalanches. Only after you have done a comprehensive search of the area and failed to find the victim should someone go for help. While waiting for help you might as well go on probing.

Using small battery operated avalanche beacons or transceivers is the best way to find someone buried in an avalanche. Ski tourers in steep terrain and some mountaineers use them but few hillwalkers do as they probably are not in avalanche terrain much of the time and the devices are expensive. If you are interested in more serious snow travel they are a good investment. They send out a signal that can be picked up by other beacons set to receive. Conducting a search with beacons should be practised in advance as it is not that easy. Beacons should be worn inside the clothing so that they cannot be ripped off in an avalanche.

ICE AXES

Whenever there is snow on the hills an ice axe may be needed. In some years this can be long before Christmas and can continue well into spring. Many walkers have been surprised at the amount of snow high in the hills in May or November. I can remember one TGO Challenge crossing of Scotland where large drifts of old hard snow made traversing Sgurr na Ciche and Garbh Chioch Mhor in Knoydart without ice axes very tricky. It certainly scared me and my companion enough that we picked up ice axes in Fort William for the rest of the trip. We needed them too. I can still remember cutting steps down into Coire Odhar from the Cairn Toul-Devil's Point col in the Cairngorms.

Designs and Materials

Choosing an ice axe is not difficult despite the initially bewildering choice. Most styles, though, are designed for snow and ice climbers not walkers. The axes to look for are usually labelled 'walking' or 'general mountaineering' axes.

The head of the axe should have a gently curved pick with a few teeth at its end and a broad adze for cutting steps, stopping a fall in soft snow and even digging emergency snow shelters. Most heads are made from a single piece of steel or two pieces welded together. The latter, while apparently not strong enough for serious climbing, are cheaper than the former and perfectly adequate for walkers. Ultralight axes, which weigh well under 1lb (450g), have alloy heads. These axes are fine for walking but not for climbing as they are not strong or heavy enough.

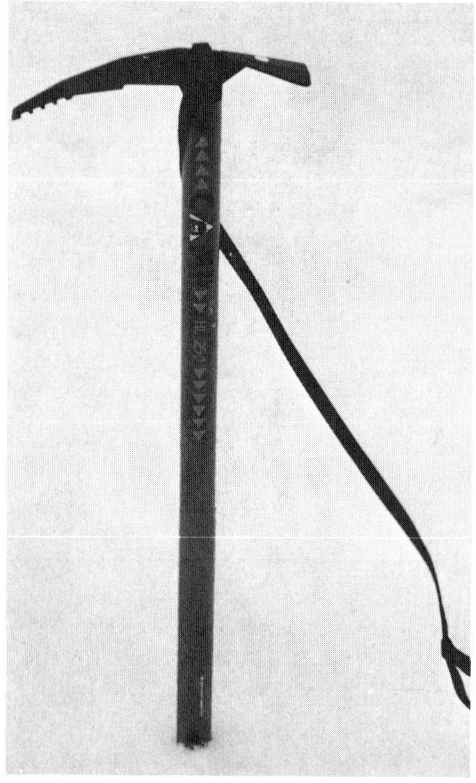

A lightweight ice axe suitable for hillwalking.

self-arrest with picks of both angles and with neutral picks (with ends parallel to the shaft) I have not noticed any difference so I would not be too concerned with this.

Metal is the standard material for shafts. It is strong and light but cold to hold and slippery when wet. A rubber hand grip or synthetic coating overcomes this. Painted shafts give a bit of grip.

Length

What length an ice axe should be is debatable. The usually recommended length is one that leaves the spike about 1in (2.5cm) above the ground when the axe is held by the side at arm's length. For most people this means one between 60 and 80cm. There is an argument that axes in these lengths are too long and difficult to use on steep slopes and for self-arrest. Those who say this, and they include experienced mountaineering instructors, recommend much shorter axes. While they undoubtedly have more experience with ice axes on very steep snow and ice than I have, my experience is probably closer to that of most hillwalkers rather than mountaineers. Having used both 55 and 70cm axes extensively, I feel much more secure with the longer axe because it can be used on relatively gentle slopes without the need for bending low over it.

Wrist Loops

Also disputed is the question as to whether a wrist loop should be used. Some axes come fitted with these and all axes have holes in the head for one. The advantages of a wrist loop are that it makes losing the axe unlikely if you drop it, that you can pull on it to take

They also blunt quickly. For the hillwalker who rarely uses an axe but needs to carry one for occasional use they are ideal. If you want to do some easy mountaineering a steel-headed axe is needed. Weights of these run from just over a 1lb (450g) to 2lb (900g).

The angle of the pick end in relation to the shaft is said to affect how it performs during self-arrest. A negative angled pick – with the pick end sloping towards the shaft – can apparently skid or drag on hard snow while a positive angled pick, with the pick sloping away from the shaft, can hook and grab as it bites abruptly into the snow, making for a jerky stop in which it can be difficult to keep hold of the axe. When practising some of the strain off your wrist, and that the axe can be suspended from your wrist when scrambling. Against that a wrist loop makes it more awkward to move the axe from hand to hand when you change direction and if you let go of the axe in a fall and it is still attached by the wrist loop it could do you an injury. I usually use a wrist loop but I am not convinced that it is really necessary and I do find it awkward to switch from hand to hand when zigzagging up or down a slope. First time ice axe users will probably find one useful.

Using an Ice Axe

Carrying an ice axe is not enough. You have to know how to use it and when to have it in your hand. Every winter I am surprised at how many people I meet on tricky terrain with their axes strapped to their rucksacks (or even with no axes at all). If I am on terrain where I think a slip might take me very far or be at all dangerous, then I have my axe in my hand, however unlikely such a slide might be.

Using an ice axe is not difficult but does require practice. Mostly, it is used like a walking stick with the spike pushed into the snow so you have a third point of contact to help with balance. When zigzagging up or down slopes the axe should be in the uphill hand, which means changing hands each time you change direction. When going directly up or down the axe is placed ahead of you. If you do slip, putting your weight onto the axe will push it farther into the snow and probably stop your slide before it has really started. Mountaineers call this a self-belay.

Most of the time you should be able to kick rather than cut steps. When

Kicking steps up a gentle snow slope. The axe should be pushed into the slope ahead of you so it can be rammed in hard if you slip.

When ascending a snow slope keep your weight over your feet and take short steps.

going straight up this is done with the toes. Aim to make a step big enough for the ball of the foot and angled slightly into the slope so you do not slip out of it. Step kicking in hard snow is tiring. In a party people can take it in turns, with everyone using the same line of steps. On steep slopes it is easier to climb in a series of zigzags. To kick steps with the side of the boot you can use a sawing motion. Again steps should slope inwards. They should also be the length of the boot and at least a third the width of the boot, preferably more if others are following. When traversing the axe should be held in the uphill hand and moved only when your feet are secure

on steps. When changing direction both hands can hold the axe while you turn.

In descent you can kick your heels down into the snow to make a platform. This is known as the plunge step. On steep slopes of hard snow you can use your body weight to really slam your heels into the snow. On softer snow and gentler terrain just walking down on your heels will be enough. The ice axe can either be carried in the self-arrest position or placed down the slope ahead of you with the shaft in the snow. When the slope eases you can just hold it by your side. On steep slopes traversing is again easier and also less intimidating. On a really steep slope,

When traversing a slope kick steps with the upper edges of your boots. The axe should be held in the uphill hand.

When descending hard snow kick steps with your heels.

which you should only be descending if there is a safe run-out below if you slip and if there is no alternative, you can face inwards and kick steps with your toes with the axe shaft thrust into the snow in front of you. This is getting into the realm of serious mountaineering rather than hillwalking.

If you cannot make more than a slight dent in the snow when you try kicking steps then you either have to cut steps or put on crampons. These days most people will do the latter. Occasionally short stretches of hard snow or ice may have to be crossed. It can be a hassle to have to put on crampons just for these. You could just keep the crampons on when you do not need them – though this can lead to problems – but if you can cut steps this will see you across the difficulty. If you do not have crampons you may have to cut steps or turn back. To cut steps swing the axe from the shoulder and make small cuts with each swing. Trying to hack a huge step in one go is tiring and likely to knock you off balance. In ice or hard snow the pick can be used to slice a V, which is then enlarged with the adze. Steps need to be a reasonable size as you have to balance in them while you cut more. They should also slope slightly into the slope. Step cutting is not as easy as it might seem and is well worth practising.

When walking on easy terrain holding the axe with the pick pointing forwards so the hand can rest on the wide flat top of the adze is very comfortable. You are also less likely to stick the pick in your leg if you stumble. But for quick self-arrest the pick should be pointing backwards so I carry my axe like this if I think a fall is possible.

The main reason for using an ice axe is for stopping slides by a technique known as self-arrest or ice axe braking.

When on slopes of hard snow or ice you should always be aware of what lies below. If there is a gentle run-out into a bowl of deep snow a slide might well be no more than a nuisance but if, as is more usual, there are crags, boulders or stream gullies in the way the result of a slip could be a serious accident. It is surprising just how quickly you pick up speed during a slide, especially when wearing smooth nylon clothing, so you need to be able to react very quickly, using the pick of the ice axe, backed up by your body weight, to stop your slide.

The best way to learn self-arrest is at an outdoor centre or from an independent mountaineering instructor. Second best is an experienced friend. Self-arrest should be practised until it becomes second nature. In a real incident there is not time to think about what to do. You just need to stop as quickly as possible.

A slope of hard snow with a gentle run-out so that if you fail to stop you will not hurt yourself is the best place for practising self-arrest. Wearing a climbing helmet is a good idea if you have one. Lie on your back with your feet downhill and push yourself off down the slope holding the axe diagonally across your body with your lower hand on the shaft near the spike and your upper hand over the head, with the pick pointing away from you. Once you have started to slide, roll sideways toward the head of the axe and onto the pick, tucking the adze in just above your shoulder so you can use your body weight to push down on the shaft. Arching your back exerts extra pressure. Do not hold the axe at arm's length as this prevents your weight helping to force the pick into the snow and may lead to it being ripped out of your hands. Make sure your lower hand controls the spike so it does not stab you in the thigh, and do not roll toward the spike or it may catch in the snow. Pulling up with your lower hand keeps the spike out of the snow and helps you arch your back. Your knees can be used as extra brakes. Although you may be wearing crampons in a real fall you should not do so when practising as the crampon points might catch in the snow and flip you over onto your back. It is worth lifting your feet well off the snow when practising as this is what you should do with crampons on. Once you are comfortable stopping at slow speeds slide further and faster then try again.

If you slip you are unlikely always to fall with your head up the slope so you should also practise self-arrest when sliding head first, both on your back and on your front. The self-arrest position is exactly the same as described above but getting into it is harder.

When sliding head first on your back, grasp the axe with both hands, then place the pick off to the side and roll onto your front while pivoting round it until your feet are downhill and you can stop.

Face-down head-first slides are harder to stop. Again with the axe held in both hands you place the pick off to the side and pivot around it to get your legs downhill. This results in the axe being out at arm's length above your head. To stop it being snatched out of your hands the pick has to be lifted out of the snow so you can pull the axe into position close to your shoulder.

With both sorts of head-first fall make sure you place the pick to the side on which it lies. Do not bring it across your body as this could lead to you stabbing yourself with it or to the spike catching in the snow. It also takes more time.

Sliding down snow slopes on your feet or sitting down is a quick way to descend and can be fun. It can also be

very dangerous. Glissading, as it is called, should only be attempted if you can see the whole slope and there is a big flat run-out at the bottom. It is easiest sitting, with the axe held in the self-arrest position. The spike can be dragged in the snow to control speed. The heels can be used for this too. Standing glissades are difficult as you are sliding on your boot soles. Ski techniques help here but many standing glissades finish as sitting ones.

Carrying an Ice Axe

The usual place to carry an ice axe is on the back of the rucksack, using the straps provided. This means you have to take your pack off when you need it unless you have a companion remove it for you. Even so, it may be tempting to

An ice axe strapped to the rucksack for transport to the snow.

push on without removing the axe until you suddenly realize you need it. An alternative and easily accessible way of carrying the axe is to slide it between your back and the pack shoulder straps.

However you carry your axe remember it is sharp and take care. People have been injured by stumbling onto the spike of an axe on the back of the rucksack of the person in front. Some form of stopper on the spike is therefore essential. Rubber stoppers often come with axes but tend to be quickly lost. The corks from wine bottles are a good substitute and I have seen the end of a toothpaste tube used. Rubber covers are also available for the pick and adze.

CRAMPONS

An ice axe can help you stop a fall if you slip on an icy slope, but wearing crampons could have prevented the slip in the first place. If you need an ice axe then you often need crampons as well. On a number of occasions I have found crampons of more use than an axe and I certainly would not venture out with an axe but no crampons.

Choosing crampons is not easy, particularly as much of the advice and information available is contradictory. It is also often more suited to the climber rather than the hillwalker as much of it is given by climbers whose idea of a winter walk is far more difficult than anything most walkers would ever tackle. I have met people with light-weight boots who have been told that they cannot use crampons with them. Believing this they have then gone out on the hills in winter without crampons. My guess is that the advice was given by a climber who knew you could not do any technical climbing in such boots. There are no boots to which crampons cannot be fitted. What is crucial is to match the crampons to the boots and then use the combination in conditions to which it is suited.

The simplest crampons are instep crampons. These have only four to six points and fit under the boot instep. Instep crampons have a poor reputation as they do not perform very well on steep slopes and cannot be used for climbing. For walkers who stick to footpaths and just need something for the occasional fairly level section of slippery ice they could be ideal, especially as they will fit any boot.

There are not many models available and some are poorly designed. The best are Grivel Grippers, which will adjust automatically to fit any boot. This is because they have short stainless steel chains that curve round and grip the edges of the boot sole when the nylon straps are pulled tight rather than rigid bars at the sides. They also have two upward facing points that lodge against the boot heel or, if the boot has a flat sole, bite into the sole itself. The combination of the chains and upper points is designed to prevent them from twisting sideways or slipping backwards, both problems with ordinary instep crampons. Underfoot they have six points, set farther apart than is usual on instep crampons.

I have used such crampons fitted to a pair of soft boots that have very bendy soles with no stiffening, and found them very effective on icy tracks. They are not suitable for climbing, but for walkers who do not venture onto steep mountain terrain they could prove useful, especially as they pack up small into the stuffsack provided and weigh just 13½oz (375g) a pair.

Hillwalkers who venture onto steep slopes in winter need full length rather than instep crampons. There are three basic types – flexible, articulated and rigid. Flexible crampons are light in weight and the right choice for most hillwalkers. They are suitable for use with walking boots because they have a flexible bar connecting the rear and front sections, which means that they can bend with your boots. Those with two forward pointing spikes, known as front points, are suitable for easy gully climbs and for going up steep slopes.

Crampons without front points have to be used with the foot kept flat on the snow. They are safer for walking, as you can trip over front points and catch them on your trousers or gaiters. Flexible crampons may have eight, ten or twelve spikes. Although they work best with boots with some degree of stiffening in the sole flexible crampons will fit most boots. Some will not fit all sizes. In particular, crampons where the middle two sets of points are some distance apart may not fit larger boots

well. This means that such crampons are ideal for smaller boots. Weights range from around 16 to 20oz (450 to 550g) for crampons made from light alloy to 28 to 30oz (790 to 850g) for steel crampons. Alloy versions are fine for occasional use but are not designed for prolonged use or for serious climbing. They are excellent for backpackers and ski tourers who want to carry a pair just in case they are needed. For more regular use and any sort of technical climbing steel crampons are needed.

Articulated crampons always have front points as they are suitable for both walking and climbing, making them the most versatile type. Instead of a flexible connecting bar they usually have a rigid bar that hinges behind the front section. This makes them best suited for use with stiffer boots. Hillwalkers with ambitions on easy winter climbing routes should consider articulated crampons.

A pair of flexible ten-point walker's crampons.

Rigid crampons – those with no hinged or flexible centre bar – are designed for rigid boots. This means either plastic climbing boots or leather boots with full length metal shanks. For hard winter climbing such boots and crampons are excellent. But rigid crampons are not suitable for walking in or for use with more flexible boots as they may either break or fall off. If you want one pair of crampons for both climbing and walking an articulated pair with twelve points is the best choice.

Attaching crampons

Perhaps the most confusing aspect of crampon selection is choosing the right bindings. Of the two alternatives step-in (or clip-on) bindings would seem ideal for walkers because they are quick and easy to fit, important for walkers who may well be putting on and taking off crampons several times a day. Strap-on crampons, the other choice, can be difficult to put on with cold fingers. Threading and fastening them takes longer too. Unfortunately, step-in crampons will not fit all boots but they will fit more than is often thought. Some people claim that they are unsuitable for use on anything other than fully rigid plastic mountaineering boots but I disagree.

Whatever sort of bindings you have crampons should fit your boots well without them. You should be able to shake your boots without the crampons coming off. The best way to get such a fit is to take your boots into a good outdoor shop and have the crampons adjusted and fitted there.

Because step-in bindings feature clips at the heel and, in most designs, bales at the toe they will only fit boots with a pronounced welt or special ridges built into the sole unit. As long as boots have either of these they do not need to be

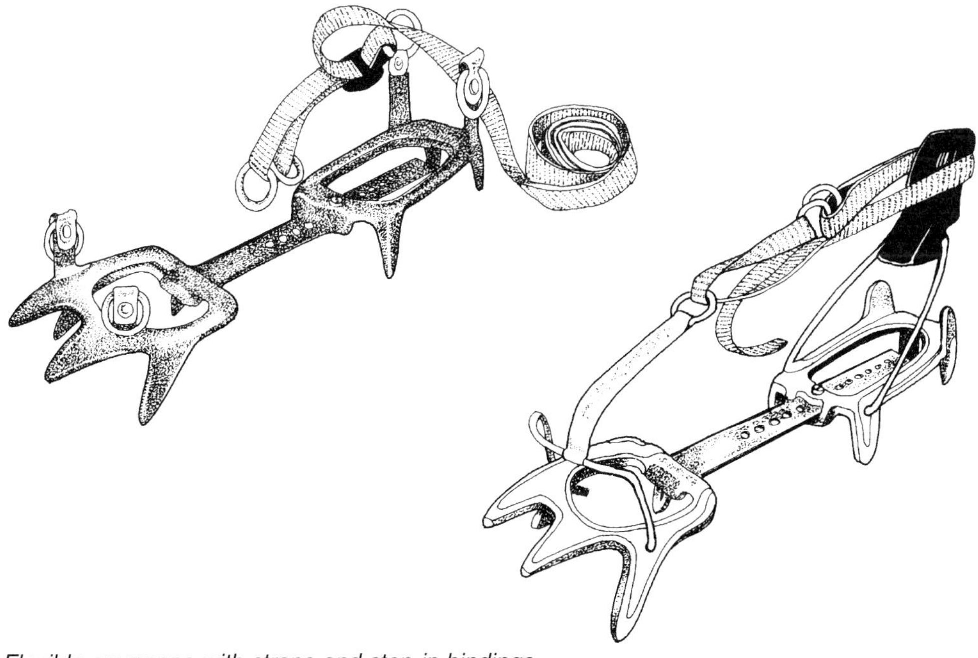

Flexible crampons with straps and step-in bindings.

fully stiffened. Most walking boots do not have these features but some do. I find step-ins so easy to use that I would not choose a pair of boots for winter hillwalking that they could not be fitted to.

Step-ins come in three styles, only two of which are suitable for use with bendy boots. The first type has a wire bail at the toe and a plastic clip at the heel, which are not connected. This type should only be used with rigid boots as the flexing of walking boots could cause them to pop off.

The second type is very similar except that the front bail is linked to the ankle strap by a flexible metal strip. In the third type the front bail is replaced by a toe strap with a central ring through which the ankle strap runs. In both these types the fact that the toe and heel bindings are linked should mean that they should not come off a bendy walking boot. My own usage suggests that these types of step-in bindings can be used successfully with walking boots but I should point out that some experts, including crampon manufacturers, say they should only be used with boots with a full length shank. What you cannot do with the combination of step-in crampons and walking boots is any technical climbing.

If your boots do not have welts or ledges for step-in crampons then you will need straps. Most crampons come with straps, and these attach in various different ways. Because you may have to put them on in a blizzard when you are cold and tired and your fingers are numb it is important that you practise doing up the straps beforehand. Straps may be nylon or neoprene. The latter are reckoned to be less prone to freezing when wet than the former and so are a better choice for British conditions.

Strap-on flexible crampons are suit-able for most boots as long as the uppers are reasonably solid. Crampon straps need to be done up fairly tightly, which could cause the circulation in your feet to be cut off or at least imped-ed in boots with soft uppers. Step-in bindings would be better for such boots if they only had suitable sole units.

Carrying Crampons

All those spikes make crampons awk-ward to carry. If you have a crampon patch on your rucksack you could just strap the crampons to this while walk-ing, though you will need to be careful when you take your pack off. Some rucksacks have large adjustable flaps on the front, sometimes called compression shields. I stick my crampons behind this flap. Rubber crampon protectors with individual covers for each point are available but they easily get tangled up and in my experience do not last very long. Better is a tough nylon or neo-prene bag that either wraps round the crampons or has a side zip. For years I have used a Cordura side pocket for my crampons. This can be carried inside the pack or strapped to the outside.

Using Crampons

Crampon technique is not difficult but it does require some practice. Once you have eight to twelve sharp spikes under each boot you have to be careful where you put your feet. Anyone who wears crampons is likely to catch them on their gaiters or trousers sooner or later but you can minimize the chances of this happening by not having any loose boot laces or gaiter cords dangling round your feet. When walking in crampons keep your feet farther apart than usual and put them down flat.

To use crampons effectively and

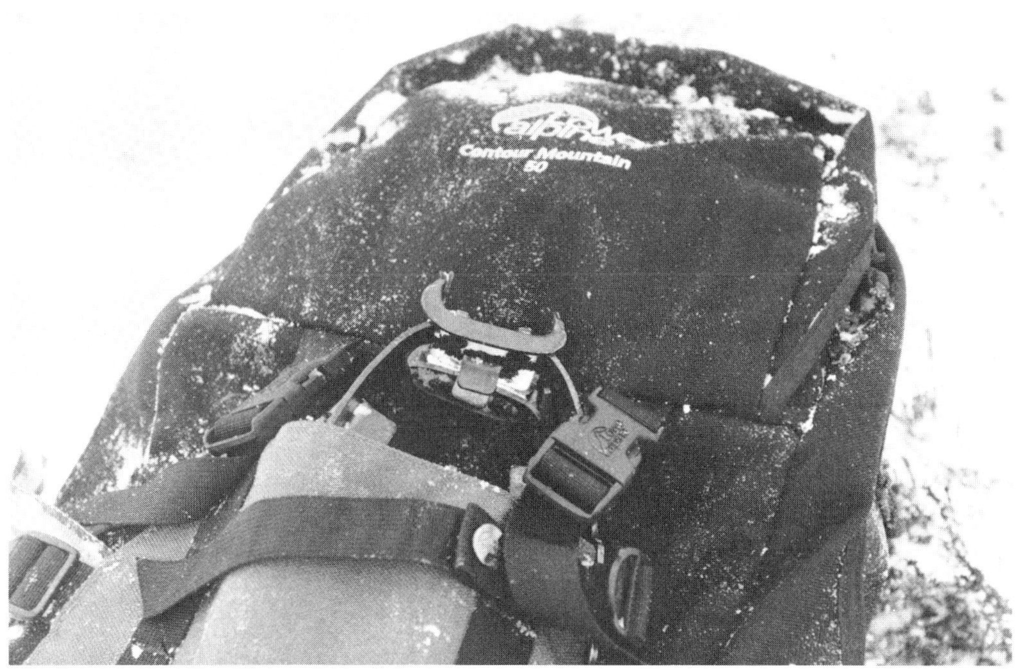

Carrying crampons behind the storage flap found on some rucksacks.

When walking in crampons keep your feet flat on the snow even when on a slope.

safely you need flexible ankles as it is important to keep the crampons flat on the snow so that all the points bite. Just using the edges when traversing or the heels when descending can lead to a slip. If your crampons have front points you can kick these into the slope and walk up on your toes, though this is not something you can do for very long on steep slopes in bendy boots. A combination technique I often use on moderate slopes is to front-point with one foot while keeping the other flat on the snow. When the first foot tires I swap feet.

Crampons are not just for use on unbroken snow and ice. They are also very useful on icy rocks and mixed scree and snow. Do not worry about damaging them – good crampons are tough and the points can always be sharpened. I once used crampons in Greenland for climbing a mixture of wet, loose scree and long ribbons of fairly soft snow. Overall the crampons were more use on the scree than the snow as the latter was soft enough to kick steps in.

Soft snow can in fact be a problem as it can stick to the bottom of the crampons creating a layer that makes walking difficult and can cause you to slip. One solution to this is to tap the side of the crampon with your ice axe every so often to knock the snow off. If the problem persists consider taking the crampons off unless you really need them.

If you fall while wearing crampons and have to self-arrest with your ice axe lift your feet off the snow so the crampons do not catch and flip you over.

SKIING

Once the snow starts to be more than ankle deep, walking becomes hard work and skis are the obvious way to travel. There are two sorts of skis suitable for hill touring: alpine ski mountaineering skis – which are similar to ordinary downhill alpine skis and which require stiff-soled plastic boots – and Nordic mountain touring skis. The latter are lighter and are used with more flexible boots, usually of leather though there are some plastic models available. Alpine gear gives the best downhill control on really steep slopes but is very slow on flat and undulating terrain and the weight is tiring. Nordic skis are designed to do everything and are the best compromise for hill touring.

Nordic skiing is the original means of travelling across snow covered terrain, and a great contrast to the mechanized world of alpine downhill skiing. It can be practised wherever and whenever a layer of snow covers the ground. That is its great advantage, especially in the UK where snow can fall anywhere, though it does not usually last for long except in the Scottish Highlands. Once it does you can just grab your skis, head out of the door and go. Skiing ability also opens up the hills in spring and winter in places where snow lies long and deep such as Scandinavia and the mountains of North America.

Once competent in basic techniques winter hillwalkers can ski across the moors and mountains, an exhilarating activity but one that requires a degree of skill and experience to do safely. You do not just need to be a good skier either. Navigation is very important as are winter survival techniques and an ability to judge snow and weather conditions. For the experienced nothing compares with the joys of swooping over pristine snow-fields high in the hills on a sunny winter's day.

The equipment for Nordic skiing is much simpler, lighter and cheaper than that for alpine skiing. For skiing in the hills metal-edged skis are needed along

Ski touring is the ideal way to explore snowbound mountains.

with mountain touring boots, which are similar to winter hillwalking boots and have rubber soles with deep treads for walking. Flexible and articulated crampons can be used with these boots but only a few types will fit due to the wide, square toe of the boots. The boots are only attached to the skis at the toe, though some bindings may wrap right round the boot. They give great freedom of movement compared with alpine boots, which are locked down at toe and heel.

The right equipment is important, so buying from a specialist Nordic supplier who can give the right advice is wise. The two leading ones in Britain are Highland Guides in Aviemore and Braemar Nordic Ski Centre in Braemar. Both have very good mail order services. Few outdoor shops know much about Nordic skiing; one that does is Base Camp in Ilkley. While Nordic skiing is not hard to learn teaching yourself is difficult. The way to progress quickly is by taking a course of instruction at a Nordic ski school or from an instructor in your local ski club. For further details see my book *Wilderness Skiing and Winter Camping* (details in Further Reading section).

SNOW SHELTERS

Not so long ago a Nordic skier was lost in a blizzard in the hills above Glenshee in the Southern Cairngorms for several days before managing to stagger out to the road, much to the astonishment of the rescue team who had never known anyone survive so long in such appalling conditions. He did this by digging a snow shelter that protected him from the weather. This was an extreme situation but hillwalkers die every winter in similar conditions. Knowing how to build a snow shelter could have saved their lives.

Snow shelters are not just for emergency use. Snow is an excellent insulator, and a snow shelter is warmer than a tent. A small shelter can even be dug for a lunch stop in stormy weather. A roomy one can make an excellent base, and it is better than a tent in snowy or blustery weather because it is absolutely quiet and still inside. I once spent 36 comfortable hours in a snow-hole in the Cairngorms while a blizzard raged outside. Travel was impossible and camping would have been very difficult and unpleasant.

High in the hills in a blizzard is not the time to learn how to build a shelter. Luckily, practising is fun! A good time to try building a snow shelter is when the weather prevents you from going far. Apart from being more enjoyable than staring glumly at the storm through a window, practising in bad weather will demonstrate the difference a shelter makes to your comfort.

Tools

In an emergency anything – gloved hands, pans, mugs or ice axes – can be used to dig a shelter, but it is much quicker and easier to use a snow shovel or, in hard snow or ice, a snow saw. I always carry a snow shovel when there is much snow on the hills but I only take a saw if I am intending building a shelter.

Snow shovels are small and light, between 1 and 2lb (450 and 900g) in weight and 2 to 3 ft (60 to 90cm) in length, and can be folded or broken down into handle and blade for carry-ing. Most have alloy blades and wooden or plastic handles. The lightest I know of is the Camp Snow Shovel, which weighs 19¼oz (550g) and has a flat alloy blade and a detachable wooden shaft. I have used it for over ten years and have found it quite tough, although the blade has needed re-riveting a couple of times. Most plastic shovels will not cut through hard packed snow but there are a few designed to do so.

Different shovels serve different purposes. A large shovel is great for shifting large amounts of snow when building a snow dome but difficult to use in the confines of a snow-hole. Curved blades are good for shaping roofs but not so good for cutting blocks or using as a stand for a stove. In a group a variety of shovels is better than several similar models so if you are buying one find out which types your companions have and buy a different one.

Snow saws are very lightweight – around ½lb (225g) – and not very sharp, blunt alloy teeth being adequate for cutting through even the hardest snow.

Snow-Holes

There are several types of snow shelter. Which is best depends on the terrain and on how urgent the need for shelter. Where deep snow is available only on banks and slopes, often the case in the UK, a snow-hole may be the easiest type of snow shelter to build.

To make a snow-hole you need a bank of snow at least 6ft (1.8m) deep and preferably much deeper. The steeper the angle the better. Such banks are often found beside streams and on the lee sides of corries. If you start part way up the slope you can throw the snow downhill, which is easier than piling it up.

Start by digging straight into the

Digging a snow-hole in a steep bank.

Digging out the inside of a snow-hole.

bank at about head height. If you have two shovels, two entrances can be started about 6ft (1.8m) apart. Dig in for about 3ft (90cm), then start to clear an area on either side at about waist height. Dig upward rather than down, but make sure there is at least 1ft (30cm) of snow for the roof or it might collapse. The idea is to produce sleeping platforms with a trench between them for cold air to sink into.

How big you make the snow-hole depends on how many it must sleep and how ambitious you are feeling. Several holes can be linked by short passages for a large group. The roof above the sleeping platforms should be high enough for you to sit up comfortably, and smoothed and rounded to minimize dripping. While one person is digging out the hole, someone else can be removing the snow from the entrance. Snow can be thrown onto a plastic bivvy bag and then hauled outside. Once the hole is complete the bivvy bag can be used as a groundsheet. Inside, a shelf can be dug out for use as a kitchen and niches cut in the walls to store small items. Be careful to keep track of everything. Gear trodden into the floor can be hard to find. Do not leave your boots in the cold trench either, they will freeze hard.

Once the hole is dug, stop up most of the entrance with snow blocks. A rucksack can be used to block the doorway to help prevent it from filling up with snow. Having the floor of the hole sloping down to the entrance is the best way to prevent snow and cold air from

Inside a snow-hole.

Looking out of a snow-hole.

entering. If you started with two entrances, fill one in completely. Occasionally you may hit rock, earth or vegetation at the bottom or back of your hole. All you can do then is try again farther along the bank or adapt the hole to accommodate it.

Ventilation is very important, so as a backup to the entrance (which may drift over in a storm) poke a hole in the roof with a ski pole or ice axe. If you leave the pole poking out of the hole you can easily make sure that it stays clear of snow. It will also act as a marker so that no one walks over your roof (do not investigate a ski pole sticking out of the snow for this reason) and to help you locate your snow-hole. Keep a shovel handy inside the hole. Snow-holes are very stable, but the entrances can get blocked with snow very quickly.

Snow Domes

Igloos are complex constructions requiring a degree of skill to build. But snow domes, sometimes called 'instant igloos', are simple to make. Their big advantage is that you do not need a bank or slope. You do not need deep snow either. But if the snow cover is very thin you will have to shift snow over a greater distance so more work and time will be needed. It may seem that some snow is too soft to be used for a shelter but snow hardens quickly when it is disturbed so just moving it will make it suitable.

Initially you just heap up a pile of snow some 12ft (3.6m) across and 6 to

8ft (1.8 to 2.4m) high. If the snow is deep enough this can be made easier by digging a circular trench around the perimeter of the heap. Once you have a big enough mound of snow tunnel into it on the side away from the wind. Then it is simply a question of digging out the inside. Despite what you may be told or may read elsewhere you do not need to wait for the snow to consolidate before doing this. I have built several snow domes from different types of snow and have never had to wait before tunnelling into them. The walls need to be at least 1ft (30cm) thick. To check this a ski pole or ice axe can be pushed through from the outside and the wall thickness measured. A wall beside the entrance uses up the snow from the inside and protects the door from filling up with blown snow.

Building a snow dome can be speed-

Building a snow dome, a useful shelter when there are no steep banks suitable for snowholes.

Digging out the entrance of a snow dome.

ed up by placing your rucksacks in a pile and heaping the snow over them. They will be recovered when you dig the dome out. I have heard of snow domes being built around two or three people standing in a huddle with their arms around each other. This is not something I would fancy doing!

Snow Trenches

A good snow-hole takes at least a couple of hours to build, a snow dome an hour or more, so they are not really practical in an emergency. A slot or sentry box big enough for one person to get out of the wind can be shovelled out in a matter of minutes. It can always be enlarged if you decide to stay put. But the best emergency shelter is a snow trench or snow grave, which can be built in a few minutes and will shelter two people. At least 3ft (90cm) of reasonably level snow is required, so this is a technique for places where the snow falls heavily and lies deep.

Start by digging a slot about shoulder width and a little shorter than a plastic bivvy bag. While one person digs, another can build a wall around the windward end with the excavated snow. Dig straight down until the trench is 3 to 5ft (0.9 to 1.5m) deep. There should now be room for two people to sit in the trench with their heads well below the rim. Insulating mats can be used as the floor. A plastic bivvy bag can be used as the roof with ice axes or ski poles laid across the trench as sup-

ports. Snow can be piled on the ends of the bivvy bag to hold it down in wind.

If you have skis with you, sliding them into the bivvy bag helps keep it in place. You can get in and out of the trench by lifting one corner of the roof and sliding in. If this is only a temporary shelter while you lunch or rest out of the wind, no more needs to be done. If you are going to spend more than a few hours in your trench, perhaps even the night, dig out the sides at the bottom to make slots you can slide your legs into so you can stretch and lie down.

The size of the trench is determined by the size of your roof. If you have a double size bivvy bag or a tent flysheet you can dig a bigger trench and stretch the roof out, weighing down each side with snow and perhaps using upright poles or skis as roof supports from inside. Such a large trench will hold more people than the grave type, but the roof is much more vulnerable to collapse. A small trench will be warmer than a big one, too, and quicker to dig. Overall, if your need is to get out of the wind quickly, several smaller trenches are better than one large one. If it looks like your stay will be prolonged, a more solid roof can be put on a snow grave by using snow blocks to make an A-frame-style roof.

When you leave a snow trench, fill it in and stamp the snow down. Apart from leaving as little sign of your presence as possible, this ensures that other people will not have an accident by falling into it.

8 Staying Out: Backpacking Techniques and Equipment

You fight every ounce of the way. (Hamish Brown, *The Last Hundred*)

Many walkers never spend a night out in the hills. To my mind they are missing much. You cannot fully experience the hills without sleeping out at times; and extended journeys where you stay out for days or weeks are the ultimate expression of hillwalking. I gain far more from backpacking trips than from day walks. Backpacking is about living close to nature, about being part of the wild world. By camping in the hills the backpacker experiences much that the day walker misses: the glories of sunset and sunrise, the wildlife that only moves when intrusive humans have gone, the vast starry skies of clear nights. Only the backpacker is able fully to leave behind our artificial world and enter the living natural world.

Being able to move on each day without the restrictions of having to find overnight shelter gives the freedom to partake of all that the hills have to offer. It enables the backpacker to

Backpacking high in Yosemite National Park. By camping out at night you can explore remote wilderness areas.

undertake long journeys, both in distance and in the mind. Wild lands are opened up in all their splendour when you stay in them all the hours of the day and night. Only by backpacking can they be fully appreciated.

Camping out at night brings a closeness to nature impossible for those who shelter inside four walls. Waking to the mist slowly clearing from a mountain lake as the first golden shafts of sunlight slant through the dark rocks is magical. But staying out also means having to cope with wind, rain and cold. However, even those days – especially those days – that dawn bleak and grey with rain hammering on the flysheet and the wind whistling overhead give you a contact with nature unknown to those who have fled the hills at the coming of night.

Venturing out into the wilds for days at a time is not something to be done lightly. It requires careful preparation and both walking and lightweight camping skills. This chapter is just an outline of how to backpack comfortably and safely – perhaps it will encourage those who have not yet ventured beyond day walking to undertake some backpacking adventures of their own. If you want to know more I have written a comprehensive book on the subject called *The Backpacker's Handbook*.

EQUIPMENT FOR BACKPACKING

A backpacking load does not need to be a back-breaking load even though you have to carry everything you need for camping as well as walking. Keeping the weight down can be done in two ways.

First, the weight of every piece of your gear, from your tent to your spoon, is important. For day walking the weight difference between, say, one jacket and another does not matter that much. For the backpacker, on the other hand, a little extra weight on each bit of gear can add up to a considerable amount on the back. If you cannot decide between two items of gear, always choose the lighter one. Most stores can tell you what a tent weighs (though not always accurately) but few know the weights of the clothing they stock. Taking along a small spring balance for weighing gear when you shop is well worthwhile. Those who intend backpacking in the future would do well to pay careful attention to the weight of any items like waterproofs they buy for day walking. Those who camp on roadside sites should do the same. It may not matter how much your tent or sleeping bag weighs if you arrive at your site by car but if you plan on using the same gear for backpacking then the weight will become very important.

Second, ask yourself if everything you are taking is really necessary. Be ruthless. If you are not sure leave it at home. Then after each trip go through your gear and see what you did not need and resolve to leave it at home next time – apart from emergency items like the first aid kit (and even here weight can be saved if you cut out some of the extra sheets of blister coverings or plasters).

As a guide, a summer backpacking load for a solo walker should weigh no more than 25lb (11kg) without food or non-essential accessories such as books or camera gear. Adding food at around 2lb (900g) a day gives a total of 30lb (14kg) for a weekend and 40lb (18kg) for a week. Sharing gear can bring this down a little. Very careful attention to weight can do so too; it is possible to get down to around 20lb (9kg) for a weekend or 30lb (14kg) for a week.

Paying such attention to weight may seem almost obsessive, but the time spent will be welcomed when out on the hill. The difference between a 25lb (11kg) and 35lb (16kg) rucksack is very noticeable. I have carried some extremely heavy loads over the years, mostly in remote wildernesses where extra gear and many days' worth of food have to be carried, but I still check the weight of everything carefully. I also know from carrying those loads – some in excess of 70lb (32kg) – that there is a direct relationship between how far you can walk and how much you carry. The heavier your load the slower you walk, the more often you stop to rest, the longer your rest stops last, the sooner your feet hurt and your legs feel tired and the sooner you stop for the day. Climbing hills is much harder too. If you want to cover the same ground when backpacking as when day walking then you need a light load. If your aim is to haul your gear for half a day to a site that you will use as a base for several days while you climb the surrounding hills then the weight of your initial load may be less important than your desire to have some luxury in camp such as fresh food or even camp chairs. Mostly, though, keeping the weight as low as possible is the way to go.

Choosing Equipment

A vast amount of gear fills the outdoor shops and catalogues. Much of it is too heavy for backpacking and walkers need to beware of being seduced by impressive features that will not be of use on the trail. They usually add weight. How many pockets does a waterproof jacket really need? A simple sweater-style fleece top weighs less and takes up less room in your pack than one with a full length zip, hood, multiple pockets and reinforced elbows and shoulders. Over-specified gear is another temptation. Do you really need a sleeping bag rated to -30°C (-22°F) or a tent built to withstand blizzards on Mount Everest? To avoid being tempted by items that are too heavy shop with a maximum weight in mind for items of gear such as those listed below. Try to find items below these weights and do not consider models above them regardless of how good they may be. Suggested target weights are shown in Table 3.

Packs

Packs are the exception to the rule that light and simple is always best. A large day pack may be fine for the occasional night out in summer but if you do much backpacking a bigger pack will be required, preferably one with a padded hip belt and some form of stiffening in the back. For load carrying comfort is paramount and complex pack harness systems are much more comfortable than simple ones. Unfortunately they are also heavier. When choosing a pack think of the weight you will be carrying. A heavy load will be most comfortable in a pack with a frame and thickly padded shoulder straps and hip belt even though such a pack will weigh more than a simpler model. A rough guide is that a pack should not weigh more than 10 per cent of your total load. So for a winter load weighing 60lb (27kg) a 6lb (2.7kg) pack is acceptable. If you only backpack on summer weekends and never carry more than 30lb (14kg) a pack weighing around 3lb (1.4kg) should be adequate. If you backpack year round and only have one pack you will be carrying 30lb (14kg) in

Suggested target weights for backpacking. If you backpack year round and have one set of gear you will of course end up carrying more in summer.

Footwear – weights shown are for a pair of UK size 9; scale up or down for different sizes.

Sports sandals 25oz (700g)
Running shoes 25oz (700g)
Trail shoes 2lb (900g)
Three season boots 2½lb (1.1kg)
Winter boots (suitable for crampons) 4lb (1.8kg)

Shelter

Groundsheet 10oz (280g)
Waterproof or breathable bivvy bag 20oz (560g)
Solo tent, three season 4lb (1.7kg)
Duo tent, three season 6lb (2.7kg)
Duo tent, winter mountain 8lb (3.6kg)
Sleeping bag (summer) 25oz (710g)
Sleeping bag (three season) 3lb (1.3kg)
Sleeping bag (winter) 4lb (1.7kg)
Closed cell foam mat 9oz (250g)
Self-inflating mat 14oz (110g)

Cooking gear

Stove (butane/propane cartridge) 14oz (100g)
Stove (multi-fuel, petrol or paraffin) 1lb (450g)
Stove (methylated spirit with solo cookset) 30oz (840g)
Stove (methylated spirit with duo cookset) 44oz (1.2kg)
Quart pot with lid 8oz (225g)
Cookset with 3 and 4 pint (1.7 and 2.2 litre) pans and lid 26oz (730g)

Summer Clothing

Synthetic T-shirt 4oz (110g)
Warm top (wool or fleece) 1lb (450g)
Shorts 6oz (170g)
Synthetic long johns 4oz (110g)
Summer weight trousers 12oz (340g)
Windproof top 12oz (340g)
Waterproof jacket 1lb (450g)
Overtrousers 8oz (225g)
Warm hat 2oz (55g)
Sun hat 4oz (110g)

Winter clothing

Synthetic zip neck shirt 8oz (225g)
Warm top (wool or fleece) 20oz (560g)
Windproof fleece (for wet-cold) 25oz (700g)
Down top (for dry-cold) 20oz (560g)
Synthetic long johns or pile trousers 8oz (225g)
Thick trousers 34oz (670g)
Waterproof breathable jacket 28oz (780g)
Waterproof breathable trousers 20oz (560g)
Warm hat 2oz (55g)
Windproof pile lined cap 4oz (110g)
Liner gloves 2oz (55g)
Warm gloves or mitts 4oz (110g)
Shell gloves or mitts 5oz (140g)

Packs
Summer backpack (60–75l) 60–80oz (1.7–2.5kg)
Wilderness expedition/winter backpacking (100l+) 90–120oz (2.5–3.4kg)

Table 3.

the 6lb (2.7kg) one.

To compare the weights of different packs you can look at the ratio of the volume to the weight. From the catalogues of the major pack makers I found that 15 to 18 litres of capacity per 500g of weight (830 to 1000 cubic inches per lb) is the average. Lightweight packs suitable for loads up to 35lb (16kg) can have ratios of 25 or more litres per 500g (1390 cubic inches per lb) but packs suitable for heavy loads are usually nearer the average. Packs with less than 15 litres per 500g (830 cubic inches per lb) are too heavy to be worth considering.

It is also important that the pack fits properly. To check this try a selection on with loads of at least 30lb (14kg) in to see how they feel. A good pack will let you carry 75 per cent or more of the weight on your hips without them feeling sore. It should not wobble when you walk or it will be very unstable on steep slopes.

It is worth taking time over your decision. Your pack should last for years and can make all the difference to the success of a walk. There is little joy in aching shoulders and sore hips.

The design of the packbag itself is far less important than the harness system. Pockets are useful for carrying small items while split compartments make organizing gear easier but they are not essential. The capacity is important and I would urge you to buy a large pack. Small packs, stuffed to bursting and with gear dangling off the outside, are uncomfortable to carry, lack stability and are hard to pack and unpack. Choose a pack big enough for the largest loads you think you might carry. You do not have to fill it. If your pack has detachable side pockets and compression straps it can easily be adapted to varying sized loads. My favourite pack, bought for ski expeditions to

A large 80 litre pack suitable for long backpacking trips. This model has a zipped lower compartment, a top pocket and side compression straps for attaching side pockets or tent poles and for snugging the pack around a small load.

The back of the pack shown in picture above. Note the wide padded hipbelt, essential for carrying heavy loads in comfort, and the different slots into which the shoulder harness can be threaded to fit different back lengths. There is an internal frame inside the pack.

places like Greenland, has a capacity of 115 litres (7015 cubic inches). I often use it as a day pack for side trips away from camp. For three season UK use a pack that large is not needed; one of around 75 litres (4575 cubic inches) should be fine.

Tents

Tents are needed for protection from wind, rain and biting insects. Unfortunately they also cut you off from the outside world and add weight and bulk to your load. If you are going somewhere where rain or mosquitoes are unlikely, do not assume you must have a tent. A bivvy bag may be all you need or, in wooded country, you could take a sheet of waterproof nylon, known as a tarp or basha, to sling between trees if the weather turns bad. On most backpacking trips you will need a tent, though – choosing one needs care and is worth taking time over.

The tent is usually the heaviest piece of gear carried so keeping its weight down is very important. At the same time comfort and stability also matter so your tent needs to be able to cope with storms and provide enough room for cooking and living under cover. A compromise has to be reached between weight on the one hand and strength and space on the other. Happily, there are a large number of top quality light-weight tents available. For those who move on every day and are keen on keeping the weight down there are tents weighing 4lb (1.8kg) or less for solo units, 6lb (2.7kg) or so for two person models. If you often camp on the same site for several nights – or feel greater comfort in camp is worth the extra weight – there are plenty of roomier and heavier models.

The lighter the tent the smaller the packed size, and any tent under 10lb (4.5kg) will be reasonably low in bulk. However, the length of pole sections should always be checked as some are too long for packing easily inside a rucksack.

After weight consider ease of pitching, weather resistance and roominess. In wet weather you want to be able to get your tent up quickly. Familiarity is important here but some tents are much easier to pitch than others. Making tents waterproof is not difficult and it is rare these days to find a good quality tent that leaks. Wind resistance is a different matter. Tents designed to withstand mountain gales you cannot stand up in are available but they are heavy and expensive. Some degree of wind resistance is required, especially if you plan on camping high in the hills. Roominess is relative and related to weight. Some people are happy with tiny tents you cannot sit up in, others use two person tents for solo use and three person tents for duos.

It is impossible to judge the wind resistance of a tent or how easy it is to pitch or how roomy inside by looking at pictures in a catalogue or holding a packed model. Ideally you need to see the tent erected and be able to crawl inside. Most shops do not have the space to do this, unfortunately. There are tent shows around the country each year, which are well worth visiting, and Backpackers' Club meetings are good places to see various models and hear some clear opinions on them.

Modern lightweight tents usually consist of a breathable nylon inner and a proofed nylon flysheet to keep off the wind and rain, though there are some single-skin waterproof and breathable fabric tents available. Sewn-in groundsheets are standard. Shock-corded poles are much easier to use than single section poles and usually a good sign of the quality of the tent. Generally, aluminium poles are stronger than fibreglass.

In any tent condensation can be a problem. Moisture from your body, from damp clothing and from cooking may condense on the inside of the non-breathable flysheet. The purpose of a separate inner is to protect you from this condensation. For two-skin tents to work properly there must be a gap between the inner and the outer in which air can circulate. If the two layers touch then condensation on the outer can dampen the inner. In theory breathable single-skin tents allow moisture to pass through the material to the outside. In practice I have found that while they do this most of the time they can become very damp inside in prolonged wet and cold weather. I would not choose a single-skin tent for a long trip in a damp area.

Condensation can be minimized by cooking outside or in the porch with the door open (also advisable for safety reasons) and by having a tent with two-way door zips or vents so that airflow can be maintained through the tent. You should also store any damp items outside the inner tent. In really wet weather, when you have to keep the tent zipped shut, some condensation is inevitable.

There are many different shapes of tent available, most of which work well.

Tunnel tents are lightweight, roomy and easy to pitch.

The real difference is usually in how easy they are to pitch, some designs going up in seconds with a minimum number of pegs being needed, others requiring extensive pegging. With any tent it is worth considering what it would be like to pitch in a storm in the dark when you are tired.

Of the many designs available single hoop and two- or three-pole tunnel tents are light, roomy and easy to pitch. Simple dome tents where the poles cross at the apex of the tent are even roomier but also heavier and not quite so stable. Geodesic domes where the poles intersect at a number of points are heavier still and harder to pitch but very stable in high winds – hence their popularity with mountaineers and arctic explorers. Three pole semi-geodesics are quite light and can be pitched quickly. All domes have the advantage of being free-standing. This makes them ideal for use in areas where pegging down a tent could be difficult.

An essential feature is a large porch in which you can store wet and muddy gear and cook safely under cover when the weather is stormy. Larger tents designed for winter use sometimes have two porches.

Although lightweight tents are amazingly strong for their weight they do require care in use. Most will withstand quite strong winds but in severe conditions it is still best to seek a relatively sheltered site. You will also sleep better if the tent is not thrashing noisily in the wind.

Groundsheets are vulnerable to

A two person dome tent at a high valley camp. Note the large porch for storing gear and cooking under cover.

A geodesic dome tent at a high camp in the Pyrenees.

puncture so clearing away sharp twigs and stones before pitching is a good idea. Take care too not to step on poles lying on the ground or poke them into rocks when you connect up the sections. When the tent is up do not pull on poles when leaving or entering the tent. Carrying a short pole sleeve and some tape to repair a broken pole section is worthwhile, especially on long trips. I have had poles break twice and on both occasions was able to continue using the tent only because I had the means for a makeshift repair.

Whichever tent you choose it is advisable to practise pitching it before

167

you use it in the hills. By doing so you will also find out if there are any defects or any pole sections or pegs missing. Always seek out as flat a site as possible in order to be able to pitch the tent as tautly as you can. On really bumpy terrain you may find it impossible to achieve a tight pitch, something you will know about when the wind picks up and rattles any loose fabric.

Sleeping Bags

A warm night's rest is crucial for enjoyable backpacking so your choice of sleeping bag is very important. All sleeping bags are rated for different temperatures but these should only be taken as a rough guide as there is no standard. People differ too: warm sleepers can often use a bag at lower than the rated temperatures while cold sleepers would be wise to go for a bag rated for colder temperatures than they expect to encounter.

How the fill is held in place affects the warmth as well as the type and amount. Sewn-through constructions where the tubes that hold the fill in place are sewn together at the edges are fine for summer but not for colder conditions as heat can escape through the stitch lines. Better for three season use, and essential for winter, are constructions that keep the inner and outer of the bag apart.

There are two sorts of insulating fill: down from geese and ducks and synthetic fibres. Down is lightweight, easily compressed (important for fitting in the pack) and has a good warmth to weight ratio. The disadvantages are cost and a relative lack of water resistance, though this last is not as great a problem as many people think. Synthetic fibres dry quickly and keep some of their warmth when wet. But they are bulkier

and heavier than down for the same warmth. They are also less durable, a factor that more than offsets the lower cost. My view is that down bags are best for backpackers as long as you always use a tent and carry them in waterproof stuffsacks. Bags with water resistant breathable outers (they are never waterproof as the seams cannot be sealed) help in resisting condensation but are not essential.

Pile bags also exist made by Buffalo. They are warm when wet and quick drying but also heavy and bulky. If you regularly sleep out without a tent a Pertex nylon covered pile bag is a good choice.

Weights of bags vary enormously but those for summer use need weigh no more than 2lb (900g) for down filled bags and 3lb (1.4kg) for synthetics, three season bags no more than 3lb (1.4kg) for down and 4lb (1.8kg) for synthetics and winter bags no more than 3½lb (1.6kg) for down and 5lb (2.3kg) for synthetics. There are many bags well below these weights so it is worth choosing carefully. Weights of pile bags range from around 1lb (450g) for the lightest warm weather versions to 6lb (2.7kg) for double winterweight models. Do not go for the warmest bag if you want to use it year round. A -30°C (-22°F) rated bag will be far too hot in summer even when completely unzipped. If you only have one bag a three season one rated to around -5°C (23°F) is the best choice as it should not be too warm in summer and you can wear clothes in it in really cold temperatures. Another option is to use a summer weight bag with a three season one in extreme cold.

Whatever the fill, except in the warmest weather some form of insulation is needed under a sleeping bag. This can be a closed cell foam mat or, for more comfort, a self-inflating Therm-A-Rest mat.

Accessories

Along with the items already carried for day walking there are a number of small accessories that make life in camp more comfortable. I always carry a small repair kit containing stove spares, a tent pole repair sleeve, sticky backed nylon patches, a needle and thread, elastic bands and lengths of cord. I also carry a toothbrush and toothpaste, toilet paper and a toilet trowel. Options include candles, mosquito coils and paperback books for reading when sitting out a storm.

THE ART OF CAMPING

Camping in a different place every night is one of the joys of backpacking. It can also be one of the horrors if you find yourself stumbling around in the rain still looking for a site long after dark, so being able to find places to camp is an important skill. It is also important to leave your site so that no one can tell you were there. This is known as minimum impact camping.

Finding a Site

For a gentle introduction to lightweight camping the novice backpacker can use organized camp sites. There are many small sites where you will not be overwhelmed by frame tents and caravans. The Backpackers' Club has a list of farm sites, available to members only.

Once they have learnt basic camp craft most backpackers want to leave roadside camp sites behind and camp wild in the hills. On long distance trails and in popular areas there are plenty of well used sites. If you look carefully at these you can learn what to look for when selecting a site. If you are in an area where there are no established wild sites you can work out from the map where potential sites might be (look for widely spaced contour lines and water sources) and then plan to reach them with several hours of daylight left so you have time to scout round for the best pitch.

A superb view is always welcome but it will not look so good if the site is not comfortable. For a good night's sleep you first need flat dry ground. If a slight slope has to be accepted it is best to pitch the tent so that you can lie with your head higher than your feet. In strong winds look for shelter from crags, trees, banks or walls. If biting insects are a problem a breezy site is preferable. Finally you need access to water, though if you carry a collapsible water container big enough for all your overnight needs you can camp some distance from water without inconvenience.

Leaving no Trace

Backpackers have more impact on the countryside than day walkers. In order to preserve our hills and leave them unsullied for future visitors and for the creatures that live there it is essential that you leave no trace of your passing. Everything you bring with you must be taken away.

If you camp where no one has camped before you should not alter the terrain in any way. This means not removing vegetation, shifting rocks or digging trenches. Rocks are often used to weigh down tent pegs, though this is not usually necessary if you know how to pitch a tent properly. If you do use rocks for extra security please put them back where they came from: rings of stones are unsightly and kill the vegetation underneath. Avoid camping on damp ground as this is easily damaged. Ideal surfaces are bare earth, gravel or

A dome tent at a high site. Finding somewhere flat enough to camp can be difficult in a rough rocky area like this.

grass. Before leaving a site check round for scraps of litter and if the vegetation looks flattened rough it up a little so that no one will ever know you were there.

In most areas others will have been there before you as good sites are not that common. If a site shows little sign of use it is best to pass it by so that it can continue to recover. A well used site should be re-used in order to limit impact to one area. If possible tidy the site up, removing litter and breaking up rings of rocks.

Setting up Camp

When you have found a site setting up camp is usually easy. The deciding factor is the weather. If it is raining or cold and windy you will want to get the tent up quickly. When possible pitch the tent with the tail into the wind. For the best storm resistance tents should be pegged out so the fabric is taut with no folds or loose material to catch the wind. Guy lines should be fully tightened. Nylon stretches when wet so in rainy weather the tent will need adjusting every so often.

Once the tent is pitched remember to fill your water containers before you strip off wet clothing and get inside. Damp gear should be left in the porch or outside in your pack or a large plastic bag. Once in the tent put on dry clothing and if it is cold slide into your sleeping bag. Do not wait until you feel chilly – keeping warm is much easier than getting warm. Next, set up your stove in the porch, making sure there is good ventilation, and get some water on to boil. You can then cook and eat from the comfort of your sleeping bag.

In good weather the procedure is the same but you can be much more leisurely about it, maybe setting up your kitchen outside and sitting and relaxing with a hot drink for half an hour before pitching the tent.

That is, if you pitch the tent at all. I view tents as a mixed blessing. When it is wet and windy or when biting insects are about a tent is essential. But all too often tents are used when they are not necessary, cutting campers off from the world they have come to be part of. On clear calm nights I often sleep out under the stars, perhaps pitching the tent nearby if I am unsure the weather will hold. And when I do sleep in the tent I only zip up the flysheet doors if it is raining, very windy or midges are about. I much

In fine weather a tent isn't necessary. The author at a bivouac site in the Grand Canyon.

One of the joys of mountain camping is waking to a view like this.

prefer to leave the doors wide open so I can watch the hills darken into silhouettes as night falls, see the black shapes of deer and other creatures passing by and then wake up to the first sun and see colour flood back into the land. A tent is a shelter from storms. Use it only when you have to.

In the morning if the weather is dry it helps to air your gear, especially your sleeping bag, before you pack up to keep it as dry as possible.

SANITATION

Toilets should be sited at least 300ft (90m) from any water. Burying faeces is best unless you are in a really remote area where no one will come across them. A light plastic trowel is useful for digging holes, which should be at least 6in (15cm) deep. Toilet paper can be burned if it is safe or buried too. Curls of soiled pink paper sticking out from under rocks despoil too many wild sites.

Hand washing is very important for hygiene but should be done well away from streams or lakes, and the water poured into vegetation. Soap should be biodegradable and you should use the minimum amount.

CAMP FIRES

Sitting beside a blazing fire watching the night sky is a romantic image but one that in the main belongs in the past. Camp fires leave scars and use up nutrients needed by the soil. This is not to say that fires should never be lit. In places where you can light one without damaging the ground (on gravel banks by rivers or below high water mark on beaches but never on vegetation) and there is plenty of fallen wood a small fire probably does no harm. Overall it is best to rely on your tent and sleeping bag for warmth and your stove for hot food.

THE BACKPACKER'S KITCHEN

One of the joys of backpacking is sitting in the tent with a steaming hot drink while the wind howls and the rain lashes down outside. Hot food is also a good way to restore morale at the end of a tiring day.

Stoves

There is a large choice in stoves but the big difference between them lies in the fuel they run on rather than the individual design. Four fuels are available: butane/propane gas in pressurized cartridges, paraffin, petrol or a purified version, such as Coleman Fuel, and methylated spirits. The last is the safest fuel and recommended for beginners. Conveniently, most methylated spirit stoves come complete with cooking pans and windshields.

Methylated spirits is also clean and easy to use and most stoves work well in the cold and in stormy weather as they come with efficient windshields. Another big plus is their reliability; having no moving parts, they are nearly indestructible. Methylated spirit is clean too, evaporating quickly if spilled. The only real objection is that it is not a hot fuel, roughly twice as much being needed for the same heat output as other fuels.

Butane/propane cartridge stoves are also easy to use as well as being very lightweight. They work fine when the cartridge is full, but as it empties the pressure inside drops and the heat output lessens. The colder it is the quicker the flame weakens. Even so, for three season use they are excellent – especially if you do a lot of simmering as flame control is very good. There is a huge choice in cartridge stoves; I have tested many of them and they all work reasonably well.

For maximum heat output unaffected by temperature, petrol and paraffin are the best fuels, though both can flare badly when being lit. Paraffin is the safer choice as it is harder to light than petrol and will not ignite if spilled. For the same reasons it is more difficult to use, does not evaporate when spilled and leaves long-lasting greasy stains.

Petrol is easier to light than paraffin and cleaner, evaporating fairly quickly if spilled, but it is also far more volatile and explosive. Overall, it is not a fuel for anyone inexperienced in stove use.

To avoid having to choose in advance between petrol and paraffin, you could buy a stove that will run on either. The best multi fuel stove, the MRS XGK II, will also run on white spirit, diesel and jet fuel, making then ideal for trips to out of the way places. The lightest weight stoves use fuel bottles as the tank and are very stable as they have low profiles. Protecting your stove from the wind is essential, so if an adequate wind shield is not provided it is worth making or buying one.

The best stove in the world is useless if you cannot light it. Matches weigh virtually nothing, so I carry several boxes in plastic bags in several places in my pack. Lighters are also worth carrying – the spark alone can light petrol or butane or propane (but not methylated spirit or paraffin). I also carry a canister of windproof, waterproof matches in my repair kit in case the other fire-lighters get wet.

All stoves are potentially dangerous and need to be handled carefully. Read the instructions thoroughly and practise outside before taking a stove on a trip.

Ideally you should always cook outside. All too often, however, the weather makes this unpleasant or even impossible. When you have to use your stove in the tent porch – you should never use one in the inner tent – make sure there is adequate ventilation: all stoves give off poisonous carbon monoxide. Also ensure that nothing flammable is within touching or melting distance. Provide a clear space of at least 1ft (30cm) on all sides, and more above the stove. Leave the door at least partly open and be prepared to hurl the stove outside if it malfunctions. This is highly unlikely but a tent fire is to be avoided at all costs. If you are using petrol or paraffin the stove should be lit outside, even if it is raining, because of the danger of flaring. Once lit it can be brought under cover.

Refilling a stove or changing a cartridge should always be done outside. Take care not to spill fuel and be sure there are no naked flames such as burning candles nearby. Afterwards, ensure that any fuel tank and fuel bottle caps are screwed down tight before you light the stove.

Kitchen Utensils

There is no need to carry much in the way of cooking gear and there are many simple lightweight aluminium and stainless steel pans available. Two should be ample; weights including lid and pot grab should be no more than 6 to 8oz for a pint size pot and 12 to 16oz for a two-pint pot (equivalent to 150 to 200g for a 0.5 litre pot and 300 to 500g for a 1 litre pot).

Solo backpackers can eat straight from the pan. Plates or bowls are needed by groups; bowls are the best choice and plastic ones are lightest. Plastic is good for mugs too, though stainless steel mugs last longer and can be used as small pans by solo campers. Large sizes mean you do not have to brew up too often. The only cutlery needed is a spoon and a pocket knife.

Water

Check on the map where water sources can be found on or near your route and carry water if there is far between them. In particular you need to be sure there is water in the area where you intend to camp. Just before dark after a long day is not the time to discover that the nearest water is an hour's walk away.

In camp a large collapsible water container will save endless trips to fetch water. Using one also makes damage to the fragile ground around lakes or streams less likely as you will only need to make a few trips.

Food

The type and amount of food you eat is determined by how much you are prepared to carry. Bear in mind that backpacking can be hard work, so more calories than usual are needed. On one or two night trips the weight of food is not too important and fresh foods such as bread can be taken. On longer trips the weight of your food can become a problem. That is when lightweight specialist dehydrated and freeze-dried foods are a good idea. These are relatively expensive though many are not very tasty. For most trips you can find all you need in the local supermarket. Foods that cook in a few minutes are best. With them you get a meal quickly and save on stove fuel. Packet soups, pot noodles and pasta meals are quick and easy to prepare for dinner while cereals such as muesli or porridge make good breakfasts. Using such foods you should be able to get the weight down to about 2 to 2½lb (900g to 1.1kg) of dry food per person per day.

Clearing Up

Please be careful when you wash your pans. A good scourer is all that is needed. Washing up liquid should be left at home. Even soap-free dishwater should be poured into the ground at least 300ft (90m) from streams or lakes. Only water should be chucked away. Food scraps should be carried out as should all empty food packets and other litter. Leave your site as you would like to find it: pristine.

WALKING WITH A HEAVY PACK

Walking is easy. Once you put a heavy pack on your back and head off into the wilds it is not quite so simple, however. You do not have to be superhuman to go backpacking, but the fitter you are the more you will enjoy it. Backpacking is about stamina rather than speed so day walking, long distance running and cycling are good forms of training. If you do not backpack regularly it is worth doing short walks with a full pack before you set out on a trip to get used to carrying a load.

WHERE TO BACKPACK

You can go backpacking anywhere in the countryside, though in lowland areas you will usually have to camp on organized sites. However, backpacking makes most sense and is most enjoyable in remote, wild areas. In the UK this means the hill country and the coasts of the north and west.

Long Distance Paths

Many people take up backpacking because they want to walk one of the famous long distance paths, usually the Pennine Way or the West Highland Way. This is a worthwhile goal but there are many lesser known long paths in all parts of the country that are well worth tackling. Many can be done in a long weekend and they are usually far less crowded than the big name routes. You can also link long distance paths to make even longer routes, the ultimate being a walk from Land's End to John o'Groats.

There are guide books to all long distance paths, and information on camp sites and facilities is easy to obtain making these routes excellent for the beginner to backpacking.

National Parks

The national parks of England and Wales are criss-crossed with paths, comprehensively covered by guide books and have plenty of camp sites for backpackers and other lightweight campers. Most of the parks are in hill country and wild camping is usually permitted once you are above the last field walls. The compact area of most parks makes them ideal for circular routes in contrast to the linear long distance paths.

Mountain Areas

Many of the best areas for backpacking

are not in national parks. These include the hills of central Wales, the northern Pennines in England and the Scottish Highlands. This last area is without doubt the finest for backpacking in the UK. It is wild and rugged and will challenge your backpacking skills. You can walk for days here and see few other people.

Europe

The opportunities for backpacking abroad are many. In Europe the Pyrenees is a magnificent area, far less developed and regulated than the Alps, and with a much drier and warmer climate than that of the UK. A fine long distance path, the Haute Route Pyrenee, runs the length of the range from the Atlantic to the Mediterranean.

Scandinavia offers many opportunities for long distance treks in rugged mountains. In Lapland there are several long distance routes including the famous and spectacular Kungsleden.

North America

The best backpacking is to be found where it began, North America. In the United States and Canada there are vast areas of spectacular and pristine wilderness that are accessible only to the backpacker. Here lie the really long routes: the 2000 mile (3200km) Appalachian Trail, the 2600 mile (4200km) Pacific Crest Trail and the 3000 mile (4800km) Continental Divide Trail. There are many shorter routes too, of which the most famous is the John Muir Trail in the Sierra Nevada in California. For the keen backpacker a visit to North America must be the ultimate aim.

9 Recording and Remembering

Mr Young was eager for news. I told him there could be no news of importance about a town. We only had real news, drawn from the wilderness. (John Muir, Travels in Alaska)

As you gaze out over a spectacular mountain vista or struggle through a blizzard straining to see ahead, you cannot imagine that you will ever forget the experience. But as the years go by and your hill days grow in number memories can become hazy. If you do not keep some form of record it can be impossible to recollect just when and where something happened. Some incidents fade completely or become changed in your memory. I am often surprised when reading an old journal to discover that my memories of an event do not accord with what I wrote at the time or even to find an incident I had totally forgotten or I thought occurred elsewhere or at another time.

As well as being a way of keeping a record of hills you have climbed or distances you have walked, a journal can be a very enjoyable way of spending long dark evenings or times when the hills are far away and out of reach. It can also be a source of ideas and information. When revisiting an area I have not been to for years I always read my journal entries for previous visits to see if there were any plans I had for future trips and how long it took to do various ascents.

KEEPING A JOURNAL

A diary of your walks can consist of nothing more than a list of hills climbed along with dates and other factual information or it can be a detailed description of each day. For the first there are now log books available with the pages divided up for different entries such as date, hills climbed, weather, time and more. Some of these are designed for any area, others cover specific ranges. They are obviously an easy way of keeping records, though I find them a little impersonal.

I have always compiled my own logs, with a small notebook for each year. Walks of several months have their own notebooks too. The front part of the books I keep for descriptions of days out, the back for log book style data. The advantage of this is that you can decide what information you want to keep. I rule the back pages of my yearly notebooks into columns headed Date, Route, Distance, Amount of Ascent, Peaks, Height of Peaks, Weather, Time and Companions. This gives me an index for each notebook as well as a quick way of finding out what the weather was like when I climbed a certain hill or how long it took. On long backpacking trips I also keep a record of where I camp each night.

I only carry my notebook on trips of more than day, filling it in at home otherwise. I normally use notebooks with waterproof oilskin covers and pens with waterproof ink so that if a book gets wet I do not lose all my records.

Small electronic notebooks could be used in place of ordinary notebooks, with the information printed out or downloaded to a personal computer at home.

PHOTOGRAPHY

Far more hillwalkers take photographs than keep a journal and many regard cameras as essential equipment. Taking passable pictures is not difficult with modern automatic cameras, but consistently taking good pictures depends on the photographer rather than the equipment. No camera can compose a picture for you!

I take photographs almost every time I go into the hills. While these are often for books or magazines I enjoy taking them and I enjoy the hills more through photography. There is an argument that photography detracts from the experience of being in the hills, distancing the photographer from the landscape. I find that the opposite is true. Taking photography seriously has helped me to see more deeply the beauty and grandeur of the hills. I am much more attuned to slight changes in light than I was before I became a photographer. If the light starts to change I notice immediately and usually head for wherever I think the most dramatic scene will be.

I also find that photographs can really capture a time and place, perhaps more than the written word. For that reason I photograph people, camp sites, signposts and bridges as well as landscapes.

Cameras and Lenses

Many people are not interested in photography itself, they just want reason-able pictures of their walks. For them compact cameras that set the exposure and focus the lens automatically are ideal as all that needs to be done is to point the camera and press the shutter. There are a vast number of these cameras around. For hillwalking those that are weather resistant or waterproof are obviously useful while the smallest, lightest models are easiest to carry and add least weight to your load. These generally have fixed lenses, however. A zoom lens that can just take a small portion of the scene or be altered to take in a larger part is more versatile but does require a little more thought when composing the picture. Zoom compacts also weigh more and take up a little more room than fixed lens compacts.

At the time of writing compact cameras use 35mm film. Smaller sizes than 35mm have been available in the past but none have proved popular due to the poor quality, but 1996 sees the launch of yet another small format called the Advanced Photo System (APS). This is backed by many of the big camera and film manufacturers and if the quality is higher than previous small formats it could be an alternative to 35mm for amateur use. Larger formats than 35mm mean bigger, heavier cameras and so are rarely used on the hills. In the hills most professionals use 35mm, as the format is capable of producing superb photographs. Only a few lug larger format cameras about with them.

Those who are interested in taking good photographs and are prepared to learn about photography need a camera that either has manual controls or automatic controls that can be overridden. There are some compacts like this, but many of them are very expensive. There is no reason why photographs taken on a compact camera should not be as high quality as those taken on a larger model. I have taken pictures that have appeared on magazine covers with a long discontinued semi-automatic compact.

Most hillwalkers seriously interested in photography will use a single lens reflex (SLR) camera – not because it will take better photographs but because a range of different lenses can be used. SLR cameras still use 35mm film but they are larger and heavier than most compacts. Some professional models can weigh as much as 4lb (1.8kg) without any lenses – a heavy load for lugging about the hills. The lightest and smallest weigh less than the biggest compacts; there are many models in the 16 to 24oz (450 to 670g) range. I use Nikon cameras because of their durability. With batteries my manual FM2 weighs 19oz (540g), my automatic/manual F801 29oz (820g).

Some SLR cameras are fully automatic with no override. These are not, in my view, suitable for mountain photography unless you just want snapshots, in which case a simple compact would be just as good. Most have manual, semi-automatic and automatic modes. Using the camera in manual mode means you can adjust the exposure settings to take account of the light, which is very important for getting the best rather then just adequate photographs. You also focus the lens yourself – essential for maximizing the depth of field when taking landscape pictures so that both foreground and background will be in focus.

Lenses are the most important part of the SLR system. Without good lenses you cannot take good photographs no matter how sophisticated or expensive the camera body. The choice of lense matters too. Zoom lenses are ideal as they allow you to vary the composition without having to move. With a fixed lens you may have to change position to include more of the scene or home in on the specific detail you want in the picture. This can be difficult, dangerous or impossible in the hills. Zoom lenses used to be markedly inferior to fixed focal length lenses, resulting in poor pictures, but these days the best are so close in quality that it is very difficult to tell the difference.

For general use a wide range zoom such as a 28–70mm is best, perhaps combined with a longer range one such as a 70–210mm zoom for picking out distant details. I also carry a 24mm wide-angle lens for photographing wide skies or including distant peaks and detailed foregrounds in the same photograph. If I am travelling light I just take the 28–70mm zoom. Wider range zooms such as 28–200mm are heavier, bulkier, harder to hand hold and lower in quality so I would not recommend them for hill use.

Film

The best film for compact cameras is colour print film as this does not require precise exposure to produce adequate results. For showing to other people prints are ideal as they can be handed round. They can also be stuck in journals or albums and reprints are inexpensive to make. The speed of the film is important, as slow speed films require slower shutter speeds and wider apertures, which can mean that fuzzy photographs due to camera shake or inaccurate focusing are more likely. Slow speed films often have brighter colours and are less grainy than faster films, though film technology has advanced greatly in recent years and some fairly fast films now produce high quality pictures. Slow speed films are those rated from 25 to 64 ISO. Medium speed films are 100 and 200 while fast films are 400, 800, 1600 and 3200. I recommend using films of 100 ISO in bright sunlight and 200 or 400 in duller weather.

The majority of the mountain photographs that appear in books and magazines are taken on colour transparency film as this reproduces with more detail and brighter colours than print film. It's also needed if you want to give slide shows – projecting pictures onto a large screen is the most impressive way to see them. However, colour transparency film is harder to use than print film as the results can be very poor if the exposure is only slightly wrong so it is best used in cameras with manual controls, especially in unusual lighting. As with print film, slow speed film is brighter, sharper and less grainy: 25, 50 and 64 ISO film produce the best results as long as it is not too dull but 100 ISO film is better for hand-held shots in all conditions. There is not a great deal of difference between the top brands of slide film, Agfa, Fuji and Kodak; the speed is more important than the make. My own favourites are Fuji Velvia, a 50 ISO film, when using a tripod and in bright conditions, and Fuji Sensia 100 the rest of the time.

Black and white film is a rather specialist medium, usually only used by the dedicated few or professionals. Processing your own film is generally regarded as giving the best results, and it certainly gives you control over the results, but good processing laboratories can produce competent black and white pictures. As with other films speed is more important than the brand in distinguishing between films: 125 ISO film is recommended for normal use and the faster 400 ISO for dull lighting conditions. The pictures in this book were taken on 125 ISO Ilford FP4+ or in dull light, 400 ISO Ilford HP5+.

Accessories

The most important accessory for good photography is a tripod. Few hillwalkers carry one, as it means extra bulk and weight and also takes time to set up and use. Most tripods are too heavy to carry far but there are some lightweight models weighing under 2lb (900g) that are suitable for hillwalking. Serious photographers tend to look down on these as not being stable enough but I have found lightweight tripods perfectly adequate with the wide angle to short telephoto lenses I use. Most of the time you can take hand-held shots but at dawn and dusk, when the best light often occurs, and in midwinter when the light is never very strong a tripod can be essential to avoid handshake ruining your pictures. Because I walk solo much of the time I also carry one so I can put myself in pictures that I think will be improved by the presence of a figure.

For landscapes a tripod has another advantage. It slows you down. You cannot grab quick snapshots with a tripod. This means you can study the scene more closely and take time to make the best composition. If you use a tripod a cable release is useful so you do not jar the camera when pressing the shutter. On electronic cameras the self-timer can be used.

Alternatives to a full size tripod are tiny tabletop models that can be set up on a rock or, with care, the edge of a cliff. There are also camera attachments that can be fastened to trekking poles or ice axes. I find they take more time than using a tripod so I prefer the latter despite the extra weight. An option that requires no extra weight is to use your rucksack as a support. This works best with a large backpacking one as you can kneel down behind it and lay the camera across the top. You can also use rocks, walls and fence posts to rest your camera on or brace yourself against.

Filters are the most common accessory. Keeping skylight or UV filters on lenses at all times is a good way to protect them; it is much cheaper to replace a scratched filter. A polarizing filter – to darken skies, bring out colours and cut out distracting reflections when used at right angles to the sun – is the most useful filter for mountain photography. After that the only ones I use regularly with colour transparency film are graduated neutral density filters, which reduce the range of light in scenes with dark foregrounds and bright skies so that details of both are recorded in the photograph. Graduated grey filters have a similar effect but those I have used have an unnatural pink cast.

These filters enable photographs to be taken that approximate more closely to the scene than they would without them. I do not use filters that add colour or special effects, as the results are unnatural.

The only colour filters I use are with black and white film. If you do not use a filter a cloudy sky will come out a uniform white or grey on black and white film. To make the clouds stand out you could use a polarizer, though this only works at right angles to the sun. I usually use an orange filter instead. If you want a darker, more stormy looking sky you could use a red filter. (Filters cannot be fitted to most compact cameras but they are available for all SLR lenses.)

The only other accessories I recommend are lens hoods for each lens. These cut out stray light entering from the side – causing flare and washed-out pictures – and protect the front of the lens from rain and snow.

Taking Photographs

There are many good books on outdoor photography for those who want to study it in depth. Correct exposure and focusing will ensure that your photographs are technically adequate as long as you hold the camera firmly

Driftwood makes for a more interesting foreground than the still waters of the lake. The eye is drawn down the lake, framed by the trees on the left and the crag on the right, to the distant peak.

This picture would have far less depth and be less interesting without the skiers as the foreground is too plain on its own.

Swirling clouds and patches of snow give drama and depth to this picture, taken from a position halfway up the side of the valley.

enough or use some form of support.

The general rule for hand-held photographs is that the focal length of the lens should not be higher than the shutter speed. A 28mm lens can be hand-held at a shutter speed of ⅟₃₀ second but a 100mm lens should not be hand-held at less than ⅟₁₂₅. It is always better to use faster shutter speeds whenever possible; most of my hand-held shots are taken at ⅟₁₂₅ and ⅟₂₅₀ whatever the lens.

Even the most technically perfect photograph can still be dull and lifeless if the composition is poor and the light flat. When you take a photograph you should consider everything that will appear in it. A common fault is to have vast amounts of uniform foreground with a row of peaks or a walker on the far horizon. If you only have a wide angle lens, the norm on many fixed lens compacts, you cannot easily cut out the foreground. What you can do is to look for an interesting object such as a rock or pool to break up the monotony and give a greater sense of depth to the picture. A person can be used for this too. It also often produces a more dramatic picture if you crouch or even lie down and take it from a lower angle. Alternatively you can climb onto a rock or bank and take the photograph looking downwards. Landscapes usually look better if the horizon is situated about one-third of the way from the top or bottom.

Moving off the footpath or away from the summit cairn can often produce a better photograph too. Rather than taking a quick shot from where you happen to be standing move around with the camera to your eye seeing how the scene looks from different viewpoints. Take several pictures too,

Here the grassy bland foreground has been kept to a minimum in favour of the more interesting sky.

rather than just one. You can decide which is best when you get the pictures back from the processor.

When a person or object such as a rock or even a distant peak is the main subject of your picture make sure they are quite large in the frame or in strong lighting so they stand out. Photos of people staring straight at the camera can be boring; it is better if they are looking at the view, reading the map, walking or even waving an ice axe in triumph at reaching the summit.

The best times to take landscape pictures are at dawn and dusk so good photographers tend to get up early or stay out late. This is because at these times the angle of the sun gives good shadows and side lighting, revealing textures and shapes. Colours are also often richer and more distinct too. In the middle of the day, between 10am and 4pm in summer, when the sun is high overhead the light is usually flat and often hazy, making for washed out looking pictures. A polarizer can help, as can a film with highly saturated colours.

In winter the low angle of the sun in northern mountain ranges means the light can be dramatic all day. But snow brings its own problems. A common complaint of winter photographers is that the snow in their photographs comes out grey and any figures are much too dark. This happens because camera exposure meters are calibrated to turn everything a mid shade of grey. In sunny summer weather this usually works well and produces properly exposed pictures. Snow is so bright that the meter closes down to let in less light and make the snow grey. This also darkens figures. A solution I use regularly is to take the meter reading off the back of my hand, without gloves on, held in the same light as the scene I want to photo-

graph. An alternative is to turn the exposure compensation dial, if your camera has one, to plus one and half or plus two. On a purely manual camera you can either open up the aperture by a stop or two or use a slower shutter speed. For example if the meter tells you to use F11 at $\frac{1}{250}$ when pointed at a bright snow scene you could stop down to F8 or F5.6 and stay at $\frac{1}{250}$ or you could stay at F11 and use a shutter speed of $\frac{1}{125}$ or $\frac{1}{60}$. You can see that there are two options in each case. One way to increase the chances of a good photograph of snow, or in any unusual lighting, is to take some at different settings. That way one frame should turn out all right.

Fully automatic cameras cannot be adjusted like this but the exposure latitude of print film is such that you will probably get adequate results in snow anyway. Some automatic compacts will take good snow photographs with transparencies too as the meter is set towards overexposure as most print films can be overexposed without spoiling the picture and makers of compact cameras tend to assume they will be used with print film.

Many hillwalkers only take pictures on sunny days yet storms can make for some of the most dramatic pictures. Black clouds backlit by the sun, figures battling against the wind or covered with snow and clouds swirling round the peaks can all make good photographs.

Those who really wish to improve their photography and learn which settings work for which type of scene or light should keep a record of the aperture and shutter speeds used, along with the film type and speed and any filters or supports used. Then when the pictures come back from the processor you can see what worked and what did

Storms can make for dramatic lighting. This picture was taken as the clouds cleared and a late afternoon sun shone on this peak in Greenland.

Waterproof padded camera cases are essential to protect against rain and snow and to absorb shocks when banged against rocks.

not and learn from this. Once you know how your equipment and favourite films work you will not need to do this in standard lighting conditions but it is still worth doing so in any dramatic lighting, especially if you have taken photographs at a number of different settings.

When you get your photographs back go through them carefully and reject those that are not good enough. Some you may want to keep because of the memories they bring back even if they are not particularly good. Before you show photographs to others you should be ruthless and select only the best. This ability to judge their work is one major difference between professional photographers and most amateurs.

Camera Protection

Cameras need protecting from the weather and from being knocked against hard objects. They also need to be quickly accessible or they will not get much use, so keeping them in the rucksack is not the answer. Camera makers' cases are usually awkward to use and not very weather or shock resistant; better are padded cases that can be carried on the rucksack waist strap or slung over the shoulder. Models are available for all shapes and sizes of cameras; my Camera Care Systems ones keep out rain, snow and dust and absorb the impact when they are banged against rocks. I find the most comfortable way to carry a camera is diagonally across my body, as it then sits snugly in my midriff. To take the strain off my shoulder I use a wide stretch neoprene strap.

I only keep one camera and lens to hand. If I carry other cameras or lenses these live in the rucksack. If I want to use them I am likely to be stopping so removing the rucksack is not a problem. Some walkers like waist packs worn round the front so they have easy access to all their camera gear, but I find such packs restrict movement and sag under the weight. Larger camera bags are too big for hill use while rucksacks designed to carry camera gear often do not have room for the other gear you need. You still need to take them off to get your camera out anyway.

Useful Addresses

Altberg, 10 Borough Road, Gallowfields Industrial Estate, Richmond, North Yorkshire DL10 4XA. Tel: 01748 850615. Custom bootmakers. I have not used any of their boots but I know experienced hillwalkers who have and who consider them to be good.

Backpackers' Club, PO Box 381, Reading RG3 4RL. For those interested in camping in the hills. Local groups hold regular meets. Please enclose an sae.

British Association of Ski Patrollers, 20 Lorn Drive, Glencoe, Argyll PA39 4HR. Organizes excellent mountain first aid courses.

British Mountaineering Council, 177–179 Burton Road, West Didsbury, Manchester M20 2BB. Covers hillwalking as well as climbing. Good insurance scheme for overseas trips.

Glenmore Lodge National Outdoor Training Centre, Aviemore PH22 1QU. Courses on hillwalking, navigation and more.

Long Distance Walkers' Association, Membership Secretary, 117 Higher Lane, Rainford, St Helens, Merseyside WA11 8BQ. Regular long walks, local groups and an excellent quarterly journal, *Strider*. Please enclose an sae.

Mountain Bothies Association, Information Officer, Ted Butcher, 26 Rycroft Avenue, Deeping St James, Peterborough PE6 8NT. Maintains unlocked shelters for the use of hillwalkers. Regular work parties. Please enclose an sae.

Mountaineering Council of Scotland, 171 King Street, Crieff, Perthshire PH7 3HB. Conservation campaigns, information, newsletters and more for hillwalkers and climbers.

Plas y Brenin National Centre for Mountain Activities, Capel Curig, Betws y Coed, Gwynedd LL24 0ET. Courses on hillwalking, navigation and more.

Ramblers' Association, 1–5 Wandsworth Road, London SW8 2XX. Local groups, regular meets, access campaigns.

Recorded Weather Forecasts

These numbers are current at the time of writing. They do change, though. Some of these reports are available by fax as well as telephone:

Weathercall: 0891 500404 (covers Dartmoor but not specifically for the hills)

Weathercall: 0891 500414 (covers the Brecon Beacons but not specifically for the hills)

Weathercall: 0891 500417 (covers the Yorkshire Dales and the Peak District but not specifically for the hills)

Lake District National Park Weatherline: 017687 75757

Mountaincall Lake District: 0891 505287

Mountaincall Snowdonia: 0891 500449 or 0891 505285

Mountaincall West (West Highlands): 0891 500441 or 0891 505329

Mountaincall East (East Highlands): 0891 500442 or 0891 505328

East Highlands Climbline: 0891 654668 or 0891 333197

West Highlands Climbline: 0891 654669 or 0891 333198

Scottish Avalanche Information Service: telephone 01463 713191; fax 0990 112202; e-mail avalanche@dcs.gla.ac.uk; World Wide Web http://www.dcs.gla.ac.uk/other/avalanche/

Index